"Amy Blackthorn has created a trove of historical, magical, scientific, and spiritual information that will deepen and enrich any practitioner's magical experience. She leads us through plant families, how to work with the spirit of the plant as opposed to (or in support of) the physical material, and offers ways to communicate with the natural world around us, encouraging us to expand our ideas of what functions the plant realm has within our daily lives on both mundane and magical levels. I wish I'd written this book, but Amy has done a much better job than I ever could have. *Blackthorn's Book of Sacred Plant Magic* is a book I will recommend to absolutely everyone."

—Arin Murphy-Hiscock, author of *The Green Witch*

"*Blackthorn's Book of Sacred Plant Magic* is an abundant garden of flavorful advice and well-rooted knowledge for practicing green witchcraft—an absolute treasure for anyone seeking to grow a powerful connection to the plant allies and their green world. Amy Blackthorn guides the reader through an extensive variety of plants, from common kitchen staples like dill to exotic botanicals, such as May Chang. She expertly discusses challenging botanicals, including cannabis, in an extensive section. Throughout this excellent book, Blackthorn offers spells, rituals, meditations, foundational recipes, and an expansive collection of detailed monographs. She wonderfully shares all of this on varying levels, so everyone—from complete newcomer to experienced practitioner—will find new ways of rendering sacred plant magic through her approach."

—Cyndi Brannen, author of *Entering Hekate's Garden*

"Scent is one of our most powerful tools for altering consciousness and facilitating both psychic and physical change according to our needs and desires. The plant kingdom has the capability to help us do anything: bolster our courage, connect to deceased loved ones, achieve success in our endeavors. Amy Blackthorn is a master green witch and plant spirit practitioner who provides the reader with accessible magical techniques for working with plant allies, as well as an expertise on active compounds and scent profiles. *Blackthorn's Book of Sacred Plant Magic* is much more than a guide to botanical aromatics—it provides the reader with tools and techniques to tap into the spiritual powers of plants and build lasting relationships through the ethereal and profound properties of natural fragrance."

—Coby Michael, author of *The Poison Path Herbal*

"While reading *Blackthorn's Book of Sacred Plant Magic,* I felt as if I had been invited into an exquisite garden club's educational afternoon tea. In an ideal teacher/student relationship, Blackthorn builds trust and a rapport with her readers while presenting a bouquet of knowledge on plant magic. I praise her decision to include cannabis, helping to reclaim, destigmatize, and renormalize this important and beneficial plant."

—Kerri Connor, author of Kerri Connor's
Weed Witch series and *Spells for Good Times*

"Amy Blackthorn knows her botanicals. *Sacred Plant Magic,* another enriching and educational addition to the Blackthorn's Books series, is full of clearly presented information and instructions designed to bring any witch or magician closer to their own plant spirit allies via a wide variety of successful methodologies, both beginner and advanced. If you have a green heart, you won't be disappointed."

—Tara-Love Maguire, coauthor of *Besom, Stang, and Sword*

BLACKTHORN'S BOOK OF

SACRED PLANT MAGIC

Spells, Rites & Rituals
for Living an
Aromatic Life

AMY BLACKTHORN

WEISER
BOOKS

This edition first published in 2024 by Weiser Books, an imprint of
Red Wheel/Weiser, llc
With offices at:
65 Parker Street, Suite 7
Newburyport, MA 01950
www.redwheelweiser.com

ISBN: 978-1-57863-830-7

Library of Congress Cataloging-in-Publication Data

Names: Blackthorn, Amy, 1981- author.
Title: Blackthorn's book of sacred plant magic : spells, rites, and rituals
  for living an aromatic life / Amy Blackthorn.
Description: Newburyport, MA : Weiser Books, 2024. | Includes
  bibliographical references. | Summary: "This book travels deep into the
  magical garden of scent. Scents can bring back memories of childhood or
  places we've visited. We experience scents not only in the here and now
  but also filtered through the lens of our past. Using the power of scent,
  we can create a sense of the sacred in our daily lives. This book shows
  readers how to bring plant spirits into their daily spiritual practice and helps
  them understand plant spirits on a deeper level."--
  Provided by publisher.
Identifiers: LCCN 2024019941 | ISBN 9781578638307 (trade paperback) | ISBN
  9781633413290 (ebook)
Subjects: LCSH: Plants--Religious aspects--Neopaganism. | Smell--Religious
  aspects--Neopaganism. | Witchcraft. | Magic. | BISAC: BODY, MIND &
  SPIRIT / Witchcraft (see also RELIGION / Wicca) | HEALTH & FITNESS /
  Herbal Medications
Classification: LCC BF1623.P5 B58 2024 | DDC 299/.94--dc23/eng/20240531
LC record available at https://lccn.loc.gov/2024019941

Cover design by Sky Peck Design
Interior by Brittany Craig
Typeset in Adobe Jenson Pro

Printed in the United States of America
IBI
10 9 8 7 6 5 4 3 2 1

*To every herbalist who has struggled to explain just
how important your plant allies are to you.*

*To the ancestors that brought me here, who lent
their strength, fortitude, and stubbornness.*

*To the future generations, including
June-Bee and Fox. You give me hope.*

CONTENTS

THANK YOU TO JUDIKA ILLES, for three a.m. convos, and your faith in me.

My agent, Natalie Lakosil, for keeping me grounded.

To the entire staff at Red Wheel/Weiser for taking my dreams and making them tangible for the rest of the world.

To my fierce and loyal friends—Kane, Janna, Brian, Krissy, Cecilia, Josh, Casey, Dave M., Melissa, and all the Shama-Llamas. I love you.

To the beloved friends who live in my pocket—Mortellus, Mat, Patti, Tiffany B., Forest, Lulu, Laurell, Ashli, and Alice K., you keep me sane.

And to you, reading this acknowledgment, you've made my deepest wishes come true.

As the bee is drawn by the linden bloom,
My heart is drawn to thee.

Slavonian Folk Song

Creating Relationships with Plants

Introduction

A man stumbled into the shop as the door flung itself open on a blustery January night in 2010. The wind chimes on the door clanged as the wind took the door out of the hand of a harried patron, a man in a staid gray suit, the wind blowing his hair askance. "Do you have any frankincense oil, myrrh oil? Please!" He was clearly desperate. Having been in the shop since its inception, the years had taught me that there were all kinds of emergencies. I walked him over to where we kept the essential oils, but we were out of frankincense.

"If you're using these magically, I'll vouch for this Witches' Brew oil; it's my favorite, a mix of frankincense, myrrh, and mugwort. If you like frankincense, we also carry frankincense and myrrh resin by the pound."

"*You do?!*" he nearly shouted. "Well, why didn't you say so?" he demanded desperately. He whirled around, spotting the resin section of our herb table. He reached for a pound of the resin blend and a few rolls of charcoal from the display and ran to the register, wisps of hair flying behind him.

I'm beyond curious as to what the heck is happening here, but I grabbed the nearest shop employee to ring him out and hoped he'd let me in on the situation as he was checking out. Who am I? I'm Amy Blackthorn, and on that windy January night I was working as a tarot reader at my local shop (RIP Mystical Voyage) and was between clients. I was always happy to help customers if there was downtime, but I'd never encountered such a frantic customer in my four years of reading at that shop.

"Is everything okay? You came in looking for oil. Can I suggest something besides the resin?"

It turns out the harried man was a junior priest at the local Catholic parish, and it was ten minutes before the Epiphany mass was supposed to start. Apparently, they ran out of incense during Midnight Mass for Christmas, and they forgot to reorder in time for that night's mass. As the staff argued, he remembered seeing the shop sign during his weekly grocery store trip and thought he'd take a chance that we'd have the oil in store. He was overjoyed to find

witches also use frankincense and myrrh, and he snagged a few extra charcoal rolls while he was at it. He came back for our Sunday coffee klatch after mass for quite some time after that, always willing to learn, a humble guest, never proselytizing, and always kind.

Even priests get panic attacks.

It is so common for us humans to search for a connection to something outside of ourselves. It's no secret that there is a link between plants with a wide history of use and humans' understanding of those plants. The cultures captivated by them laid their own understanding upon those materials, forever linking groups, cultures, and experiences with those botanical allies, much to the chagrin of the young priest who found himself in a witchcraft shop.

Though our religious practices are different, we were able to establish a baseline connection for the priest that allowed him to open a door he might not have otherwise allowed himself, and it connected two different communities along the way. Roman Catholics from that parish were able to learn that just because our traditions were different, and our gods unfamiliar to them, didn't make us the enemy.

In this book, I hope to help open your eyes to the connection, the relationships that can be built, and the friends you'll likely make along the way. We'll talk about who to build botanical relationships with and why—as well as how to find the magical attributes for plants that aren't listed in your favorite magical tomes. It is up to us to reach out to foster those connections, and what's better, plants don't much care about what your religion is. I'm writing this book from the perspective of a Witch, but these techniques can foster a deeper connection to your faith, no matter your pathway.

Join me, as we discover the relationships that can be built with our plant allies. We can explore how our memories color our experience of scent. Look deep within to help develop our relationship with plants as empowered beings with agency of their own. We'll learn how to create custom botanical treatment plans complete with flower elixirs. There is a section on understanding the relationship between plants in botanical families and how that can work to boost your magic, your understanding, and perhaps shed light on the reasons we experience plant allergies. We'll work together to create divination tools with our plant spirit allies and understand what role scent plays in religion. We'll journey into our inner landscape to create connections with plants in the realm of Spirit. Creating scent activations gives us an instant ally for creating change in our bodies, minds, and spirits. That's all before we get to our A to Z listing of plants that can be allied with in the form of essential oils, perfumes, and hundreds of spells. Thanks for coming with me on this journey of mind, body, spirit, and the divine plants within all of us. You'll be glad you did.

In Her Service,
Amy Blackthorn
12/29/2023

SCENT, MEMORY, AND PERSONAL HISTORY

1

What is scent anyway? We learn from such a young age to beware of certain smells. Kids go through that phase where every smell is gross or funny. Adults have built a forty-billion-dollar industry around smells. We crave the perfect perfume, the right plug-in room scent for the bathroom, and even more, just the right candles for the living room, family room, and kitchen. Why? Why is scent so important?

When people talk about the history of aromatherapy, folks have a tendency to zone out and picture women in leotards drinking cucumber water or imagine rooms filled with bland wall art talking about their feelings. Instead, we are trying to evoke a response though scent, whether the response is processing grief, sedating after a stressful day, or opening the sinuses after a rough cold. Our sense of smell isn't a lone wolf. The sense of smell is a trip down memory lane, every time we inhale.

People take for granted that we recognize smells nearly instantly, but there is a lot happening in those hundredths of a second. The information collected by the nose has to speed through neural pathways created over a lifetime of building a scent catalog in the brain. Before the lavender information can land on the space provided for lavender it has to pass through the memory center of the brain and spin through the catalog of scents experienced during life. This happens in the hippocampus. The electronic signals that equal lavender will speed past danger scents, animal scents, and mechanical scents before landing in the floral arena and proceeding to the square marked "lavender."

However, along the way it is more likely to trigger memories of times when lavender was experienced. This helps speed the process of understanding whether lavender smells like danger or not. This is called relational memory. This is also why smells that were encountered during a traumatic memory are burned into our sense memory. When in the midst of a dangerous situation, our thinking gets turned off because it's using too much energy, just like our blood vessels constrict to limit blood flow to extremities and keep the vital organs safe. By turning off our thinking mind and giving the reins over to the muscle memory, we aren't doubting ourselves, we're just doing what we can to survive. It's a totally different system, which is why we can't just *think away* a traumatic flashback that's caused by a sense memory like a specific cologne. The feelings that are brought up by sense memories are not just to torment or entice. Human ancestors like *Homo erectus* used their sense of scent to detect danger, just as we do today. If a Neanderthal were to wander into a new territory in search of food and encountered berries, they would smell them first to see if they recognized the smell of the berries. Are these berries something that have been experienced before? If not, do they smell bitter? Bitter signals the possibility of poison to the brain. The brain wanders through memory in order to then proceed to recognition.

Memories through Time

What was your first memory? Watching dust motes filter through dappled sunlight while lying in a crib? Was it playing with siblings or friends? Perhaps it was enjoying a favorite toy or game. What was your first scent memory? The smells we experience as children often have a stronger impact on our emotional connections because we have been traveling those neural pathways much longer.

This also affects our sense of time. You know how when you were a kid, summer seemed to last forever? Remember the warmth on your skin, the smell of ozone and petrichor after a thunderstorm? Those days seemed to last forever, while the most recent summer memories are so fleeting. Our memories work on a timeline, but not the way you think. We experience memory and time in relation to our entire lifespan, not calendar months, or days. Humans have had memories much longer than calendars have existed. When we are young, we experience a single day as related to the scale of our lives. It is the legend to our map, so to speak. If you have been alive exactly eight years, you have experienced 2,920 days. Any one day out of that many days will seem much larger than one day out of 10,950 days, or thirty years. This makes time feel like it has sped up, when really only the perception filtered through our memories has changed.

Picture a race. Each day you have lived is a square in the race. They are all the same size squares, but every time you have to run back to a particular square you run back farther for every day added. The memory square has not moved, only your distance from it. While this is true, you continue running over the same squares each time you have to go back to a different memory.

GREAT MINDS THINK ALIKE

Just as we have our sense memories, our family and siblings do as well; however two people experiencing the same exact events won't necessarily respond the same way, making the idea of trauma very personal. Two siblings raised in the same home, at the same time, can still have two very different experiences with the same parents, leading to two different reactions to the same smell.

As a young child there was a particular day, probably during the summer between second and third grade. I'm one of four girls in my household and my two younger sisters were misbehaving that day. Who knows why. I'm sure there was a reason. My mother warned, "If you don't behave, I'm telling your father when he gets home." It had no effect and by the time my father arrived home from work, my sisters were standing in the corner as punishment for arguing. My father had come home with a box of chocolate-covered Oreos and since my sisters had been naughty, they weren't allowed to partake. My older sister and I were made to eat the whole box in front of our sisters to punish them. I was so sick that night that, to this day, I can't stand the smell of chocolate-covered Oreo cookies. I had a sense memory of this while discussing it with one of my sisters, and they didn't remember it. Punishment seemed frequent so it didn't surprise me that a specific instance didn't stand out in their mind.

Since trauma leaves imprints similar to fall leaves staining a sidewalk, some events are a mere shadow on the clear gray cement (bad memories), and some are perfect outlines of the horrible event that linger for years (post-traumatic stress). Some are faint outlines that repeat over and over until the whole field is stained with brown shadows (complex post-traumatic stress). With the process of introducing new experiences to familiar scents, we are gently sweeping that sidewalk until all the leaves have gone, and the memory of the shadow is all that is left. Trauma therapy doesn't erase the awful thing, but it gives us the tools to deal more effectively with the stains that remain.

DEVELOPING PLANT SPIRIT RELATIONSHIPS 2

It's been a long morning, and I think I need a mug of peppermint tea. I stand from my desk, and my sweet dog Millie perks up, hoping I'm headed to "Where the Treats Live." I keep a countertop water heater so that I'm always ready to have tea, and I grab a large bag of peppermint from the cabinet along with my tea infuser (infusers allow the leaves to develop more than a tea bag or a tea ball). When I reach into the cabinet, my hand finds my favorite cauldron-shaped mug. A few short minutes later I'm straining peppermint tea into my mug with a little sweetener and taking a seat in my living room.

But what about those lonely peppermint leaves in the kitchen? I'll compost the leaves and say a word of thanks to the spirit of Peppermint for the joy I have found in my mug. You see, the plant matter I'm drinking from has done its job. I might have re-steeped the leaves for a second pot or not, depending on my mood, but no matter how many mugs of this comforting brew I drink, I can never drink enough mint tea to damage the spirit of Peppermint. Peppermint endures, as anyone who has ever grown it in their garden can attest.

> As long as there are people who know mint, grow mint, flavor candies with mint, or can identify mint, mint will endure.

The spirit of Peppermint is the one I give thanks to because the physical plant that created this plant material is not available to me. I can't give it fertilizer to thank it for its hard work. I don't know the plant that this material was harvested from, but I do know that spirit. The analogy that I'm working with is that the peppermint from my garden is like my neighbor down the street who is Catholic. We meet, we chat about things, they learn about me, and I them. The spirit of Peppermint would be more like the Pope, head of the Catholic Church. They're both Catholic, or in this case, peppermint, but as empowered beings with agency, a will of their own, they may have different experiences, slightly different views or thoughts from each other. They are still peppermint.

Nature or Nurture?

Say we have two oak trees: one is from my childhood block in north Baltimore and one lives on an organic farm outside Denver, Colorado. Botanically speaking, because of the difference in altitude, soil composition, temperature, and a number of other factors, their leaves might contain vastly different chemical makeups. But they are still both oak trees.

To take it a step further, if one oak was grown in a swamp, full of decay and rot, while the other was on an organic farm, they are going to have two different chemical makeups, and due to these differences, they can have two different magical personalities. The swamp oak might be great for breaking down barriers to your success, or banishing things that no longer serve you. The oak from the organic farm might be well suited to magic of renewal, growth, new beginnings, and vibrancy.

When I make my morning tea, I might blend something from my tea garden. I might blend a rooibos from South Africa or an Assam from India.

- ❈ If the plant material is from my garden, I'll have explained that it's time to give the haircut and what I'll be doing with the plant material I will be taking away, and obtain their consent.

- ❈ If it's a tea that's already been harvested and dried, then I can't ask for the plant's consent.

- ❈ But I can thank the spirit of the plant for nourishing my body.

That's what we're talking about here; we're looking to the thought forms or spirits of these botanical allies. We are building relationships with them just the same way we build relationships and friendships with people in our daily lives. Imagine if Peppermint and I met at a party. I might introduce myself by saying, "Hey, I'm Amy and I write books; how about you?"

Blackthorn's Book of Sacred Plant Magic

Peppermint might respond, "Oh, great to meet you, Amy, my name is Peppermint, and I'm anti-inflammatory and can bring clarity to your magic." If we part ways and bump into each other at the grocery store a month later, I might recognize their face, I might remember their name is Peppermint, but forget the tidbit about their anti-inflammatory properties. Building these relationships takes time, energy, and effort. Likely more so, because these aren't beings that you bump into at the water cooler in the office. (Or at least, if you do, I want to visit you at work!)

The Santa Effect

My eight-year-old niece came to me with a seriously furrowed brow. "Aunt Amy, I have a question, and I know you'll tell me the truth. Is Santa Claus real?" I looked into her eyes, filled with defiance and a light she didn't yet know how to harness and said, "Yes, but not in the way you think." I explained that when enough people believe in something, with their whole hearts, they can create that thing, that spirit, that energy. It's called a thought form or an egregore. Over a long enough period of time, it takes on a life of its own, powered by that belief, and it can become part of the collective spirit. I continued to explain that even if Saint Nick wasn't based on a real person (an effective saint who lived in what is now Turkey and is the patron saint of brewers, sex workers, sailors, students, and children, among others), the energy of all of that belief, prayer, letters, and joy would have made him into a real being. It might not be real in the case of a currently living, breathing person she could meet at a local mall, but his energy and life would endure as long as there was a single person alive to pass on the legend of Santa.

Connecting with Plants around You

The closest plants to you might be closer than you know. We tend to think of the big showy plants near us like trees or landscaping florals. But the easiest plants for you to connect with as you're beginning your journey toward kinship with plants are the indoor plants, the houseplants, the ficus in your apartment building's lobby, the spider plant your mom gave you when you moved out, the pothos you rescued from a big-box hardware store because it was too sad to leave it there. Each of these plants has an experience that shapes part

of your life. The snake plant (*Dracaena trifasciata*) that you picked up after a breakup, to brighten your mood? It knows how you cried the first month in your home. The tree out front of your apartment that shades you as you wait for the rideshare in the morning has heard you vent about the petty coworker plaguing your break room.

Because of the close proximity, you're already building relationships with these plants every day. Every time you water them, every time you lean on the tree outside, even just breathing in their space is feeding them the carbon dioxide that they need for photosynthesis and creating oxygen. The hard part's already done; now you just have to do what people have been doing since we had speech: talk to the plants.

Plants respond to people, they feel pain, they cry out when they're hurt (for example the smell of cut grass contains a pheromone that signals danger to the other grasses around them), they grow more thickly and lushly when they're played music. We don't have to rely on a taker mindset for developing relationships with plants. They aren't here to serve us merely because we have a central nervous system and they don't. We can develop understandings and relationships with plants as a way to understand the world around us better.

A Spirit Is a Spirit Indeed

For those of you experiencing doubt, think of this as being akin to mediumship. Mediumship is the work involving communication with spirits of the deceased. In this case the spirits are living; with plants, we just have different language and communication styles. We are connecting at a level of higher consciousness, and the more we work with plant spirits, the more we understand them, and those relationships get to be as familiar as our friendships with people and spirits of the deceased. When I speak to the dead, for example, they aren't always the best at elocution. Some spirits are weaker and come through on a time delay, with static, or sounding like they're underwater. Some spirits come through clear as a bell, live, and in color. Some spirits speak languages other than mine. The spirits who have a harder time emoting or speaking with clarity can instead show you images. I had a client last week who wanted to know if any of her family was coming through, and when I asked the spirit his name, instead of getting "his name starts with an S sound" I got a video clip of a Steve character from a popular sitcom when I was a kid. "Who is Steve?" I asked her. "Oh, my god, that's my dad."

Reaching Out

Developing relationships with specific plants in your home can do so much for you as a magical practitioner as well. Plants, like dogs, like having a job to do. You might ask a peace lily (*Spathiphyllum spp.*) to remind you to give everyone a good water in the winter when it's dry inside and cold outside. You might incorporate your indoor plants into your magical wards for the home. (More on that in my previous book, *Blackthorn's Protection Magic.*) The harder part in all of this is allowing yourself to be vulnerable, to open yourself to the possibility that life comes in many, many forms. And that it just might feel silly the first time you sit down to have a heart-to-heart with a fern. But. It's. Worth. It.

CONNECTING WITH PLANTS IN THEIR ABSENCE

What does this have to do with our botanical allies? The idea of a thought form or a spiritual connection to our plant allies means that I can call on the spirit of Peppermint without having to reach for the mint tea in our earlier example. I might print a photo of peppermint from an internet image search, or I might save the illustration from my favorite box of mint tea to connect with that spirit of Peppermint.

This opens a whole new avenue of connection to the plant world. By connecting with the essence of the plant, you have access to an understanding and a relationship that otherwise wouldn't be possible. You can connect with plants outside your geographical region, outside your price point, or even outside your epoch. This also removes the barriers to magical communications. If someone wishes to be a green witch, they aren't required to garden. There is no licensing bureau. No one checks.

How to Connect

Sadly, we don't have the morphological map to drive us to the closest peppermint plant to ask for their help. However, in Spirit we don't really need a map if we can "call them on the phone," so to speak. Instead of looking for them, we'll ring them up and see if they can help.

Building Your Virtual Inner Landscape

The first step in getting to know the spirits of these plants is to create an inner landscape from which to venture forth. Think of your inner landscape as the Start screen on a video game. Every time you venture there, it has the same start screen. No matter where you end up, you can always go back to the start and begin anew. Your start screen can be anywhere, any time. After all, you're the architect of your virtual world. You could start in a field, inside a castle wall, or inside your own bedroom—the important part is that this is a place where you feel safe and in control. Allow your inner landscape to develop just as any other landscape does. Meadows evolve, forests evolve, and so should your landscape. You can add different touches, banners, posters, trees, flowers, anything you can imagine. Some things will stay for decades, some things change with the seasons; it's all up to you, as you are the god of this arena.

Getting Started

Sit or lie comfortably. Start relaxing each muscle in your body individually, starting at your toes and working up to the top of your head. Is it physically possible to relax every muscle? No, we're going for major muscle groups, to the best of your ability. This exercise is about your needs, not about making you question your corporeal form.

As a neurodivergent Witch, I find active visualization more engaging and easier to do than the sit-and-think-of-nothing style of meditation, but honor your energy where you find it. I will use an application on my phone to record a new visualization if I need a prompt to keep me on task. If I've got the time to do it, I'll just visualize where my attention takes me. If I'm stuck on the grocery list, I can visualize the things I need to get from the store and move on, whereas if I try to ignore it, I might waste more time trying and failing to steer my attention back inwards. If you need to do this in smaller time chunks, that's okay. Rome wasn't built in a day, and your inner landscape doesn't have to be either. If all you have the energy to do is pick out the drapes and wall color, so to speak, that's great, and enough for one day. You are enough.

By the same token, if you have aphantasia and cannot see or visualize inside your head, that's okay too. There are plenty of blind and visually impaired magicians and it doesn't make them any less a magician/witch.

In this book, "witch" is used as a gender-neutral term, as is "magician." The difference pertains to the style of magical practice, rather than the gender presentation of the practitioner.

Once you've relaxed as best you can, it's time to move inward. Everything starts in darkness; it's our job to create the light. This first question is, within your inner landscape, are you inside or outside? That'll determine the texture of the light that surrounds you. You're inside? Great, now, what are the walls surrounding you made of? Drywall? Stone? Mud? A cave wall? Anything goes, and it can change at a later date if it is no longer satisfying.

If you're outside, what's under your feet? Dry grass? Limestone? Sand? What kind of sand? Sand is largely comprised of the materials in the water surrounding it, so each kind of sand has its own wholly unique makeup, color, structure, and feel. The black sand beach of Reynisfjara, Iceland, is different from the pink sand beach in Moriya, Japan.

What is overhead? A blue sky? A green sky? A purple tapestry? Acoustic tile? You get the point.

Once you get to the point that you feel you've got a good starting place, it's time to journey. Standing in the center of your inner space, it's time for the next step. If you have a spirit guide that you work with, you can meet them in this space to talk about your plan to meet plant spirits to aid you in your magical practice. No spirit guide is required; you don't even need to believe in spirit guides. This goes at your own pace. Spirit guides are there for anyone who would feel more secure in their practice with one.

You may choose to meet the head of the Rosaceae family, or you might choose a plant you know. If you're not sure where to start, choosing your favorite plant is a good place to start. If you don't know any plants, look to your spice cabinet. There may be some great allies there waiting to meet you, like garlic, paprika, or cumin. Just because they're not green and growing in a pot doesn't mean that you don't have help if you want or need it.

Your plant spirit could appear as a green, growing plant, or they may choose a humanoid shape to more easily relate to you. They may speak to you, or you may receive telepathic impressions. You are building a relationship with the spirit of this plant, just the way you would human friendships, offering information about yourself, listening to the things they share, and getting to know each other. As with human relationships, getting to know someone enriches our lives.

Getting to Know the Spirits

When meeting the spirit you've chosen to interact with, try to have some pre-planned interview-style questions ready. Not every spirit you want to meet with will have the time for you that you have for them. Some may be impatient, some may speak more slowly than you're used to, merely due to the fact that their physical existence is on a different timescale than you're used to. Trees for instance have a much different scale of time than you or I are used to. Their slow response is great if you're looking for magical longevity, say in your prosperity work. A tree will think in years and decades rather than minutes and seconds.

Your interview questions may sound similar to this:

- How can I best work with you?

- Do you have any plant allies that can also assist me in this work?

- Would you be willing to introduce me to this spirit?

- Is there anything you'd prefer I not do while we work together?

- Is there any way I can show appreciation for our work together?

Remember that modern science understands only so much about the world we inhabit. If they talk about being older than your understanding of them, that's okay. If you don't understand everything they talk about, ask clarifying questions. You're building a relationship together.

Because we are building relationships with plants that don't rely on their physical presence, we can develop magical relationships that *don't rely on their physical presence*. Read that again. We can work with plants outside our ecosystem. We can work with *extinct* plants. We can work with plants that are prohibitively expensive or otherwise hard to obtain.

Relating to the Spirits of Plants

When looking to connect with a physical plant, it is beneficial to find the queen tree/plant/fungi in the area, as they'll know the area best. What is a queen tree? This in many cases is the oldest tree in the stand (a geographic grouping of plants), the first specimen in the area. In other cases, it might be the strongest tree, but in either case, they're in charge of their domain. For this purpose, it's the oldest plant in a stand of your plant ally. Look to the center of a stand of plants you see, and try to find the tallest, oldest specimen. Examine it with your inner eye, and see if it feels to be the oldest plant in the area. If it's safe to do so, consider meeting this specific plant in your inner landscape and asking if it is indeed the oldest specimen in the area, and if they'd be willing to answer some questions. Manners will get you a long way; just remember to approach them with respect.

Extinct Species

In Ancient Rome, there lived a plant that was supposed to prevent disease, act as a contraceptive, make food taste better, cure nausea, remove corns on the feet, and even break a fever. How can one plant do all of this? Well, we don't know, *yet*. It was such an important plant that the image of it was inscribed on Cyrenian (modern day Libya) money. Sadly, it was so important that it was considered extinct before the fall of the Roman Empire. However, in August 2023 a scientist in Turkey believed he'd found the plant. Silphium is the name of this miracle plant, and if it has resurfaced, it could mean a series of incredible discoveries is just around the corner. But can any plant live up to this amount of hype? The *Ferula drudeana* that was discovered on a rocky hillside a thousand miles from where it was last seen has antitumoral effects that have already been documented. Whether this is the famed Silphium plant bears further research and testing. You might try connecting with this member of the *Apiaceae* family to see what they have to tell you.

INDIVIDUAL PLANTS IN MAGIC

Talking to the spirits of plants and their heads of families is a great way to get to know them, but don't discount the physical plants that grow in your physical space. The maple tree on the corner, the dandelion growing between the sidewalk sections in front of your apartment building, the stand of tulips you pass on the highway each spring—they each have something to offer you, if you're open to talking to them.

My younger sister B had a friendly relationship with the second maple tree in our childhood yard. She talked about the maple as though they were her imaginary friend. B even went so far as to sneak into our home to steal a paper plate from the pantry and give her tree friend a face for B to talk to. Adults who caught wind of a child talking to a tree might have small smiles and a pat line about how imaginative children are, but Witches know the truth. Children don't have their connection to the Other stamped out of them by society yet.

Individual plants have the ability to form connections, just as the arch spirits of those same plants. Just as you can form relationships with a Catholic friend, and you can write a letter to the Pope, they're both Catholic, but they aren't the same person. For instance, if you have a plant that is associated with protection, you can task it with protecting your home and property. It's a two-way street; offer something to them to pay them for their time. Fertilizer and care are popular offerings.

Affinity with Botanical Allies

Have you ever been in a plant nursery, hardware store, or even a big-box store and noticed a plant that you knew you just had to purchase, take care of, and get to know? When you feel it in your bones, you know it's time to get to know that plant, whatever it is. The plant you find can tell you a lot about yourself or your magical needs—and the remedy is that plant. As a teen I fell in love with a sweet-smelling landscaping shrub. Its flowers were sweeter than jasmine; it had beautiful black-green foliage and it would get big enough to make hedges out of. As I moved into my own home, I wanted to track down that incredible plant, so I went back to the nursery where I found it the first time and smelled that incredibly heady fragrance. I bought some for my home and looked it up in my magical herb texts. Wouldn't you know that it was a magical herb famous for protective qualities. I didn't make the connection before then because in the nursery we used Latin binomials and in most magical texts, they used the common name.

Plants that you're meant to develop relationships with will let you know. And if you don't get the message the first time, maybe they'll come back around to ask again.

Creating a Magical Intention Oil

1. *Decide your intention*—The most important step is deciding to do the working. Once you've committed yourself to the idea of a working, you start building your reserve of energy that'll be dedicated to the working you intend: money, protection, peace, whatever you settle on. It needs to be specific enough to be attainable, and specific enough that you then know when the goal has been reached. Money isn't a specific enough goal. "I need $98 before next Tuesday to pay a parking ticket" is a pretty specific goal. "I need Bob to repay the money he borrowed, because I need $98 before next Tuesday to pay a parking ticket, and I want to receive it in nickels and dimes" is a little too specific.

2. *Write the spell*—It's time to figure out just exactly how much effort you're going to put into the spell, by writing it. Start by searching for the broad category of magic and the plants involved. Narrow that by application. If Suzy doesn't have a bathtub, only a shower, then making her a bath oil is pointless. Remember, every moment of looking up correspondences, colors, looking at your apothecary's supplies, deciding what type of application or carrier oil to use, the shape of candle to use, is powering the spell you're writing. Think of it like you're choreographing a ballet. You've got to decide everything from where the candles go, to what incense you're burning (if any), as well as how long to chant or what safety precautions you use.

3. *Gather supplies*—Now it's time to gather your supplies; every moment of time you spend on this intention is stored up in the intention to power the spell you're writing right now. That includes the energy in the form of money you spend on supplies if you have to run out to the local witchy shop to find just the right ingredient.

4. *Bless your supplies*—It's common to see candle blessings included in spell-work before the actual spell begins, because it's important to transform the item, say, a candle, from a mundane item into a magical one. In this

case the candle was poured in a warehouse, shipped to your local shop, unpacked by a clerk of the shop, possibly handled by customers, and on and on. You want to remind the candle that it is a magical tool and that its aim is to help you attain your spell's end goal. But first you've got to bathe the candle so it forgets the lousy day the delivery driver had and the grief of the candle's pourer and everything in between so that it can concentrate on your goal without excess interference.

5. *Do the thing*—It's time to do the spell you've written. Just like cooking, the *mise en place* or "putting in place" before you start the spell means that you don't have to jump up, scare your pet, knock over supplies, or potentially risk a hazard while working your working. By having everything where it needs to be before you start, you can fully concentrate on where you're going and what needs to happen. It's especially important for magical workings because you're trying to raise energy, and stopping to run to the shop because you forgot the candle you needed before you started means all the energy will evaporate like helium from a second-day balloon.

6. *Evaluate*—Now it's time to see how successful you were. I usually give a full twenty-eight days to give my final ruling on how successful or un- my working was so I have a full picture of just how much work was accomplished. Instant results are amazing and the stuff of television and movies, but most magic takes time to evolve and things to fall into place before they're ready to go.

Let's try it together:

7. *What am I doing?*—My friend Suzy has suffered a loss, and I'd love to be able to support her in her time of grief. I don't have a specific timeline as I know grief is malleable and goes through cycles.

8. *Writing the spell*—How can Suzy use the gift I'm preparing? She's crying a lot, so something to help her meter her breathing is a good idea. I'll make her a nasal inhaler tube that can provide comfort and soothing. So, I look up some of the plants associated with grief. They are: basil, cassia, citruses, cypress, frankincense, geranium, grapefruit, lemon, lime, Melissa, rose, sandalwood, vetiver, ylang-ylang. I know that Melissa (lemon balm) aids in processing the physical symptoms of grief, the pain, the anxiety, the sadness, so I know I want to include that. What from this list is going

to smell good with lemon balm? High-quality frankincense has a citrusy note to it, so that'll be lovely, and it has antidepressant effects as well. May Chang (*Litsea cubeba*) is uplifting and associated with prayer, centering, and strength. I know that'll be important in the coming days. Cypress helps us accept loss and calms anxiety, and its scent is evergreen and will pair with the citrus theme of uplifting.

9. *Gather supplies*—I needed to reorder nasal inhaler tubes from my supplier, but luckily they're close by. I make sure I have all the essential oils on my list, as well as a 2 ml bottle. I blend the oils in the bottle, because it'll work better to make sure the blend works as is and it'll provide a uniform experience for Suzy as the end user.

10. *Bless your supplies*—I blessed the nasal inhaler tube and 2 ml bottle, as well as a pipette and other tools. I asked the spirits of the essential oils to lend their help to guide me in the creation of the oil. Had I gotten a "no, thanks" feeling from any of them, I'd have traded out that oil in favor of something else. They know their limits better than I do.

11. *Do the thing*—I started with the lemon balm because I feel like it should be the star of the show, as the physical symptoms of grief are a) the hardest to deal with and b) get the least attention. I started with 20 drops of lemon balm. Frankincense was next for the spiritual support and antidepressant effects, so I added 10 drops to the 2 ml bottle. The uplifting of the May Chang and strength are going to be needed in the background as she has immediate family involved in the grief and she wants to support them as much as possible. Five drops of May Chang went into the 2 ml bottle, because it's a strong scent, even with the creamy lemon aroma. Because cypress is also pretty strong I didn't want to overpower the citruses so only 5 drops went into the bottle.

I put on the lid and rolled the bottle between my palms to mix it and then placed a drop on a plain tissue to see how it came out. Oxygen is the important factor here, as you need air to properly smell the blend created. It was perfect for the needs of Suzy, and once the blend settled, I added about 1 ml to the cotton that I had placed inside the nasal inhaler tube. I placed the end cap and labeled it for Suzy with directions and ingredients in case anyone else wondered what it was, as they might have allergies. I kept the original bottle of magical oil as well in case she loses the first one or it helps so much that she'd like to continue working with the scent in the future.

12. *Evaluate*—I'll check in with Suzy after twenty-eight days to see if she's needing anything different. She may not use it at all, she may have different needs a month from now, anything can happen. If she doesn't use it, there are plenty of reasons why that might happen, and I won't take it personally. She may have negative associations with citrus-like scents. She may have lost it in the shuffle of loss and grief. Remember, those who are undergoing the grieving process will have difficulty with memory as their bodies are taking over the daily care tasks, as the emotions and mind are somewhere else. The evaluation will come when Suzy is ready to, and I trust her to let me know what her needs are at that point, when she'll be in a better place for a more in-depth personal consultation. In the meantime, I know she has what support I can give her. Update: She was incredibly touched and felt that the blend I created was exactly what she was looking for. In a follow-up discussion we added a bracelet that acts as a focal point to her inner work.

From a Sacred Plant Magic perspective, this is already a success because I was able to connect with each plant in the magical perfume, and each one let me know they were willing to work magic for Suzy's benefit with her consent. Even if one had communicated that they didn't want to help Suzy, I would have called it a success because I got the feeling in my heart that they communicated their wishes. Remember, the point in here is that plant allies are spirited beings with their own agency, even if they aren't "people" per se.

BUILDING BOTANICAL RELATIONSHIPS 3

GETTING TO KNOW ENERGY IN PLANTS

Getting to know plants by their energy signature is learned just like any language as children. We look at pictures, associate the picture with a word, and we repeat until it's so ingrained that there's no thought process; it's an immediate one-to-one correlation. This can be difficult if you have no background in working with plants, but it's never impossible. You can start with the spice cabinet. What we're doing is exploring our minds for memories or experiences that had an impact on who we are, to see how they might shape us as people. We are also creating a scent vocabulary for further exploration of perfume, ritual oils, and other botanical allies.

Spice Cabinet

Take a look inside your kitchen cabinet and you can take a trip around the world. Each spice, herb, and flavor has a rich history of use in medicine, folklore, and witchcraft. No matter where you start, you can't go wrong. No matter your experience, there's going to be some history in that cabinet, even if the only things you saw were salt, pepper, and take-out menus.

EXAMPLE

Black pepper has a recorded history that goes back to mummification in 1279 BCE. Think about the contributions to history that a plant has with that length of service. It was used as currency in ancient Rome. It was such a common occurrence that the city of Rome was held hostage in 410 CE and one of the demands was three thousand pounds of black peppercorns. The use of black peppercorns as currency continued to occur until the 18th century, and the drive to find the spice that bolstered the world economy was one of the driving forces in European colonialism.

WHAT TO DO?

Take a spice jar (in our example, we're doing black pepper, but you can choose anything in your spice cabinet) and find a comfortable place to sit with a notebook and pen. Close your eyes, and take some cleansing breaths. Open them, and take your spice jar in your nondominant hand (sometimes called the receptive hand) and give a nice long smell. If it's a strong smell or something potentially irritating, use the waft instead of a direct inhalation. There are a lot of really lovely smells in the spice rack, but we don't need it lining our sinuses. Notice the aroma itself, as well as any associated shapes, colors, symbols, or memories that come up when you smell it. Repeat the smell inhalation two more times. This gives our nose and brain time to collaborate and make sure they've dug up any really important memories from the depths of your mind and experience. Write down anything that comes up after these smells. Feel free to break it up into sights, sounds, colors, shapes, and other things that arise so you can compare it to other scents and spices you try next. Building your scent vocabulary can help strengthen connections in your mind between allies you already know and ones you're learning as we go through this book together. Mine might look like this:

> Black pepper: Smells sweeter than I expected. The spice is there, but it's warm and round, instead of sharp and hot like other peppers. Reminds me of gray wool sweaters.

First, we established the name, black pepper. Then we experienced the aroma. Bonus points if it's a spice that you have the essential oil counterpart to for comparison.

> Black pepper essential oil: sweet, tangy, warmer than the spice, but still not as sharp as expected. Perfumy.

We've connected your present sense of smell to the plant name, and hopefully we've connected you with any sense memories that stand out.

(Feel free to come back to the journal entry if any memories come back in the next days.)

Dialing in That Connection

Now that you have experienced that plant material in recent memory and have a connection to that plant spirit, I'd like you to try to connect to the spirit of that plant.

We've talked about your inner landscape and how to furnish your "mind palace"; now we need to populate it with friends you've invited to the party. If you were calling a friend on the phone, you'd dial their number, and that secret code would connect your phone to theirs. Unlike texting, it would require someone to pick up on the other end, instead of waiting in your text inbox for the messages to be picked up. In the spirit realm, your secret code is the name of the plant spirit you're hoping to establish a connection with. You can use the Latin if that feels more formal, respectful, or clear, but the connection is the important part.

1. *Enter your sacred space*—with a notebook and pen, whether it be your bedroom, a spare room, a closet where you've got some safe feelings, wherever you feel magical. Sit or lie comfortably.

2. *Close your eyes*—Center yourself in your physical body. Feel the scattered energy lingering in fingers and toes coming into the center of your body. Send any excess energy you're not using into the earth, where the planet can use it much more efficiently. Bring up small amounts of energy into your being if you're feeling low energy.

> **Pro Tip:** The earth isn't the only celestial body. If you've practiced grounding/earthing enough to be an advanced practitioner, consider picking a celestial body. Venus and Mars are the next closest celestial bodies after the moon; try one of these three bodies and see how that energy changes how you feel. Make sure to record your findings for later.

3. *Start relaxing*—By going muscle by muscle we can build in enough repetition to allow you to enter a trance state. Start by relaxing each and every toe individually. Then relax your calves, knees, each muscle in your thighs, all the way to the top of your head. (You'll be surprised how much tension you carry in your ears alone.)

4. *Picture (or feel) yourself in your inner landscape*—however you've decorated and built your space to be your sanctuary. Whether a castle, a college dorm room, an open meadow, or your local witchy shop, your inner landscape is the virtual start screen for any journeys we undertake to meet the spirits of the plants we will be working with.

5. *I always include visualizing a walking meditation*—on a set of rainbow stairs to help move my brain from the physical (red) to the spiritual (violet). I reverse this visual when returning to my body after the journey is complete.

6. *If you work with a spirit guide in your inner landscape, feel free to invite them to join you*—If this isn't a part of your practice, that's okay, too. The important part is your feeling of safety and security. If you'd like to work with your spirit guide but haven't met them yet, feel free to add that into this journey, or build in time at another point to meet them.

7. *Speak the name of a plant you are hoping will meet with you*—Or ask that a plant spirit who has a message for you to come forward.

8. *If no spirit comes forward, go for a walk to explore your inner landscape*—Look around to see if there are any plants making an appearance. They should surprise you; you shouldn't be trying to see anything specific if they didn't make an appearance when requested. Remember, this is a cooperative relationship. We have no authority to order any spirit to appear in this place and time. That's a different style of magic. (Not better or worse, just different.)

9. *If a spirit comes forward, have some low-energy interview-style questions for them*—"How best can I work with you?" "Is there anything you need from me to best work together?" "Is there anything you'd prefer I not do while we work together?" On the first meeting, don't expect to get all the secrets of the universe; we're building a relationship on the first meeting. Subsequent meetings will make it easier to ask difficult questions and to be able to receive the answers in your heart. If no spirit comes forward and you go to walk about, make note of the plants that appear (trees, ivy, bushes, and so forth) so that you can figure out their meaning when you're back in your body (so to speak).

Working with New Allies

Linden—Linden is a loving plant ally to signal to the universe that you are ready for a new loving relationship. Working with the spirit of Linden encourages respect, both for you to show, and for respect to be shown to you. Linden inspires calm and allows us to recognize our needs, especially the ones we have neglected in favor of others. As a loving ally, linden helps find lovers who are faithful and have relationship longevity in mind, and is also a plant associated with protection magic, so it can help find a relationship that is safe for your heart and body. This working can work to bring both new platonic and romantic relationships, because both are important for happy, healthy humans.

The Spell

Supplies:

- Choose a candle (white, pink, or red depending on intended outcome, or all three!)

- Candleholder

- Ballpoint

- Enough jojoba oil to anoint the candle

- Linden flowers, leaves (dried linden from a bulk herb website is also okay)

- 1 handful salt

The white candle signifies purifying those past behaviors that you'd like to overcome, as well as feelings of loss, fear, depression, and the like that you already overcame. The pink candle represents the ability of the Witch (you) to understand and embrace the love they have for themselves. Move lastly to the red for blossoming love and understanding with a new potential partner, whether romantic or platonic.

A flat surface like a plate or serving platter is ideal to place your candleholders on to keep the spell contained for easy cleanup. Carve the word "linden" into the candle surface that you choose with a ballpoint pen. Anoint the candle with jojoba oil for removing blockages to your desired goal.

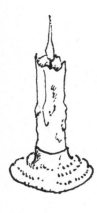

Place the candle in the center of the space in the candleholder. Next, mix one handful of salt (purification) with one handful of linden flowers and leaves. You can do this in a bowl or with a mortar and pestle. We want to incorporate the two as best we can. Once they are mixed well, sprinkle the mixture in a line to form a small circle an inch or two away from the candle.

Add more linden to the salt mixture and do a second ring.

Add more linden and make a third ring.

The center ring will have the most salt, the outside ring, the least. Think of it as a multistage water purifier. We are taking the energy that the candle is putting out and forcing it through filters of love, protection, and respect.

When it is time to light the candle, picture the emotions you have overcome to make room for a new person in your loving relationships. Remember, there are so many types of love—love for family and siblings, love of your teammates, love for your home; each is different.

We are growing and moving through our lives as loving adults. You may have heard some (toxic) adages about not being able to love anyone if you don't love yourself. Please understand that this couldn't be further from the truth: we all deserve love. Sometimes we didn't receive the love we were meant to in our homes as children, so it can be hard to know what loving relationships look like until someone shows you how to love appropriately. It has nothing to do with your ability to recognize feelings directed at yourself. You're an incredible person, and I can't wait to see what you do with this life.

Connecting with Plants outside the Physical

Working with plants as spirit beings means that we can work with and develop relationships with plants that we might not otherwise have access to, due to time, distance, cost, scarcity, and a number of other factors. In this case, it can be important to interact with that plant as a spirit being using your inner landscape rather than interacting with the plant itself.

One such example would be to interact with the spirit of a plant that you're allergic to. It isn't safe to handle plants that you're allergic to, but it can be a fulfilling experience to meet that plant ally on the spirit plane to ask what you're supposed to learn about that plant through your allergy. There could be a message in it. There could *not* be. But you don't know until you ask.

1. Enter your sacred space.

2. Relax your body.

3. Count down from ten to one to settle your mind further.

4. Feel yourself enter your inner landscape.

5. Invite a plant you are allergic to, to meet with you in sacred space. Ask them what you can both learn from each other through this allergy. For example, if you're allergic to plantain, a common weed found in grass, you might learn that you avoid healing parts of yourself that you see as not being too bad or not bad enough to warrant treatment. Where does this understanding come from? Plantain (both broadleaf and narrow leaf plantain) is an anti-inflammatory, a vulnerary (wound-healer), and astringent (draws out poison, venom, and irritants like bee venom, spider venom, and the like).

6. To discern the meaning in any botanical associations, you can check field guides, herbal books like *The Modern Herbal Dispensatory: A Medicine-Making Guide* and magical herbals like *Blackthorn's Botanical Magic* and *Cunningham's Encyclopedia of Magical Herbs.*

   Quick note: folklore is a vast and varied subject, but some Beings (with a capital B) can get offended if you thank them. If you feel strongly about showing your appreciation, ask them how they feel about the words "thank you" and if there's anything they might ask of you in return for helping you. Debts are a funny thing. Make sure it's something you can 100 percent do, as breaking your word to spirits can have disastrous consequences.

7. Once you have the information you need, exit your inner landscape, and write down everything you can remember. You may have more vivid than usual dreams, and parts of your journey may come back to your memory hours or days after a journey. That's completely natural, just write it down when you can, as you remembered it for a reason.

Just make sure to get a nice grounding meal afterwards and plenty of rest that evening.

FLOWER ESSENCES FOR ALLYSHIP

4

In the late 90s, I joined my first coven. In this tradition, each coven chose a specialty to benefit their community, and as the high priestess was an emergency room nurse and many of the members were in the medical field as doctors and nurses, it seemed a very fitting calling. As a part of that coven, we were trained in so many healing modalities, from color therapy to Reiki, aromatherapy, massage therapy, and, lastly, to Bach flower remedies, which are a form of flower essences. But what are these essences and how are they a benefit to witches?

Let's start at the beginning. Samuel Hahnemann (1755–1843) was a German physician who in the course of his study railed against much of the modern medicine of his time. He saw that bloodletting and other techniques taught in medical school were doing more harm than good. After all, what good is it to treat the disease if it kills the patient you are treating? He left active practice in 1784—a year after he married—and devoted himself to chemistry and the study of medicine to further the cause of medicine, rather than the practice of it. It was during these studies, in 1796, that he came across a piece of information he found interesting. The bark of the Peruvian tree, cinchona (a member of the coffee family), was listed as a remedy for malaria. Hahnemann decided to test that material for himself. He soon noticed that this cure for malaria quickly produced the same effect as malaria in the curing of same. He became entranced with the idea that if you could find substances to cause reactions similar to the ailment, you'd found the cure for that ailment. Another hallmark of Hahnemann's work was the theory that dilution of the elixir or essence had the opposite effect from what you might think. Instead of the dilution of your essence making the elixir weaker, homeopathy states that it's concentrating the spirit of the botanical you're hoping to build a relationship with.

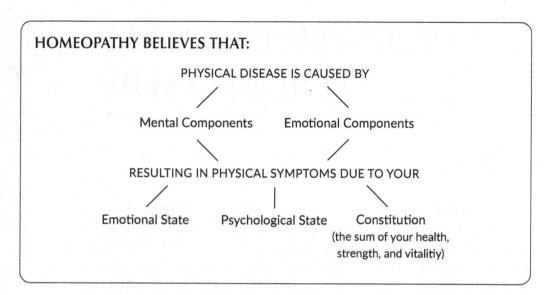

HOMEOPATHY BELIEVES THAT:

PHYSICAL DISEASE IS CAUSED BY

Mental Components   Emotional Components

RESULTING IN PHYSICAL SYMPTOMS DUE TO YOUR

Emotional State   Psychological State   Constitution
(the sum of your health,
strength, and vitalitiy)

So homeopathic practitioners and holistic doctors won't ask about your allergies or your peptic ulcer. They're going to ask about your daily life, your emotional state, stress level, and mental state to see where your baseline is. They're going to treat you like a person, rather than a list of symptoms. An initial visit could be multiple hours rather than a fifteen-minute prescription dash.

Because there is no identifiable plant matter in these flower essences, the results have been mixed as far as scientific, peer-reviewed, double-blind studies go. Some show the results consistent with the placebo effect, and some show slightly better outcomes. However, because there are no measurable quantities of plant matter in these elixirs, they can't interact with medications you're already taking. They generally have very few side effects (allowing for placebo and an occasional negative dip in well-being when elixirs are first utilized). Not only can they be made by practitioners but also pharmacists and drug companies.

The interesting thing about homeopathic remedies is that, if they claim to treat ailments and diseases, they are regulated (in the United States) by the Food and Drug Administration (FDA). The FDA started regulating homeopathic remedies in 1938, so this isn't a new fad. Keep in mind that dietary supplements, herbs, minerals, vitamins, and other supplements are *not* regulated by the FDA, because they're considered food, not drugs. If you claim that your product diagnoses or treats ailments, you have to have the regulation of the FDA.

Hahnemann wasn't alone in his theories. Paracelsus (1493–1541) came up with a similar theory in the early 1500s called the doctrine of signatures. The idea he posited was that God's divine plan included a cause and effect or a design for every plant known to man. This divine plan included ways to let people know what the intended use was for each leaf, seed, and flower. The instructions are on the box, so to speak. It depended on a complicated series of observations about the flower or leaf based around colors, shapes, and other physical characteristics. For instance, the leaves of the lungwort plant would be used to treat asthma because the leaves were shaped similarly to that area of the body. Carrots have an eye in the center of the root, so they would be designed to support eyesight. Yarrow would be used to treat liver function because the yellow flowers are aligned with the yellow color of bile. This has been largely disproven in the medical field, but it lends itself to an easy way to decipher the needs and uses for magical materials including spellwork. If red candles are used for passion, then flowers good for magic surrounding passion could be red as well. The color green is associated with healthy and vibrant plants, and therefore also prosperity magic. Eyebright is used in preparations for the eyes and clear sight, so it is also magically sound to use it when you need clear perspective.

Following in these footsteps, we have Dr. Edward Bach, a medical doctor and a homeopath, who developed thirty-eight flower essences in the 1930s. These essences are part of the reason the FDA wanted to start regulating homeopathic remedies. It was the heyday of the homeopathic movement, and creating a remedy for whatever ails you has always been appealing. To this end, Edward Bach took a blend of five elixirs to create a mother bottle of the master remedy he dubbed Rescue Remedy for soothing anything that's ailing you emotionally, from panic attacks to depression. The five elixirs he used in Rescue Remedy are Cherry Plum, Clematis, Impatiens, Rock Rose, and Star of Bethlehem. Bach was the one to bring the widely publicized remedies to the Western world, but information exists that other groups and practitioners experimented with Paracelsus and Hahnemann and others' material before Bach's seminal work.

These essences now allow people to alleviate emotional symptoms of trauma with the plants best suited to them, without concern for comorbidities, illness contraindications, or drug interactions. Today, the list of flower essences extends to the furthest limits of your imagination. If you'd like to work in concert with plants' spirits, their flower remedy makes a great starting point, especially if it's a daily or long-term working relationship.

What Does All This Mean?

Homeopathic medicine is a fascinating practice and makes an incredible ally in the search for wellness. For the sake of this book, we'll be talking about flower essences as a means to connect with the spirits of plants without the risk of physical interactions.

Here's the original list of thirty-eight flower remedies, from the Bach Centre.

Agrimony—mental torture behind a cheerful face

Aspen—fear of unknown things

Beech—intolerance

Centaury—the inability to say no

Cerato—lack of trust in one's own decisions

Cherry Plum—fear of the mind giving way

Chestnut Bud—failure to learn from mistakes

Chicory—selfish, possessive love

Clematis—dreaming of the future without working in the present

Crab Apple—for not liking something about ourselves

Elm—overwhelmed by responsibility

Gentian—discouragement after a setback

Gorse—hopelessness and despair

Heather—talkative self-concern and being self-centered

Holly—hatred, envy, and jealousy

Honeysuckle—living in the past

Hornbeam—tiredness at the thought of doing something

Impatiens—impatience

Larch—lack of confidence

Mimulus—fear of known things

Mustard—deep gloom for no reason

Oak—the plodder who keeps going past the point of exhaustion

Olive—exhaustion following mental or physical effort

Pine—guilt

Red Chestnut—over-concern for the welfare of loved ones

Rock Rose—terror and fright

Rock Water—self-denial, rigidity, and self-repression

Scleranthus—inability to choose between alternatives

Star of Bethlehem—shock

Sweet Chestnut—extreme mental anguish, when everything has been tried and there is no light left

Vervain—over-enthusiasm

Vine—dominance and inflexibility

Walnut—protection from change and unwanted influences

Water Violet—quiet self-reliance leading to isolation

White Chestnut—unwanted thoughts and mental arguments

Wild Oat—uncertainty over one's direction in life

Wild Rose—drifting, resignation, apathy

Willow—self-pity and resentment

How to Make Your Own Essences

To dwell in the presence of your chosen plant spirits, consider making your own essences. While Bach concentrated on flowers and leaves, other plant material can be utilized to different effect. Roots might be more grounding, flowers more airy. Think about the energy of the plant before you decide that you'll use it.

You'll need:

1. *Sun*—A sunny day makes the process infinitely easier and quicker to execute. It's not absolutely necessary, but it'll take less time to infuse. We aren't exactly making sun tea here, but the light helps speed the process.

2. *A field guide to your area*—If you aren't working from plants you know or have grown yourself, make sure you have a way to verify the plant you are talking to. Peterson Field Guides are a reputable resource here in the states, but you'll need to ask around for suggestions in your area. There are plenty of poisonous look-alikes, and poisoning yourself is the opposite of our goal here. A word of caution: if you aren't 1,000 percent certain what a plant or flower is, do not put it directly into your water, but rather alongside the glass vessel so it can charge the water. (This is also appropriate for a plant who would rather you not cut its blooms.)

3. *Consent*—We are discussing ways to work with the agency and spirit of plants, so it stands to reason that if an individual plant doesn't want you to cut its blooms, and you do so anyway, that's a shortcut to a bad start with your new potential ally.

4. *Water*—We're going to use the medium of water to extract the spirit of the plant material.

5. *A glass bowl and jar*—Only one needs a tight-fitting lid.

6. *Sharp scissors*—Dull scissors will do more damage to the plant than sharp ones. We want to harvest the material with as little harm to the plant as possible.

7. *Colander or cheesecloth*—To strain out the plant material.

8. *Preservative*—This will be the medium that will preserve the water we're using and will keep mold or bacteria from growing within and making you sick. Traditional remedies use brandy, which has a particular flavor, but many people have sensitivities to alcohol, are in recovery, or frankly don't like the taste. Vegetable glycerin and apple cider vinegar both make great substitutes for the brandy. (I prefer the vinegar flavor, however you are the captain here.)

9. *Labels*—I harp on it for a reason: we always believe we will remember what went into that random amber glass bottle, but I promise you, it's easy to forget. Even if you remembered, will friends or loved ones know what it is if you ask them to grab something, if they investigate on their own, or have another reason for looking?

10. *Two-ounce amber glass bottles*—These are the perfect bottles for storing your elixirs, as they protect them from sunlight and have a handy dropper included.

11. *Notebook*—It's important to write down any messages you get from plants as soon as you get them; like a dream, those messages can disappear from your memory quickly.

12. *Optional: gloves*—If you're in the weeds, wandering the woods, or encountering plants you're not familiar with, consider wearing gloves. Some practitioners worry that it'll lessen their feeling of the energies in the plants they talk to, but some flowers have toxins that can be absorbed through the skin. It's not worth the risk of poisoning yourself. Make sure to check your field guide to look for the poisonous/venomous/irritating culprits in your area. Poison ivy, poison sumac, poison oak, stinging nettle, and others are important to know on sight. Even if you work with the spirit of Nettle, you don't want a sting you aren't prepared for.

To Create Your Mother Bottle Essence

First thing: decide what kind of project you're undergoing. If you have a garden, a patio planter, a window box, or the like, this is a great place to start because you know if they've been sprayed with chemicals that could be harmful to your body or the spirit of the work. Say you grow your own lemon balm and it's starting to flower. Normally you'd want to harvest the blossoms at or before the time they start to flower, because the point of this plant is its lemony aroma and sedative properties, and flowering will lower the quality of both. Since this is an essence we're looking to create, I might choose that plant to work with first. The first foray being close to home means I don't have to drag all of my equipment to an abandoned field in the middle of nowhere.

Advanced students: Once you've done some plant communication and know what to listen for, let your intuition guide you to plants that will be more willing to talk to you.

Be careful if you intend to go foraging for materials to use in your elixirs. Don't wander into someone's yard without their permission; no elixir is worth getting hurt or arrested over. Be wary of well-tended public parks as they may use chemical sprays to cut down on manual labor.

Once you've decided on a plant whose energy you'd like to get to know, talk to it! This can be out loud or not, just establishing communication. For a first-time meeting, or if you haven't done a lot of nonverbal communication with other beings so far, you might only get an impression of yes or no, and that's okay. Plants that aren't around people don't really get a chance to learn the language of those people, so they might communicate in pictures rather than words. You might feel sunshine warmth for yes and shaded cold for no. If their communication is not clear, and therefore their consent is ambiguous, take it as a *no* and move on to another plant. As with all consent, clarity is important, and a *maybe* is a *no*. We're striving for a "yes means yes" rather than "no means no" because non-action should be understood as a no. If they can't consent, it's a no.

If this is a plant that you don't know, consider taking a photo of it for later reference with a professional.

Once you have your answer, ask the plant if they have any messages for you. They may tell you what their essence may help you with. If they didn't want their flowers used, they might tell you why. Since *no* doesn't mean "convince me," just let them know you're here for any information they may want to share. For instance, they may say no because they were sprayed with a chemical and are dying; you just can't see it yet. Whatever the reasons, thank them for taking the time to talk to you. If you got radio silence from the plant you've chosen, there's probably a reason, and it's a sign to move on to a different plant. If three or more plants in a row refuse to talk to you, I'd move to a different site, as there could be an environmental problem in the area affecting the flora, and you don't want that in your body anyway.

Once you have consent to cut, take no more than 30 percent of the plant's material. If you're specifically aiming for flowers, take a few from multiple plants (who all consented) so that the seeds that result from these flowers can create more flowers for someone else. Cut the flower as close to the base of the flower or cluster of flowers as you can. All that energy the plant was devoting to creating flowers will still be heading toward the end of the branch, and it'll push new growth for the next set of leaves to produce new branches. In horticulture this is called "pinching."

Fill your glass bowl with clean water. Place cut material in the bowl as soon as possible after cutting, because the spirit's tie to its plant starts to die the moment the plant is cut. So as much as we'd like to cut down on the things we carry, don't cut your material and then take it home to make an elixir. If you're tight on time or concerned about safety, bring a clear glass jar with a tightly fitting lid rather than a bowl, so you can place your plant matter on the go.

Let your elixir sit in the sun for 4 hours (a sunny window is fine) while you record any information in your notebook: helpful hints from the plant you took the material from, experiences with plants you met along the way, especially if anything unusual happened. You want to be able to refer back to this in a year if another plant has a similar experience, if the elixir is producing some interesting effects, and so forth.

Strain your plant material out of the water. The plant material may or may not be appropriate to compost on your property. Use your own best judgment. Place your strained water into another container and reduce by one half with the preservative of your choice. I use the giant bottle of apple cider vinegar from the bulk store for cost-effective measures. If you use 1 cup of water, you will need to add 1 cup of apple cider vinegar. (If you're using vinegar, make sure that it's 5 percent acidity or more. In order to produce cost savings, some brands are now offering a 4 percent acidity vinegar, which will not preserve your water safely.)

Place this new mother elixir that is 1 part charged water to 1 part vinegar in a clean amber (color doesn't matter) glass bottle, as clear glass will allow more UV light to get into your elixir and degrade it over time. Label your new bottle. I recommend: plant common name, Latin name if you know it, date of creation, and location of harvest. Feel free to include the intent of the plant material if the plant gave you any specific insight. You've created your mother bottle of this elixir.

Creating Your Elixir

Once you have your mother bottle established, you'll need 1 ounce of water and 1 ounce of apple cider vinegar per 2-ounce bottle that you would like to create. So if you're making five bottles, you'll need 5 ounces of water and 5 ounces of vinegar; mix these in a pitcher. Line up your 2-ounce bottles along with a small funnel. Drop in 5 drops of your mother elixir per bottle. Then using the funnel, fill each bottle to the shoulder with the water/vinegar mixture (leaving enough room for the dropper without spilling) and cap with your dropper top. I prefer to have my labels written out before filling, so I don't forget to label. Once I get creating, it's chaos in my kitchen. Make sure the bottles are completely dry before attempting to label; it's going to make the process much less frustrating. Make sure to include the name of the plant spirit in the bottle (at the very least) and perhaps what the elixir does for the person and date of creation.

What Do I Do with It Now?

It's fun to create new remedies, but don't get eyeballs-deep in botanical mad-scientist mode before you know what to do with these, or you'll wind up with more than you'll ever use. (Ask me how I know!)

A single plant spirit elixir can be used to create a desired effect very simply. If you're working with a plant and aren't quite sure what that relationship can bring you, it is time to do some research. This can be done in a number of ways:

Head to your local library and check out the botanical information on the plant.

Start with the witchy books in your personal library to see if you spot your new ally. Books like *Blackthorn's Botanical Magic, Cunningham's Encyclopedia of Magical Herbs,* and Pearson's *Flower Essences from the Witch's Garden* are great places to start.

Get comfortable and visit your inner landscape to meet with the plant spirit you are developing a relationship with and ask them directly. If your mind is focused on the creation of the botanical elixir it might be difficult to be in the right mindset to hear the advice given out in the field. Also, a key piece of information may have slipped your mind until they bring it up again in your journey.

Visit your local greenhouse or landscaping company to see if their employees know the plant there. They might not understand your discussing energies with them, so probably stick to any horticulture information they have; there may be a nugget of wisdom in there.

Visit your local witchcraft shop, and see if anyone there knows the material you've found and what they might do with it. It might be a traditional use you could find in a book, or it might be an insight the practitioner has themselves that'll open up a new world inside your understanding of this plant.

Lastly, try a drop of the elixir in your water and observe the effect it has on you.

To experience that plant spirit, you can place the elixir itself under your tongue, add a drop to your water or other drinks, or add it to lotions (like with our scent activation work; see that chapter for more information) or aromatherapy diffusers. The list of experiences is endless.

With two or more elixirs in one bottle, this remedy is as customizable and personal as each practitioner. For the original thirty-eight that Bach cultivated, there are tests to help you understand which elixirs are best suited to your needs. If you're creating your own, I like to think of it as a math problem: Plant + Plant = Overall Feeling, or Feeling + Feeling = Plant (depending on your needs).

Examples:

Elixirs of basil and patchouli wouldn't go well together as an essential oil synergy, but as botanical elixirs, they can do wonders!

Basil—develop abilities, prevent abuse, connect to inner assertiveness

Patchouli—strengthens the body, defenses, and happiness

This sounds like a winning combination for handling a bully at school or in the workplace.

Helichrysum—clarity, healing trauma, self-realization

Davana—counterattacks, divination, initiation, uncrossing

Yarrow—strengthen psychic ability, bless marriage, defeat chaos

This elixir could help ease the pain of divorce, loss of friendship, or leaving a coven.

Apple blossom, geranium, or vervain—happiness

Azalea, cedar, pomegranate, or tangerine—clarity

Papaya—clarity in romantic relationships

This is a great blend of options to help find relationships that are romantically healthy.

Create a custom elixir, once you've figured out which elixirs to blend. I'd suggest no more than five elixirs in an accord (two or more elixirs in a single container) or it'll sound like too many radio stations playing on different devices at the same time. Add a drop or two of each elixir to a clean 2-ounce bottle and fill the rest of the way with your water, apple cider vinegar solution. Then label it with the desired effect first (to differentiate at a glance between single botanicals and accords) and the botanicals it contains second; and don't forget the date. Make sure to write down the formula for the accord in your notebook for recreating later.

You can work with these elixirs:

- for the short term to get through difficult situations
- for a month to get to know a single spirit better
- for a year of ritual action with a specific intention
- until you finish a bottle, then you can reevaluate what you need in your emotional bank right now
- you can blend flower essences with gemstone essences to create a truly custom treatment plan
- the sky's the limit

Check for further ideas in the Botanical Divination chapter!

Further Reading:

Hennessy, Alena. *The Healing Guide to Flower Essences*. Birmingham, AL: Sweet Water Press, 2020.

Pearson, Nicholas. *Flower Essences from the Witch's Garden: Plant Spirits in Magickal Herbalism*. Rochester, VT: Destiny Books, 2022.

Stein, Diane. *Healing with Flower and Gemstone Essences*. Twin Lakes, WI: Lotus Press, 2012.

PLANT SPIRIT FAMILIES 5

Connection

Our interconnectedness with the plant world can offer so many benefits. Not only are we getting to know the plants as spirits unto themselves, with agency and consenting minds, but also that reciprocal information can be lifesaving.

Before becoming an author, I was the head of security for two high rises in Delaware. With such a high-pressure job, I was working a lot of hours, and in and out of the office at all hours of the night putting out literal and figurative fires. Before taking over my post, during training, my first day we had a bomb threat, a death threat, and a suspicious package. We'll say it was a high traffic job, which as you can imagine didn't leave much time for my Craft. I felt like the longer I was there, the less connection I had to "Amy the Witch," as "Amy the Head of Security" took over every waking moment.

Everyone has times in their lives when their magic seems out of reach; it's natural in such a busy, harried culture. I was looking for a reconnect. The full moon came and it was time to venture out into my yard to connect with my land spirits and let them know I hadn't forgotten them. As I gathered my libations and tools, I had a feeling of peace I hadn't experienced in a while. This is what I had been missing.

I set off around the yard pouring libations and singing to the spirits. As I came around the first corner of the yard something caught my eye: the purple-green of young poke plants. They had sprung up between the last moon and this one. Uh. Oh. You see, poke (*Phytolacca americana*) is toxic. It's used for food and medicine, but all parts are toxic and have to be prepared in a specific way so that they're not harmful to people. That's the thing about magical associations and plant spirits. If it can protect itself, it can protect you. So, all of the "nasty" plants with thorns, barbs, urticating (irritating, hives-inducing) hairs, toxic sap, and all the rest? They're great allies to have in your protection magic.

I came upon this stand of poke in my back yard. In my practice of green witchcraft, presence, location, and proximity are all important factors in understanding the message our spirit allies are bringing us. It's not like they can take out a billboard, so you've got to pay attention. So, I have a stand of a protective plant in my back yard. What is it I *need* (urgency indicated by multiple plants) protection (poke) from that I can't see (behind me)?

I had to go through my life with a fine-tooth comb to parse out the danger. It turns out that my day job had brought me to the attention of a dangerous man. If I hadn't gotten the warning I needed from my friends, Poke, I might not have lived to tell the tale. That makes it my job to help you connect with the plants around you, so that you can understand the messages they're sending and what they mean.

LANGUAGE OF THE SPIRITS

The interesting part of all of this is that Spirit and spirits (including plant spirits) can only tell us things that we'll understand because of the ways our minds work. They can yell all day, but if it's in a language we don't understand, we can't get the message, so it's in their best interest to find common ground for the language spoken. That's why plant spirits (among others) don't speak in words so much as images, pictures. "A picture is worth a thousand words" indeed. It might be harder to interpret the messages sometimes, but you'll get there. The hardest part of the interaction isn't the listening, though most people expect listening to the spirit of a plant to be the hard part, it's the interpreting that can trip us up.

For example, a few years ago I was driving on a busy highway and in my mind's eye, I got a video message showing a spinning tire hitting gravel and gravel scattering. I turned to my traveling companion and asked, "I have a bottle jack under the back seat, right? I didn't take it out for anything right?" More to double-check myself than to them. I knew my mechanic always checked on my spare when I took my vehicle in for an oil change.

"What's up?" they asked. I told them of the visual I'd just gotten from the spirits. "Yeah, it was still there when we went to IKEA. We're good." It was then that the car in front of me hit a patch of gravel and spun its tires. I braced for what I expected was a blowout, when a rock hit by the car in front of me jumped up and smacked into my windshield—*crack*. It had played out exactly as my guides had warned; the fault was in my interpretation. That's where many of us trip ourselves: the interpretation of the images we see. The only remedy for that is practice. As with any new skill, the first few times you do it, it'll be decidedly not great. That doesn't mean you shouldn't do it. We often learn more from mistakes than triumphs.

When writing down your spirit encounters, whether in your Book of Shadows or a separate journal, try to be as literal and descriptive as you can. You can include your interpretations of the literal symbols being used, but make sure to include both, because upon further review you can learn a lot about the language being used by your spirit guides (whatever you may call them) through repetition and review. Think of it as a Magical After-Action report.

PSYCHIC TRAVEL AGENCY

In a class with ten other psychics, we were working on establishing our reach. The further out you look, the less likely a certain outcome is, so practice is vital, even for psychics who have been reading forever. In our outlook we were looking specifically at travel for our reading partners in the next six months. I got two symbols that didn't mean anything to me at the time. I had to sit with them a moment before relating to my practice partner, "They're showing me my index finger and a brown and white sign with a Jeep on it." My friend Laci's face was then tacked on at the end and it all clicked. "OH! You're going to Michigan. They use their hand as a state map. You're going to right here," indicating my index finger. "There's a state park here, hence the sign with the Jeep on it." My practice partner was shocked. Her father has a cabin on the edge of a state park in Michigan. She had a lovely time.

As an intuition client, she might never have gotten the message if I'd just stopped with "Finger" and "road sign." We've got to go on that journey with them. Our spirits need us to feel out that connection to make sure we're getting where they're hoping we follow.

Spirit's Scientific Names

What does any of this have to do with plant spirits? We need to understand who we are speaking to, and why. I knew the intuitive input I was getting was coming from my spirit team, because we have worked together for thirty-plus years. However, getting to know a new plant spirit can be difficult if you don't know with whom you are speaking.

I was working on the section on bergamot, when I was writing *Blackthorn's Botanical Magic*, and seeing associations like commanding, compelling, confidence, and good fortune with a rulership of Sun and fire. However, one book I was checking as a potential source listed a rulership of Mercury and air, and said things like soothing magic including beestings, and academic success. I was flummoxed. It took a bit of work, but I figured out what the problem was. The magic I'd been working on was for *Citrus bergamia* and the book I was attempting to check as a source was talking about the other bergamot, *Monarda didyma L.* Monarda, also called bee balm for its ability to calm beestings, is a member of the Mint family, while our true bergamot is a member of the Rue family. This is why we use scientific names, rather than common or colloquial names. Regional differences, common features, and a host of other problems arise from using common names. For instance, do you have any idea how many redbud tree species there are? A lot.

So, what are scientific names? Otherwise known as Latin binomials, they're the two-part name given to recognized species (as they can't have a Latin binomial if they're undiscovered). The Latin binomial can give us a fair bit of information, like who its close relatives are, and often an identifying part of the plant. This system is referred to as binomial nomenclature. It includes the family tree of the plant. This family tree is known as taxonomic rank. When talking about plants, it includes kingdom, division, class, order, family, genus, species, and sometimes variety. For example, *Salvia spathacea* is a Salvia species that's popular with hummingbirds. So, because Salvia is such a huge group, it could be referred to as *Salvia spathacea*, Hummingbird Coral. The important part is binomial nomenclature creates clarity across regions, countries, and languages. Latin binomials contain the genus and species of the plant.

Lavandula angustifolia and *Lavandula spika* were cross-pollinated to make *L. x intermedia* or lavandin. Just calling something "lavender" leaves out a lot of the story.

While lavender (*L. angustifolia*) is a great healing ally for burns, lavandin doesn't have as much of the chemical makeup for healing, but it is great for disinfecting. In Great Britain it is used to disinfect hospitals because it is so good at its job. In perfumery, lavandin is used almost as much as lavender. It has a more pronounced green note and is often called green lavender, citrus lavender, or lemon lavender. If a casual observer saw a label saying lavandin, they might assume it's a typo. Using the Latin name illustrates knowledge of the plant as well as its hybrid status (that's what the *x* means). First, we need to understand how magical associations are determined, and then we'll talk about where they go.

How Are Plant Alignments Determined?

The traditional model for understanding the magical alignment of plant allies comes from Paracelsus' doctrine of signatures. The idea was that God (He/She/It/They) put a road map for the usefulness of each plant into the appearance of that plant so that humans would understand why they were created. The doctrine of signatures originally included the medical uses for plants as well, but science has largely discounted that. For example, the dual circles of the interior of a carrot may look like an eye, so carrots can be utilized in magic for clearly seeing the reality of a particular situation. Lungwort looks like ulcerated lungs. It doesn't hurt that species of butterflies and moths use lungwort as a primary food source in spring.

The plants that we seek to align with carry a dedicated lineage of use going back thousands of years. However, printed records don't always go back that far due to time, effort, prejudice, cultural issues, and more. So, when you come upon a plant that you don't know personally and cannot confirm their planetary associations, there are a few ways to determine their alignment. Botanical spirits rely on several aspects, from the growth habit to the nature of the root system, the aroma, or toxicity.

Sun—Plants that boost immunity and/or align themselves with happiness and vitality, like citruses.

Moon—Plants that are shade-loving, milky, consume a lot of water, or grow in muddy spaces are aligned with the moon. Think lotus flowers.

Mercury—These plants will be light and airy and imply movement even while still, like dill.

Venus—These plants are showy, soft, and luxuriously scented and have Venusian qualities, like roses (*Rosa spp.*).

Mars—Thorny, itch-inducing, or aggressive plants are Mars attributed, like poison ivy and wineberries (*Rubus phoenicolasius*). Mars also rules the immune system (imagine white blood cells carrying spears), so if it's strongly immuno-supportive it can have Mars attributes.

Jupiter—If your plant ally produces a prolific amount of seeds or nuts, Jupiter is their ruler, like walnut.

Saturn—Deeply rooted plants, poisonous plant families; commonly are perennials.

Botanical Families

The Mint Family

The first family we're talking about is the Mint Family (*Labiatae*). It's a *big* one. Under this minty umbrella there are 236 genera (plural of genus) within the family. To fit under the same family umbrella, each plant has to meet certain criteria. This highly debated topic can lead to the name change of plants, no matter how long the history of a plant includes the previous name.

One such example is rosemary getting its binomial changed from *Rosmarinus officinalis* to *Salvia rosmarinus* in 2017. Before this name change, it was the only plant in its genus, and it took both a structural look and a DNA test to convince the governing board to change the name. Angel's trumpet, *Brugmansia*, is another. Experts argued for years as to whether it was a *Datura* or not and it changed hands several times.

Going in order, some of the genera found in the mint family are *Agastache*, where we find the minty-spicy anise hyssop, which is related to true hyssop but has morphological differences that place it in a different family. The family includes *Lavandula* and all the lavenders, as well as *Melissa* or lemon balm. The family is named for *Mentha* because the variety of mints is so vast. Just look at a seed catalog, and you'll find there are over four hundred varieties of mint from classic peppermint, to Corsican mint (the leaves are smaller than the head of a pin and it is so small it grows like minty moss), chocolate mint, orange, apple mint, and the list goes on. Here's the sneaky wild bergamot, *Monarda* or bee balm. *Paravitex* is the mother of chaste tree berry, *Vitex agnus-castus*, or Monk's Pepper. The *Perovskia*, commonly called Russian sage, falls into this family as well. *Pogostemon* is the mother of patchouli but there are ninety-two *Pogostemon*s in the family, so don't lump them all in with *P. cablin*, patchouli. The fragrant oil associated with the hippie movement is the result of fermenting patchouli leaves, so if you'd like to work with the plant, but are put off by the earthy aroma, fret not as the plant isn't quite so fragrant.

One of the debated genera in this family is Salvia. The sage genera has over 987 accepted species of Salvia. Rosemary (*Salvia rosmarinus*), garden sage (*Salvia officinalis*), clary sage (*S. sclarea*), white sage (*S. apiana*), and diviner's sage (*S. divinorum*) are just a few and they vary wildly in size, shape, and effect on the human body, so simply calling something "salvia" is ambiguous at best, and not best practice.

MAGIC OF MINT FAMILY

While the magic of an entire family will have outliers, the point of introducing you to this system is to give you a general way of discerning the magical character of a plant for those times when you encounter a plant that isn't in magical tomes derived from a 15th century magical system (for example). New world plants won't be in those books. Plants that hadn't been discovered yet won't be in those books. Plants native to the Americas might not be there either.

The element associated with the mint family is air, and you can see where that association comes from, with airy leaf structure and floral arrangements on the stem. The planet associated with these plants is Mercury, which makes the day associated with them Wednesday.

Magical uses for the plants in this family tend towards purification, clarity in communication, good luck, uplifting the spirit, gain of material objects, physical healing, psychic power development, the release of negative emotions, magic that spurs action in communication, divination, and relaxation. Many of the plants in the Mercury magical realm can also be utilized in magical oils to remediate the effects of Mercury retrograde that quarterly wrap up of all the outstanding projects on your to-do list.

Another family with Mercurial/air associations is the Poaceae family, or grass family, where we find lemongrass.

Another route for magical associations comes from their history. Patchouli (*Pogostemon cablin*), for example, which was being recorded for medicinal use in China around the 5th century CE, began its journey from India and made a stopover in South Africa before heading to England. It was the saving grace of the trade route for precious Indian textiles that were stored for months at sea in the hulls of ships, which, by the time they arrived at their final destination, were moth-eaten, moldy from all the water, and rat infested. Something had to be done to protect the investment during the months at sea. Enter the brave patchouli. These precious textiles were layered with patchouli leaves to keep them safe from mold and pests. When the ships reached their final destination, all the cargo was unloaded. The Kashmir fabrics, later called cashmere, were hung on clotheslines to sell, and the patchouli leaves were piled on. Well, with all the time and money spent to ship these leaves, they had to be worth something. So, they were used for another good that was shipped in the hull: India ink. India ink gets its signature scent from the patchouli leaves that once guarded the fabric at sea. The markets became famous for their beautiful perfume, as the textiles carried the scent of the patchouli they'd been stored with for months at a time. It became the perfume *de rigueur*. For the rest of the Victorian era, patchouli was considered to be the height of sophistication and glamour. Since these markets were where money came to be earned and spent, people associated the scent of patchouli with money, and the magical association continues to this day, even if our society has forgotten *how* it came to be.

The Citrus Family

The citrus family has a history of recorded use that goes back seven thousand years in India and in China since 2500 BCE, and contains more than sixteen hundred subspecies. In that time it has had seven major divisions in the ancestral species. *Citrus reticulata*, the mandarin orange, is the mother of most of the citrus family. The other citruses: the citrons, kumquats, papaedas (makrut lime is in this group), Australian, and New Guinea species are all a part of this parentage.

Citrus maxima, the pomelo, is the next core species. If you haven't had the pleasure of eating a pomelo, picture a grapefruit with a thick white rind that takes it from the size of a softball to a volleyball. It's well insulated from the cold. Most "oranges" (*Citrus sinensis* varieties) are a synthesis of *Citrus reticulata* (mandarin) and *Citrus maxima* (pomelo). It has been a process thousands of years in the making. Each subsequent new fruit has been cross-pollinated with other members of the family to get the sweetness, firmness, color, and flavor that we understand today.

MAGIC OF THE CITRUS FAMILY

The element associated with the citrus family is fire. The solar associations come from the observation of the citrus plants, as it takes a lot of direct sun to transform those orange blossoms into fruit. So, all fruits will have the inherent magic of transformation, due to the lengthy process it takes to go from flower bud to juicy orange. The day of the week for the citrus family is going to be Sunday. The other magical associations are abundance, affection, antidepressant, creativity, fertility, beauty, business assistance, change, charm, harmony, innocence, joy, memory, overcoming problems, persuasion, power, prosperity, purification, and strength.

The magical outlier in the citrus family is lemon (*Citrus limon*), which carries both the solar aspects of the Citrus family and the lunar aspects. This pairing of lunar and solar identities is what leads it to be associated with the full moon.

Grapefruit demonstrates the magic of all hybrid species, as it has the magical power and association of both parents' lineage.

The Rose Family

The Rosaceae family, or rose family, started as six subfamilies and further divided from there. One of the six most commercially significant agricultural plant families is without a doubt the rose family, which includes the crop plants: almonds, apple trees, blackthorn sloes, cannabis, hawthorns, quinces, strawberries, rose hips, and roses.

MAGIC OF THE ROSE FAMILY

The magic of the rose family is air and Venus. The Venus association aligns these plants with Friday. That Venusian influence means a magic involving love, wisdom, and intuition of the heart. Beauty, compassion, harmony, other planes, banishing, antianxiety, awareness outside the body, clarification, communication, confidence, creativity, hex breaking, honor, inspiration, and gentleness all exist here. Venus imparts an inherent magic in dealing with luxury goods, so if you have a want as opposed to a need, and this luxury item is outside of your budget, doing magic with any of the above listed fruits, say, on a Friday, has a great chance of success.

As with our Citrus friends, all fruits have the inherent magic of transformation, due to the lengthy process it takes to go from flower bud to fruit. If your spell calls for a Venusian flower and you're allergic, look to the fruits of the rose family and try to find something you're not allergic to, like apples.

The Myrtle Family

The family Myrtaceae is home to allspice, clove, guava, and the eucalyptus plants. The family came about around 60 million years ago and since then has developed a wide following. In the eucalyptus genus, there are over 420 species used in aromatherapy alone. More varieties will be discovered in the future. Because it is a new-world plant, it can be hard to find magical material because it wasn't around in England in the 1400s when a lot of herbals were being written and the groundwork laid. Luckily, we have the rest of the Myrtle family to help carry the magical torch, so to speak.

MAGIC OF THE MYRTLE FAMILY

The magic of the Myrtle family is of the earthly element, and of the planet Venus, which means its day is Friday. The magic of the Myrtle family involves

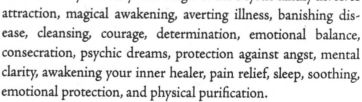

attraction, magical awakening, averting illness, banishing disease, cleansing, courage, determination, emotional balance, consecration, psychic dreams, protection against angst, mental clarity, awakening your inner healer, pain relief, sleep, soothing, emotional protection, and physical purification.

So, what do you do if you don't know about the botanical family of the plant you've just found on the side of the road? Can you still do magic with it? The short answer is, yes.

Blackthorn's Book of Sacred Plant Magic

Doctrine of Signatures in Magic

Paracelsus (1493–1541) developed the concept of the doctrine of signatures, writing that "Nature marks each growth . . . according to its curative benefit." The idea there was that God would have wanted to show men what plants would be useful for. So, the road map that God created would have been in the plant itself. His original plan for the Doctrine was intended for medical application of herbs, and while that has been disproven largely by modern science, it still applies to the magical and ritual use of plants.

For example, carrots' inner circle of the root looks like an eye, so we could use it for magic concerning the health of the eye as well as for intuition or far seeing and the like. Although the carrot didn't exist as we see it in grocery stores today, it has depictions in a 6th century copy of the 1st century pharmacopeia by Dioscorides. Eyebright was used for eye infections, owing to the supposed resemblance of its flower to an eye. This can be used in magic for revealing hidden sights, seeking the truth, or clearing up confusing situations.

So, if you don't know what plant you're dealing with, look at the plant—colors of flowers, shapes of the flowers, and leaves are telling. Needles are protective, pink flowers are loving, blue flowers are calming. Heart's ease and pansies both have heart-shaped "faces" so they're popularly used in love spells to ease a broken heart. If you're unsure, the doctrine of signatures can help. Rosemary has flowers that look like vulvae, so it can be used for marriage, courage, release, wisdom, fidelity, passion, beauty, comfort, determination, purification, and so much more. It also has needle-like leaves, so it can be used for protection, confidence (projection of self-image), strength, stimulation, vitality, and willpower.

If you find you know even a little something about a plant, it can help. If you can, look up the Latin name and figure out its familial connections. Chances are it'll be related to something you do know, and is listed in the books.

Family Matters

Heads of Families as Intercessors in Your Rites

Now that we understand where the Latin comes in, we're going to talk about the heads of these plant families, and how getting to know them can help you discern for yourself what the magic of a certain plant is, if it doesn't have a listing in your favorite magical herbal. If you don't know the magical attributes of a specific plant, you can always go up the ancestral line to the head of the plant's family and ask them for the boon you seek. For example, if you're allergic to apples, try going up the ladder until you get to *Rosaceae*, where the Rose family originates. The family contains all manner of flowering plants, trees, herbs, and shrubs, so it's a wide-ranging family with over three thousand species world-wide. While you might not have a single plant to point to in the morphology of *Rosaceae*, you can invoke the spirit of *Rosaceae* in your inner landscape and ask them to help on your behalf, either in the magic itself or on behalf of the more available species—in this example: apple. Simply visit your inner landscape and ask for the help you seek from the spirit *Rosaceae*.

Upon a first meeting with any spirit, plant, or otherwise, it's polite to introduce yourself and try to get to know that spirit, as best you can. In developing the friendship/relationship you can understand how best to work with them, as well as give them opportunities to learn about you, and humans in general. They may have never met or spoken to a human before. When answering questions as an ambassador for the human race—whether I like it or not—I like to begin in general terms and then move into specifics about myself and my feelings, beliefs, and experience secondly. While this book is devoted to working with the plant spirits, remember that all life has the overarching spirits with which you can develop a relationship, from the spirits of the worms in your garden, to the ancestor spirit of dogs. When you reach out to the spirit of the worms in your garden, think of it as the worm king, who can help communicate your needs: "I'm tilling today when the sun is directly overhead, if you'd like to move out of the way of the earth mover." You could ask the spirit of the Arch Dog to help keep your canine best friend safe during a stressful time.

I first encountered this idea around 1994–95 when I found a copy of *The Findhorn Garden* by The Findhorn Community and William Irwin Thompson in a friend's home library and was entranced with the idea of being able to communicate with beings outside myself that weren't mammals, or even vertebrates.

BOTANICAL DIVINATION 6

Whether utilizing essential oils or flower essences, or finding an ally to work with, divination can be an important guiding light to finding the correct ally for any given situation.

Divination is defined as the attempt to foretell future events but has been expanded to include attempting to divine information through other means. Water-witching for a good spot to dig a well? That's divination. Using a wedding ring as a pendulum to determine the sex of a baby in the womb? Divination. Growing up, I'd hear my aunt talk about the woman in her Catholic neighborhood who would read greeting cards for the neighbor women because using playing cards or tarot cards was forbidden. The point is that divination can absolutely fit into your life, wherever you make room for it. Patricia Telesco, herbalist, folk magician, and author of *Magick Made Easy*, teaching you how to make a tarot deck made from the coupons in the Sunday paper? Super accurate. A handful of shells from your trip to the beach three summers ago? Great for emotional connection to your querent.

Essential Oil Divination

In this take on sortilege (any divination by lots), bottles of essential oils are our lots to cast.

Choose Your Own Divination

This method is derived from an older style of divination, based on ideomotor movement, or involuntary movement caused by a thought. This is the belief that our intuitive sense, inherited by all people, knows what we need best and is often employed in choosing between flower essences. The querent closes their eyes and the person facilitating the reading hands the client two different bottles of essential oils. They quickly choose the one that feels energetically right. This process is repeated for several essential oil bottles, forming the story line of the reading. The bottles never need to be opened if there is a fear of a medical situation (like migraines), allergic reaction, or overstimulation. It can certainly be a part of the reading's story to incorporate them, but need not be.

EXAMPLE:
Client was handed two bottles at random: marjoram essential oil and galbanum oil. They chose galbanum.

Galbanum
Magical Meaning: Spirit counsel, divination, exorcism, sensual, sacred.
Sortilege Meaning: The time has come to listen to your inner voice and connect with your spirit guides, ancestors, and inner desires to see the way forward.

This pair and pick process can go on for as long as needed to tell the story and answer the querent's questions.

Pick Three

In keeping with the theme of agency, if you don't have a friend who can hand you essential oils to test, place the essential oil bottles on a surface like a plate, at random. Close your eyes and spin the plate until you can't remember where any of the oils were placed. Pick three oils at random and place them in front of you in a past, present, future reading to see what you've gotten.

EXAMPLE:

Benzoin: Past
Magical Meaning: Exorcism, peace, wisdom, confidence.
Sortilege Meaning: In the past you've cleaned house to make room for growth and gotten rid of anything that took away from your peace of mind or ate away at your confidence.

Myrtle: Present
Magical Meaning: Death, preparation of the dead, marriage, fidelity. Good fortune.

Sortilege Meaning: In the present you've made sure to stay true to yourself, and processed and released any sorrow related to your benzoin past, and made room for good fortune.

Rosemary: Future

Magical Meaning: Confidence, happiness, hex-breaking, strength, transformation.
Sortilege Meaning: Your future is pretty bright! You've moved through the Tower Card energy of myrtle, and now the sun is coming out to greet you. You're stronger than before, but you had it inside of you all along.

Recipes as Divination

You can replicate this style of divination by using recipe cards as a divination tool, as well as grabbing actual bottles or writing down feelings recipes inspire on Popsicle sticks and casting them onto a cloth. I use the center of the cloth as home base, or the significator representing myself. Feel free to play around with the format. I've used the box of 2 ml bottles of perfumes from *Blackthorn's Botanical Magic* for these examples to tell a divination story. You can pull three bottles like in our previous example:

PAST: TIME TO LEAVE THE NEST

Magical Meaning: Self-control, benevolent power, peace, protection.
Sortilege Meaning: Hey, it's a good thing you got out when you did. You're at the height of your personal power; you read the writing on the wall and got out while the getting was good. Great job.

PRESENT: NEW BEE

Magical Meaning: Awakening, balance, centering, spiritual development.
Sortilege Meaning: You're in your *element!* Everything is lining up your way, you've got all the tools you need to BEE your best self, and now it's time to seize the moment.

FUTURE: LUNAR LOVE OIL

Magical Meaning: Love purifying, lust, sex, healing the past.
Sortilege Meaning: You're deserving of love, and past relationships don't define who you want to be in the future.

Casting of Recipes

I lay out a round cloth that I use to carry divination tools in. The center has a gold star embroidered in it. This represents me. With my eyes closed, I pick five oils at random, jumble the tiny bottles in my hands, and cast them onto the cloth, where I hope the center of the cloth is. I open my eyes and see the closest to the center (me) is . . .

LUCK LUSTER OIL

Magical Meaning: You're golden. I interpret this as the Sun card in the tarot. Optimism, joy, friendship.

Sortilege Meaning: The energy closest to me is the love of friends, and they are my strength.

The two bottles close together: *Mabon* and *Self-Improvement*.

MABON OIL

Magical Meaning: Strength of character, renewal, calm focus, reduce impact of past trauma.

Sortilege Meaning: Mabon (the perfume oil) is a testament to your personal strength, and seeing it paired with Self-Improvement means that you've dedicated yourself to being a better person, not just for yourself, but for the people you surround yourself with.

SELF-IMPROVEMENT OIL

Magical Meaning: Releasing negative emotions, striving for balance, and transformation.

Sortilege Meaning: Seeing Self-Improvement with Mabon shows that you understand how hard dedicated improvement is, but how worth it it is to have the sense of renewal that comes from the pruning stage.

The last two oils bounced off the reading cloth, so I discarded them from the reading space.

With the recipes as divination tools, you can physically make the recipe in question, or pick a few of the notes from all three recipes to create a talismanic perfume that resonates with your reading and the outcome you want to encourage.

Decks, Both Tarot and Oracle

There are so many beautiful tarot and oracle decks that are devoted to plants, it is a veritable cornucopia of ways and means. You could use a deck of plant allies to choose whom you work with for a day/week/month/year. It's a very empowering practice to find an ally to work with for your liturgical year (Samhain to Samhain) or a calendar year (2040).

My ally for a year was Mugwort. It taught me about how to let go of some of my anxieties that are out of my hands, to be purposeful and avoid accidents, and that we can resolve anger with the dead through communication and divination.

Sample Allies

ALLSPICE

Magical Meaning: Attraction—physical, courage, fear—to overcome, good fortune, kindness, determination.

Sortilege Meaning: You're a desirable person, because of both your physical appearance and your ability to overcome the fears that have come against you. You're due for some good luck.

ANGELICA

Magical Meaning: Let other people help you. Manifesting desires, exorcism, psychic protection.

Sortilege Meaning: You have the protection of the Archangel Michael, whether or not you've ever worked with him. Angelica also protects children, helps attract friends and helpers, instills harmony, and releases negativity. So make sure to leave the past in the past, while keeping your boundaries solid.

BERGAMOT

Magical Meaning: Ask for help, concentration, encouragement, improve mood.

Sortilege Meaning: Hey, you've got a *lot* going on right now, but you've got your life under control. It's just time to do some magical and physical housekeeping. If you have too many tasks, objects,

or goals, it's time to trim the list down as best you can, so little things aren't slipping through the cracks.

CYPRESS

Magical Meaning: Ancestor remembrance, assertiveness, centering, clarity, harmony.

Sortilege Meaning: Bring your energy back to center. You can gain clarity on your questions if you ask your ancestors, both familial and your oldest friends. They're here for you because you're always there for them.

DILL

Magical Meaning: Protection, averting aggression, defensive magic.

Sortilege Meaning: Lean on Mercury and any Gemini friends you've got in your pocket to make sure that your protection and wards are the best they can be. It's time to duck and cover.

ELEMI

Magical Meaning: Grounding, peace, magical skills.

Sortilege Meaning: Trust in your process: you've prepared for any eventuality; things are never as bad as they appear at first glance.

FRANKINCENSE

Magical Meaning: Meditation, banishing, strength, psychic awareness.

Sortilege Meaning: Things are in balance right now; you've got the strength of magic and the intuition of your situation to rely on. Don't go borrowing trouble.

GERANIUM

Magical Meaning: Renewed joy, uplifting, awareness of situation, healed relationships.

Sortilege Meaning: You've put in the hard work; now it's time to reap the rewards. Stop and smell the (Rose) geraniums!

HELICHRYSUM

Magical Meaning: Immortality, self-realization, memory, longevity.

Sortilege Meaning: You're healing generational trauma and making it look easy. You've got the power to go the distance; just make sure not to neglect your self-care routine.

JUNIPER

Magical Meaning: Protection, uplifting, awareness of past life, transformation.
Sortilege Meaning: You have covered every conceivable base, contingency, and potential problem. Allow yourself to rest, too. Hypervigilance is exhausting, and you've already done the work needed.

LINDEN

Magical Meaning: Love, encouragement, recognizing your needs, sleep, strength.
Sortilege Meaning: You have stability in your love life and you have the longevity to make your goals a reality. Protect your relationships as best you can; they are your community support.

MANDARIN

Magical Meaning: Calm, clarity, defense, purification.
Sortilege Meaning: Time for a magical cleanse; take inspiration from the plants and fruits around you. They've been doing this a lot longer than you have. They're now masters at defense.

NUTMEG

Magical Meaning: Good luck, strength, clairvoyance, hex-breaking, visions, focus.
Sortilege Meaning: You're on a hot streak, and everything is going your way. Just make sure not to lose focus when you realize how much hard work you've put into your success.

OAKMOSS

Magical Meaning: Money, forest spirits, divination, long-acting magic.
Sortilege Meaning: Trust your divination; there's something lurking on the edges of your energy. Make sure to fortify your wards and ground any harmful energies heading your way. You are in charge of your own space, and no one has the right to it but you.

PEPPERMINT

Magical Meaning: Clarity, uplifting, happiness, healing, psychic power, release.

Sortilege Meaning: Make sure you're not holding onto anything that doesn't serve you; it's easier to rise above without anything holding you down.

ROSE

Magical Meaning: Luck, clairvoyance, beauty, divination, spiritual awakening, courage, protection.

Sortilege Meaning: Your protection isn't what people think of first, but it should be. You're a force to be reckoned with when you need to be, but you prefer to show the world your sweet face and save the difficult work for only a last resort.

SUNFLOWER

Magical Meaning: Protected growth, conception, harmony, improvement, money.

Sortilege Meaning: The fertility of Sunflower is applying to be your new best friend, bringing all kinds of new friendships along with them. Cheerfulness and expression are yours for the taking.

TANGERINE

Magical Meaning: Uncrossing, power, releasing nervousness, bringing prosperity.

Sortilege Meaning: Consider whether you need a magical cleansing or to take some deep breaths. Is it intuition or anxiety?

VETIVER

Magical Meaning: Harmony, calm, win in court, releasing negativity, confidence.

Sortilege Meaning: The outcome looks great; you've got everything in place. Center yourself and move forward with purpose.

WITCH HAZEL

Magical Meaning: Heart healing, protection, emotional support, uncrossing.

Sortilege Meaning: It's been a long winter. It's time to come out of your shell, revel in the hard work you have done, and soothe any frayed edges.

YLANG-YLANG

Magical Meaning: Love, raising vibrations, strengthening spirit, peace, relaxing.
Sortilege Meaning: It's the Sunday afternoon sunshine bunch here. It's not time to start any new projects just yet. It's time to revel in the things you have accomplished thus far. Great work!

Take a moment to think of some plants you encounter regularly, in the kitchen, the garden, or even an office. Research their magical meanings and decide what they indicate for their sortilege meaning.

Plant:
Magical Meaning:
Sortilege Meaning:

Plant:
Magical Meaning:
Sortilege Meaning:

Plant:
Magical Meaning:
Sortilege Meaning:

Plant:
Magical Meaning:
Sortilege Meaning:

I RECOMMEND:

✦ For divination, *Kitchen Witch's Guide to Divination: Finding, Crafting, and Using Fortune-Telling Tools from around Your Home* by Patricia Telesco.

✦ For tarot, *Seventy-Eight Degrees of Wisdom: A Tarot Journey to Self-Awareness* by Rachel Pollack.

✦ For flower essences, *Flower Essences from the Witch's Garden: Plant Spirits in Magickal Herbalism* by Nicholas Pearson.

✦ For essential oils, *Blackthorn's Botanical Magic,* and *Essential Oils for Emotional Wellbeing* by Vannoy Gentles Fite.

- For crystals, *Love Is in the Earth* by Melody and Julianne Guilbault, and *The Book of Stones* by Robert Simmons and Naisha Ahsian.

- For herbs, *The Green Mysteries* by Daniel Schulke and *Wild Witchcraft* by Rebecca Beyer.

- For pendulums, *The Book of Pendulum Healing: Charting Your Healing Course for Mind, Body, and Spirit* by Joan Rose Staffen.

- For incense, *The Big Book of Magical Incense* by Sara L. Mastros and *Sacred Smoke* by Amy Blackthorn.

- For candle magic, *The Big Book of Candle Magic* by Jacki Smith and *Candle Magic Journal and Handbook* by Patti Wigington.

RITUAL MINDSET: 7
USE OF SCENT IN
TODAY'S RELIGION

The cultural implications of cleanliness and scent in cleansing

The culture that we live in is made of so many moving parts. There isn't really one culture when you look closely at any one person. We are walking Venn diagrams. I am Amy, a Witch, an author, disabled, neurodivergent, and so many more labels. Each of us walks around within the spiral of those Venn diagrams. As we walk through life, our circles intersect with the people around us in varying ways. I can go out to dinner with a Witchy friend, I can run into another author at the bookstore, I weave in and out of those circles, relating my experience to each person in an attempt to understand them, to empathize, sympathize, and connect.

However, our commonalities do not empower us to know that person's entire life experience. So then why do we assume that we know what their struggle is merely because we carry some of the same labels? We can only know what we know. That might feel reductive but everything we experience falls within the scope of its relation to our own experience. We can try to imagine what someone else is going through, but it really cannot match their lived experience.

When schools reopened in Florida, following lockdown related to the COVID-19 pandemic, a paraprofessional friend of mine noted that the teacher and the parent of one of her students were locked in battle. As they story goes, the teacher and the parent both wanted this child to be as safe from illness as possible, as any good parent and teacher would. What that meant was that this child would come home from school and have his backpack and lunch box scrubbed with cleanser to make sure he wasn't bringing any germs home and so it smelled clean to Mom. He would come to school, and his teacher would be concerned about the level of cleanliness and would again clean his book bag and his lunch box with *her* cleanser. The problem was that Mom used the cleanser that she was familiar with in her house growing up, and the teacher would use the cleanser that *she* grew up with in her house as a young person. To each person these cleansers meant clean in their home culture.

To Mom, the scent of clean is Fabuloso. To the teacher it wasn't clean until it smelled like bleach, so while this child had the cleanest backpack in the history of elementary school, both adults wanted to be *right*. Now, they are both right; they're both cleaning, that's the job of cleansers, but this struggle with perspective left this child confused as to what the *right* answer was.

I feel that, in the witchcraft community, we spend more time arguing over *what* clean smells like instead of doing the work of cleaning.

There are a lot of really beautiful botanical allies available to create relationships with that are looking to form relationships with us. When choosing your botanical allies, it isn't a matter of which one smells like bleach and which one smells like Fabuloso, it's a matter of your home, culture, understanding, and to some extent the access you have, at any given time. It's more important to do the work than to argue over which one is better. I want to help you, dear reader, understand the implications of both options, the bleaches of the world and the Fabulosos of the world, and empower you to make your own choice. The associations of the smells that you grew up with will have a greater impact on your magic than the ones someone *tells* you to have, as they're ingrained in our minds, hearts, and culture.

KITCHEN SPICE RACK

Uses of Plant Material with a Dynamism/Animist Mindset*

The botanical allies that most of us begin our journeys with and that are closest to our hearts live within the spice rack, in the kitchen. Before we have access to candles, or incense, many of us start that botanical journey through

---

* Animism is the belief that nonhuman entities have a soul or spirit that inhabits them; some include a personality. Dynamism on the other hand is the belief that those entities or objects confer magical power, for example adding dried basil to a love spell.

the food that we consume, both with family and on our own. When *Black-thorn's Botanical Magic* was first released, it was very common to hear, *I can't be a green witch. I kill all my plants.* I'm here to tell you that's not the case. Growing your own plants is beautiful, is empowering, but it isn't for everyone. Some people's lives are not conducive to watering the plant, to fertilizing the soil, or to getting in touch with the ground. Some people's lives involve working in a cubicle, way too many hours. Phobias of dirt, insects, outdoors, and more can keep your magic indoors. This does not make you bad at being a Witch. This does not mean you can't work with plants. The spice rack in your kitchen and the spice aisle in your grocery store are great places to start finding which allies are hoping to work with you. When we examine our daily lives, they are built around rituals: breakfast with your family or cereal with the news, showering before bed. These rituals mark important spaces in our lives. It isn't only bank holidays, Thanksgiving, and big religious festivals. It's about the day-to-day life that you cultivate with intention. Roasting garlic to be enjoyed with friends, chopping parsley for the potluck, each of these activities still matters. In many minds, and in common vernacular, it is common to think of herbs as fresh from the garden, and spices as dried in the cabinet. While people have been arguing about the difference between those two words for far longer than I have been alive, both options are valid when cultivating a relationship with the spirit of a plant.

Frankincense and Myrrh

POPULAR INCENSE AS A BRIDGE TO WITCHCRAFT?

Earlier, I mentioned the story of how *Blackthorn's Botanical Magic* came to be. The smell of incense during a family funeral transported me to the ritual room with my first coven at eighteen years of age. My story and my experience are not wholly unique.

Incense is a beautiful ritual practice across many religious communities. From Witches to Catholics who bond over frankincense and myrrh, Nag Champa has graced the shelves of so many witchcraft shops over the years. Incense as a religious practice divides time into discernible pieces linking our scent memory with long-term memory storage. When you smell your favorite incense, you are transported to a meaningful time in your practice. When you're just starting out, incense helps divide space from time and location from space. It divides the waking world from the realm of the Witch, within from without, time without time, in place without a place.

Incense is one of the practices that can most rapidly renew the faith, practice, and emotion of a Witch experiencing burnout. It signals to our bodies that it is time to embrace the ritual side of ourselves that has to be neglected in favor of earning a living, food, shelter, work, and practical attentions. It is no wonder that we respond so distinctly when presented with our favorite smells. Each incense pairing, each match lit, is a gateway to the next realm. It is no wonder that incense is one of the most appealing pieces to the witchcraft puzzle.

In high school, a dear friend's mother saw us buying incense at a local shop. Her first question was, "You girls aren't smoking pot are you?" My friend's older sister answered from across the store, "They aren't smoking pot; they're just witches." Half of the store laughed, and that broke the ice. For those of us who come to the craft seeking bodily autonomy and increased agency, the practice of utilizing incense gives us permission to alter our state of mind merely with a strike of a match.

This is one of the reasons that creating a Sacred Smoke practice that is based on your lived experience and not cultural appropriation is so important. You can build ritual experience into your long-term memory, but using experiences you already have in your long-term memory is a heck of a shortcut.

The Role of Incense in Ritual Magic

PERFUME AS GLAMOUR MAGIC

When a friend from out of town stayed with me a few years ago, she remarked how lovely it was that every time we got in and out of my vehicle she had a renewed sense of the perfume I was wearing. She was very thankful that I didn't wear any scent that her family history had ruined. She had a traumatic memory that she had confided to me, that she had a negative experience with a particular scent; we will pretend it is pine. When I knew she was coming to visit, I took all of my perfumes, located all the pine fragrances, and set them aside until she left. I wanted to make sure that I did not accidentally cause her any emotional distress by wearing something that might harm her emotionally even if she did not realize it. She may have merely felt ill at ease, and my job as her friend was to prevent her discomfort if I could control it. When she realized that I had gone out of my way to remove any perfumes that could be upsetting for her, she was very thankful. My comment was that I had plenty of perfumes without pine and that I was happy to create a safe environment for her. She later joked on social media that I could create a perfume to put someone at ease or to disturb them, just as easily. Understanding the people around us and their history is privileged information. This is information that could be used to their detriment in the wrong hands.

SECTION II

Deeper Connections

CONNECTING WITH THE SPIRITS OF PLANTS

8

Dedicating part of your spiritual practice to connecting with the spirits of *individual* plants is a worthy magical pursuit, but the *how* can be the most daunting part to some practitioners.

Who is going to do this?

Hopefully you, as you're reading this book, but who is going on this journey with you? I'd say the sky is the limit but in magic, there aren't a lot of hard and fast limits. So that leaves the plants around you. The indoor plants in your home. The plants in your neighborhood, on your street, and all around the world. That also includes plants that are no longer a part of this world, like extinct plants, plants from other epochs, and more. (*Note:* fungi are also inspirited beings with agency, but as they have more in common with *Homo sapiens* than the plants of this world, they deserve their own time and attention, and I could not do them justice.) If you have questions as to which plants to connect with, I will be interested in meeting and working with you.

What to do.

The mere act of connection has as many paths through the metaphorical weeds as there are people on the planet. What inroads we learn to make with our best friend won't apply to the kind fellow who works the deli counter in your grocery store. Plants are much the same. One of the best things we can do as practitioners, especially animist or dynamist witches, is think of plant spirits as individual people, in that they have their own personalities, cultures, and philosophies. Just because they aren't vertebrates doesn't mean they don't have thoughts or feelings and so forth. You just have to get to know them. To do that, you've got to make space for them in your life, just like any other spiritual practice or hobby.

Making Room for Plants in Your Spiritual Practice

1. **Make physical space**—To start with, you've got to make sure you have a space that you can make your own. Then you can make space for a plant spirit in your life. If you're getting to know plant spirits in general, consider making a check-in space for them. While it might look like an altar, this check-in space can be a physical reminder to connect with the particular plant spirit you're working with at that time. Just like friendships, a plant spirit can come into your life for a reason, a season, or a lifetime. If you're shopping around for allies, consider devoting any spare moments for a specific length of time, say a month, to learning about a single plant spirit. Say you like the smell of lavender. Your check-in space could consist of a lavender plant or photos/drawings of lavender, a plain tea light, and a lavender-colored scarf. I didn't mention a lavender-scented candle, because most commercial candles don't use essential oils for their candles because of the volatility of the candle fragrance, the amount that evaporates with the heat of the pour, as well as the potential flash point temperature. It's cheaper, easier, and in some cases safer to use synthetic fragrance in candle making. If you're interested in working with the plant's aroma and there are essential oils available commercially, consider making a spray of your own, rather than hoping the end use product has essential oils within. These check-in spaces are not designed for worship, so much as they're designed to give us a physical reminder of the work that we're doing. Think of it as the difference between a god's devotional altar and the workspace where you do spells. This could be the same physical space, or it could be separate because that work is separate. It all depends on the amount of space you have available.

2. **Make emotional/mental space**—I saw a quote on social media once, *A libation without a prayer is just a spilled drink.* —Sam Webster. Lighting a candle by itself may keep you warm, but unless you make space in your life for the plant you're getting to know, it's just a spilled drink. By making a dedicated time for the practice of getting to sit with the spirit of that plant, you're making space in your life for that energy too.

Finding Your Own Way

I used to volunteer for a question-and-answer website for experts on individual topics. I volunteered as an expert in witchcraft, and I got a lot of teens asking for love spells. Most adults would blow off a teen who asked such a question, but as the resident expert, it was my job to make sure they got good information. So, I'd send them my favorite love spell. They were expecting to hear something out of a horror movie, I suppose, that would make Johnny Doe fall madly in love with them. Instead what they got was, "Go to the local garden center, and buy soil, basil seeds, and a clay pot. Plant nine basil seeds in the soil and water them in. Nine is sacred to the goddess, and basil is sacred to Aphrodite. Then spend a little time each day talking to the basil pot; tell it about your day, ask how their day went. Water it only when the soil is dry or the leaves start to wilt."

"Then what," they'd ask.

"Then you keep doing it."

"When does the spell start? I don't have time to talk to a plant."

"If you don't have time to dedicate to taking care of a plant that needs only water, and you don't have the time to sit and tell them about your day because you're too busy, how will you have time to care for and nurture a relationship with another human being, who has complex needs, thoughts, fears, and agency of their own? By being able to pay attention to the soil, to the texture of the leaves, and to talk to the plant about your day, you're showing the universe, the gods, whoever, that you're ready for a relationship with another person. Then the right person can find you." This isn't about violating and abusing someone else's free will and agency. We don't develop these relationships merely for whatever extractive reason we might need something. It's not about the big, grand gestures. It's about the relationships we're building and nurturing in small ways every day.

Location, Location, Location

We've talked about the ways we can connect with the overarching spirits of plants, and the benefits we can find from developing personal relationships with specific plants.

It's important to discuss the environment for the plants that you're developing a relationship with. Whether it's a harvest for magical purposes or a long-term investment, the location of the plant will have an energetic overlay for the energy being brought into the plant's energy. For example, an oak tree has the magic of life, vitality, strength, and wisdom. How can this wisdom be interpreted or changed by being harvested in a suburban development, versus a tree in a field, a tree in a swamp, and a tree in a busy city? Just like wine's character, or even botanical chemotypes, environment plays a big part in what the end resulting product looks like. So, each leaf is going to have strength, wisdom, and more as its primary factors, but the secondary factoring of the plant's location is going to be impacting that specific material in some way.

If the acorns (transformation, fertility, prosperity) are harvested in a boggy swamp, perhaps it carries the energy of the decay of that plant material that gives swamps their signature scent and can be useful for causing someone's bank account to sour. If leaves (new growth opportunity) are harvested in a city, could they be used to speed up the process (the energy in the city's hustle and bustle) of a slow contract signing?

We are the architects of our magical apothecary, so you can be as in-depth with your materials as you enjoy. The best part of being your own arbiter of your magical collection is that it encourages you to understand plants that grow in your own area, even on your own land, as the best first practice. Absolutely support your local witch shops, because without them we lose a vital piece of our community space and visibility in the community, but knowing which street your oak leaf came from or that you grew lemon balm during a sticky summer when nothing would grow, gives it a more immediate connection to you and your magic, and a vested interest in making that magic manifest.

For example, one day, as a new witch, I needed orris root powder for a spell. It's called by various names in folk magic including Queen Elizabeth's hand root and is also used for love magic. So, I scoured the listings for herb shops and craft stores and finally found a place that sold it. The owner of the shop cautioned me that the root was poisonous if ingested, and I started to worry about our cats knocking over the ornamental jar I was going to keep it in. I certainly didn't want anyone getting hurt. So, I sealed that frosted glass globe shut with sealing wax, sigils, and intent. It was beautiful. Only I should have been more specific in my intent because I was never able to open that jar again. It's moved houses in different states with me, and never broken, and never opened. The protection spell was abandoned and the reason for calling around faded. The knowledge about orris root never waned, though, and once we learn lessons with stories like this attached, they never disappear. If I'd stayed with something locally grown and harvested myself, perhaps I'd have felt more empowered to use that material, to do that spell.

Another benefit of having such specific magical apothecary items is that it offers us a chance to experiment, observe, and record. Due to the nature of the learning experience being largely solitary, we get used to finding our information in books; our spells come from books until we gain the self-confidence to create them ourselves. Gathering your own magical ingredients is practically a golden ticket to developing your own magical practice, because it's based on what is available to you—here and now.

Why?

Well, I *hope* that the why is evident throughout this book; the why is manifold. We do this to enrich our lives and the lives of those around us, to create magic, to process our lives up to this point. To understand the universe better. To change our perspective on life, the universe, and everything. For you. For me.

Here are some plants that might be dangerous or taboo to work with, so you can get to know their resume before deciding if you'd like to get aquainted with the spirit of the plant.

Common Name: Angel's Trumpet

Scientific Name: *Brugmansia spp.*

Botanical Family: Solanaceae

World Origin: South America

Plant's Oil: Not applicable

Scent Description: Heady, floral, sweet

Evaporation: Not applicable

Scent Impact: Sleep

MAGICAL CORRESPONDENCES

Application: Not applicable

Element: Spirit, Fire

Day: Friday

Magical Uses: Ancestor communication, angelic visions, channeling, divination

Planet: Venus, Pluto, Saturn

Astrological Sign: Scorpio

Suggested Crystal: Celestite—Ruled by Gemini—mental acuity, divination, angelic visions

Deity/Spirit: Theia—goddess of visions in the Greek pantheon

Warnings: Contains potent tropane alkaloids (atropine, scopolamine, and hyoscyamine); poison can be ingested by touching the plant, smelling the flower too closely, or eating any part of the plant; therefore physical work is best left to adepts only. Outside the physical, spirit work is recommended instead for the below magical properties.

HERBAL LORE/USES

It is said to be the tree Rip Van Winkle slept under for a hundred years. The flowers of this tropical beauty range from white to orange and red, and can reach 50 cm/19.5 inches. The sleep of the Brugmansia is deep indeed, as simply smelling the flowers too deeply can lead to hallucinations. Exposure to any parts of the plant can lead to coma and death. Seeds and leaves of this gorgeous tropical plant are the most dangerous as they contain high amounts of toxins. The first sign that you have entered into the realm of the angel's trumpet is an intense thirst, followed by light sensitivity, a bright blush on the cheeks, headaches, nausea, and lightheadedness. Even the sap can cause blindness if it gets into your eyes. A chance encounter with the smoke can cause respiratory distress, especially in those with asthma.

Brugmansia species are high in scopolamine, a drug with a history of a walking twilight state where people have been talked into emptying their bank accounts and other actions they would never do outside that influence. Hospitals report an increase in poisonings among teens and children among those looking for a high, similar to teens whispering about the hallucinogenic effects of their botanical cousins, the Datura. The intoxicating power of the genus is so potent that a town in Florida once outlawed new plantings of Brugmansia due to the number of poisoning cases among children.

There are seven plants in the genus, all from South America, and all having their distinct trumpet-shaped flower. That trumpet has caused arguments in the botanical world 220-plus years, as they look as though they are related to the Datura species (they are). In 1973 the morphology was finally settled and Brugmansia were moved to their own genus and it was named after the Dutch naturalist, Sebald Justinus Brugmans.

With all of these warnings about poison, is it even worth establishing a relationship with such a plant? Yes, it absolutely can be. The magic of this plant is incredible for overcoming fear, grief, loneliness, and healing the spirit, especially the relationships with the dead and especially if you've experienced the disconnected pain called "disenfranchised grief." Disenfranchised grief can include: the link between the lost and the bereaved, the death itself or loss, and the bereaved's capacity for bereavement (for example, the sadness of a loss of someone for whom you had unresolved feelings). The Brugmansia species can be a true angel for helping to resolve feelings associated with the death of an abusive family member or other complex/complicated relationships. Those who work in the intuitive arts (especially professionally) can benefit from a spiritual rapport with angel's trumpet.

SPELLS

Ancestor communication—Meeting angel's trumpet in your inner landscape, ask the spirit to connect you with ancestral spirits with whom you can develop a personal relationship.

Angelic visions—Meditation on the image of the trumpet's flower can induce visions of angelic beings who are capable of aiding humans in their journey.

Banishing fear of death, of change—Find a floral incense that you enjoy, and burn it in place of the Brugmansia flowers, while concentrating on the shape, color, and texture of the flower, creating a space for you to accept your own mortality, release the grief of previous losses, and release those fears as you work through complex feelings.

Channeling—Through meditation, invoke the spirit of angel's trumpet to aid you in channeling the spirits of the deceased, angels, or ascended masters, before intuitive readings of any kind.

Clarity, intellectual—Understanding the links between two or more points is the hallmark of the angel's trumpet because of the spiritual nature of this plant. It helps us relate to the people, ideas, and perspectives of those involved for a clearer, more stable understanding that doesn't rely on the emotions involved. The Venusian influence of Brugmansia allows us to consider the emotional impact of actions as they relate to Venus' realms, not just love, but beauty, the arts, and anything luxurious. It's not emotions in the realm of emotional survival, like the Moon can be, it's the fulfillment of emotional wants instead of needs.

Dream visions—Meet the Brugmansia in your inner landscape while lying in bed before sleep to encourage psychic visions in your sleep, to answer questions, connect with ancestors, and solve problems in your waking life.

Fame—Fame can be had with the helping hand of the trumpet; however, angel's trumpet is associated with Pluto and the dead, so the fame you can find with Brugmansia can be volatile and short-lived, but it's a hell of a ride. Think of it as a devil's bargain (no, not the literal devil, think Faust). You'll be a soaring comet, but the deal will come with rumors, innuendo, and secrets, and a big finale ending. Robert Johnson, the Blues man, is a good example of Plutonian fame: overnight success, lore, stories, and fables, and a splashy demise.

Graves found—Ask the spirit of angel's trumpet to guide your hands. On the index finger of your dominant hand, balance a bone. Deer ribs are big enough and have a flat spot for balancing. Walk the land where you think there may be a grave. The visualization I use is fingers shifting sand underneath my feet, combing through the land underneath me. When the bone loses balance and falls to the ground, you've found a grave. "Grave" is pretty broad for this method of divination. I've found everything from squirrel remains to long-dead human remains.

Healing—The Plutonian associations of healing with angel's trumpet align with invasive surgery. This means that angel's trumpet is a heavy-lifting ally that can aid with cancer recovery, especially for those who underwent both surgery and chemotherapy or radiation or both. The healing can be protracted, but it is lifesaving work.

Inspirational speeches—If you need a rousing speech (especially if the fame link is present), especially for celebrity charity fundraisers or political action, angel's trumpet can help you dig deep and find the roots of the spark that helps lead others to their own truth.

Love charms—Ask the spirit of angel's trumpet to bless a love token (such as a stone or jewelry) to present to your loved one to help your love grow.

Public speaking, both clarity of speech and overcoming fear of—You might have guessed from the inspirational speeches above that public speaking is a bonus feature of this gorgeous flower, but being able to release what can be a debilitating fear for some people means that it opens doors to your professional life that might have otherwise gone without exploration.

Revelation of the hidden—Especially beneficial on a Tuesday (victory in lawsuits and arguments). Ask the spirit of angel's trumpet to bless your endeavor as you carve "Revelations" into the surface of a candle. Anoint with olive oil (abundance) for physical evidence or evening primrose (psychic revelations) for confirmation of suspicions. Burn until complete.

Spirit communication—Draw a trumpet or write "Angel's Trumpet" on the surface of a purple candle (psychic intuition) with a pen. Ask the spirit of Brugmansia to open the door to the realm of spirits seeking to communicate with you.

Tarot—As tarot is an ongoing practice, I suggest dedicating a seven-day jar candle to the spirit of angel's trumpet to burn during readings. You can write the common name or the Latin binomial, print a photo of the flower from an internet image search, or create a sigil for the spirit of the flower that you use to call upon that spirit. Because of its association with all forms of divination, don't be surprised if you get a little overlap from different forms of divination, like clairaudience with your clairsentience, and the like. Think of this practice as placing a large antenna on your cell phone for better reception. It won't change the information itself; it'll just make it easier to access.

Transformation—All life is marked by change. What doesn't change, dies. To honor the changing seasons in our lives, ask the Brugmansia to ease the pains of transformation, both physical, mental, and spiritual. This can be done on a small scale by a candle spell with a chime candle, or on a larger scale by setting up an altar space, check-in spot, or other such long-term working, depending on the length of time expected for the change needed. If it is breaking a habit like smoking, that's going to be a longer intention, than, say, smoothing the transition from one job to the next as you apply for a new position.

War to win, or divination of—With the connection between Pluto and Mars (Scorpio's ancient correspondences were to Mars, and later to Pluto after its discovery, so think of them as in-laws for this exercise), it is easy to tap into this connection for divination of the path of events in a war, or the outcome thereof. Take a red (war) or purple (intuition) candle and carve the glyph for Mars onto the surface of the candle. It's the one with the circle and arrow, commonly referred to as the male symbol, to complement the Venus female symbol. Anoint the candle with sunflower oil (long-term goals) if possible. Write out the name of the conflict on a piece of paper. Place the paper under a candleholder and place the candle inside. Burn until complete. Best if done on a Tuesday. Pay attention to your dreams and other sources of intuitive input.

Common Name: Cannabis

Scientific Name: *Cannabis sativa, Cannabis indica, Cannabis ruderalis*

Botanical Family: Cannabaceae (Rosids)

World Origin: Central Asia and the Himalayas, Iran

Plant's Oil: Not applicable

Scent Description: woody, loamy, skunk-like, largely dependent on terpene content

Evaporation: Not applicable

Scent Impact: relaxing or stimulating, depending on terpene content

MAGICAL CORRESPONDENCES

Application: Not applicable

Element: Water

Day: Friday, Saturday

Magical Uses: clairvoyance, creativity, healing, inspiration

Planet: Venus, Saturn

Astrological Sign: Libra, Capricorn

Suggested Crystal: Sulfur—Ruled by Leo—removes distracting thoughts

Deity/Spirit: Diana—Roman/Etruscan—Primordial goddess of the marginalized, women, enslaved people, and immigrants. Goddess of magic, of children, of freedom.

Warnings: Legality is a tenuous condition, as it varies from state to state, region to region, and country to country. Magical information is provided for informational purposes only. Interaction with the spirit of this plant does not imply interacting with the physical plant. Follow applicable laws.

HERBAL LORE/USES

Cannabis is one of the most contentious plants in the world today, as those lobbying to legalize and those dedicated to prohibition are fighting it out in individual states of the United States, in Congress, and around the world. While much is known about this plant, there is still much we do not know, and may never. Because of the profitability of this member of the Rosaceae (rose) family, it is being hybridized at such a rapid rate that attempting to give hard numbers to its varieties would be pointless, as that number would have increased by orders of magnitude by the time this book went to print. Instead, let us look at the essential oil content of the plant material and the link it provides to the rest of aromatherapy.

The primary components of some essential oils are called terpenes (monoterpenes and sesquiterpenes), and they are what give cannabis its distinctive aroma. Terpenes are found in plants all over the globe, not just cannabis. There are over two hundred thousand terpenes found in plants, and around twenty are currently found in cannabis. As mentioned above, those numbers are subject to change as the science progresses. With the number of places decriminalizing and legalizing adult use, it's getting easier to be able to do research into the facts around this impugned plant. Terpenes give essential oils their signature fragrances. Even among different cannabis strains there are different chemical makeups for each strain, similar to how essential oils have chemo-types. This is how each strain has its own unique scent and flavor profile. Depending on the source of the cannabis, you may receive a label that tells you the terpene content of the botanical ally that you have access to. The labels that inform consumers of the tetrahydrocannabinol (THC) percent, the name of the strain, weight, and more, may list the terpene content found within.

Thyme is one plant with varieties varied by chemotype. The genus *Thymus* has 215-plus, species under its heading. Six major chemotypes are produced by *Thymus vulgaris*: thymol—(kills germs and fungi, eases muscle pain), linalool—(soothes irritated skin, relaxing for the mind, primarily found in lavender), carvacrol—(antioxidant), geraniol—(cardiac restorative, neuroprotectant), a-terpineol—(inhibits growth of tumor cells), and thuyanol—(eases muscle stiffness, nonirritating on the skin). Each one will have a different fragrance and therapeutic goal. The determining factors in what chemical components are found in two plants of the same genus, species, and variety often come down to temperature, moisture, and growing conditions like available sunlight, soil content, and related environmental factors.

Whether monoterpenes or sesquiterpenes, these chemical components are produced by the plant and have inherent beneficial aspects. While the word "chemical" was a buzzword for a while, there is nothing artificial about these compounds. Monoterpenes are emotionally uplifting, pain relieving (especially in muscles), antiseptic for the air, antiviral, bactericidal, expectorant, relaxant, and stimulant (while it may be confusing to see relaxing and stimulating next to each other, it's common in nature, and it is found in everyday items like beer). Monoterpenes are found in essential oils like lemon (*Citrus limon*), marjoram (*Origanum majorana*), and bergamot (*Citrus bergamia*).

Sesquiterpenes are analgesic, antifungal, antiseptic, anti-inflammatory, antispasmodic, bactericidal, hypotensive, and sedating. Essential oils high in sesquiterpenes are geranium, helichrysum, patchouli, and ylang-ylang.

While it's important to talk about the terpenes present in cannabis, to understand the inherent therapeutic benefit, it's also important to note there are over 150 terpenes that have been identified in cannabis, but more are being discovered every day. While their effects have likely been studied in different plant materials prior to their discovery in cannabis, studies into cannabis are difficult to conduct due to the prohibition on marijuana sales that started in the United States in 1937.

Some terpenes found in cannabis and their actions:

Borneol—(minty) pain relieving, anti-inflammatory. Found in rosemary and garden sage.

Camphine—(conifer needles) antioxidant. Found in bergamot, cypress, nutmeg.

β-caryophyllene—(spicy) pain relieving, anti-inflammatory. Found in black pepper, cinnamon, and oregano.

Eucalyptol—(herbaceous) Alzheimer's, support pain relief. Found in rosemary, mint, tea tree, mugwort, and sagebrush.

β-eudesmol—(loamy soil) liver protective, gastric emptying, mosquito repellant. Found in aniseed and cypress.

Geraniol—(rosy) neuroprotectant, pain relief. Found in geranium, responsible for rose scent.

A-humulene—(loamy soil) appetite suppression, antitumor. Found in hops, basil, cloves, and garden sage.

Δ-limonene—(lemony) sleep aid, energizing aroma, uplifting, antianxiety. High limonene content usually denotes a Sativa-based strain. Found in citrus fruits.

Linalool—(lavender-like) antidepressant, anti-seizure, pain relief. Found in lavender.

β-myrcene—(clove-like) pain relief, antispasmodic. Found in basil, hops, and mango. Eating mango can intensify an experience with cannabis.

β-pinene—(piney) soothe asthma and bronchitis, expectorant, mental acuity. Found in rosemary, parsley, and pine needles.

Terpinolene (woody) cancer/antitumor, ease symptoms of heart disease, pain relief. Found in cumin, garden sage, parsnip, and rosemary.

MAGIC OF CANNABIS

I suggest grabbing a white (all purpose) seven-day jar candle and inscribing it with the name, a flower, a sigil, or something to represent the spirit of the plant you want to work with, in a check-in space so you can work with any of the below intentions as well as get to know the spirit of the plant you're forming a working relationship with.

Clairvoyance—Intuition is a human trait; it's allowed our survival as a species thus far. Whether you chalk it up to your gut instinct, a variety of environmental factors, or your spirit team, clear seeing is just the first step. There are more "clairs-" to explore. Ask the spirit of cannabis to allow yourself to move past the limitations of the ego to receive the information you're looking for.

Consciousness, higher—Attaining higher consciousness isn't just about your intuition, it's about connecting with the eternal you who knows that the limits of our bodies aren't permanent and that greatness is attainable. Invoking the spirit of the cannabis plant is part of the attainable understanding of this connection that is possible within the limited scope of piloting this ghost ship through our day-to-day.

Creativity—To appeal to the spirit of cannabis for aid in your creativity is to look to release the imposter syndrome that plagues many creative people. It can give you the ideas to create, but more readily, it can give you the freedom to explore your own ideas without the lens of judgment turned inward. Light a candle to invoke the spirit of the plant, connect with its energies, and attempt to create. Anything. If you're a painter, paint something. If you're concerned that you are too self-critical (this plagues all creatives as we/they level up—once you've been creating long enough to understand what good work looks like, your already high standards grow even higher), try something in a medium that you don't have much practice in. If you're a painter, try to sculpt something out of paper-mache, or air-dry clay. If you write books on witchcraft, try a horror short story. The thing you don't want to do is stare at a blank page or canvas because that's when the demons of self-doubt can get louder.

Desire—Cannabis is anti-inflammatory and can help separate our bodies from the pain and stress of operating a body full-time, and connect us with the sensuous nature of existence.

Destiny—We all long to connect with the purpose of our life. Capitalism tells us that the things we do for money are our destiny/raison d'être rather than the way we occupy our time as a toll to exist upon the earth. "What's your dream job?" Plant spirits remind us not to dream of labor, rather to dream of something that fulfills us and our soul's purpose. Some lucky people get paid to do what they love (sports figures, actors, other celebrities, and the like), but the spirit of cannabis reminds you that the joys we seek are the reason we're here, or at least partly. We're not humans having a spiritual experience, we're spirits having a human experience. I know this because astral projection is possible. If it were all about being embodied, we wouldn't have that ability. Plants wouldn't have arch spirits, and there wouldn't be entire branches of folklore devoted to animal spirits and ghost dogs.

Emotions, to release—All too often in our society are we as children taught "boys don't cry/only babies cry/be strong, don't cry/a lady doesn't get overly emotional." Bottling emotions doesn't improve their "sell by" date. It molds your insides to hold in your tears. Expressing your emotions is healthy and allows us to move through and past the emotion. Working with cannabis as a spirit ally reminds us that the emotions we experience do not have to control us.

Funeral Rites—The ability of the spirit of cannabis to create levity, soothe emotional wounds, and nourish hearts makes it an ideal ally for funerary rites. It's associated with Venus so it'll hold space for the love lost with the person who crossed over. Saturn reminds us that we all have the limitations of the physical, so be careful. Pluto reminds us that death isn't a stopping point, rather an evolution.

Healing—Many strains of cannabis have sedating, antitumoral, and soothing properties, giving this plant the ability to relax and receive the healing of our bodies. Whether short-term illness or chronic, this plant is dedicated to creating space for you to heal, even if there is no cure for what ails you.

Imagination/Inspiration—Ask the spirit of cannabis to enable you to free yourself of harsh criticism and imposter syndrome. Try pairing the spirit of cannabis with diffusing an essential oil for creativity, like cardamom, ginger, or grapefruit.

Love, self—It can be decidedly difficult to truly love yourself as there are billion-dollar industries dedicated to making sure we doubt ourselves. Ask cannabis to help clear the air enough for you to truly let down the walls and let you love yourself. It can be especially hard if our parents didn't model healthy affirmations of love, so don't despair if you're not great at it yet. It takes time and practice, and that includes letting others love us for who we are. It's worth the time and energy dedicated to learning to love you, so that you know how you deserve to be loved.

Lust/pleasure—Working with the spirit of cannabis puts us in touch with our senses, while removing the pain (both physical and mental) that holds us back from being in touch with our bodies. This opens the door to the spirit of lust, making it kind, warm, and sweet to remember that you too are deserving of lust.

Meditation—Breathing exercises are physical as well as emotionally healing and regulating. By invoking the spirit of cannabis before meditation, and possibly diffusing an essential oil for meditation, like angelica, cedarwood, clary sage, or frankincense, you allow your body to forget its limitations for a few moments out of its day and experience peace. Meditation with a plant spirit isn't "sit still and think of nothing," rather it's an inner conversation with a trusted friend that allows you to reaffirm your own thoughts, feelings, and desires by quieting the other parts of body, mind, and spirit.

Pain relief—The pain-relieving energy of cannabis often comes in anti-inflammatory changes in your body, as well as antitumoral effects in strains containing A-humulene like Lemon Haze or GSC (also called Girl Scout Cookies but shortened so as not to imply any connection to the organization doing cookie fundraisers). These strains also have sedative properties because pain can make it difficult to sleep, even though all we want is to sleep. Carve the name of the strain or cultivar into the side of a chime candle asking to have your pain relieved, your sleep restored, and have peace from the pain. If it's a chronic condition, we already know that magic isn't going to suddenly and permanently resolve it; however, the reduction in pain and the ability to sleep are worth it.

Perception, change—Many a problem can be solved by taking the time and energy to change your perspective to find the solution. By asking the spirit of cannabis to change your point of view, you can see ways through tough times, tough issues, and tough situations. The ability of all plant spirits to share their perspective often leads to not just a change in point of view, but also fundamental changes in the way we see the world.

Reality, to see beyond—To see beyond the veil of daily life and glimpse realms beyond our experience, ask for the aid of the spirit of cannabis, anoint a blue (peace, exploration) chime candle with diluted anise seed oil (astral travel), and burn on a Wednesday (communication) until complete.

Sexuality, enhancing—Take a red (lust) or pink (romantic love) candle and anoint with diluted basil (lust, sacred to Aphrodite) essential oil. (If there is a history of seizures or migraines, use diluted cardamom essential oil instead of basil.) Ask the spirit of cannabis to enhance your sexual experience and allow you to come into harmony with your physical body. Pair with fire opal for sensual desires or carnelian for pleasure enhancement. Burn on a Friday (lust, beauty) for best results.

Sleep—To increase sleep, cannabis helps release the tension we carry in our bodies. Stress, fear, fatigue, and more create bunching in muscles. As those muscles are deprived of blood (and oxygen) it can create pain, stiffness, and knots, making it hard to drift off to sleep. Take a pale blue (sleep) candle and anoint it with diluted bergamot essential oil, to increase peace, allow sleep, and banish nightmares. Ask for the aid of cannabis to release any fear, tension, or pain keeping you from sleep. Burn on a Monday for emotional well-being or any time you're having trouble sleeping.

Tension, to release—Anoint a black (banishing) candle with diluted neroli (diffuse tension, physical and emotional) and ask the spirit of cannabis to help release the tension in a safe, whole-making way. Burn until complete, on a Saturday (endings) or anytime needed.

Trance—A trance state can be induced in a number of different ways. The action of the spirit of cannabis is to remove the awareness of the physical body that casts a negative light (pain, stiffness, tension) and replace it with a soft awareness that empowers the inspirited (someone working with a particular spirit), such as awareness of breath, breathing, and breath patterns that support and nurture life without stressing out the other systems. It leads to an awareness of the body that is more wholistic instead of symptom-focused. Anoint a purple (intuition) candle with diluted bay laurel (trance state) essential oil and ask the spirit of cannabis to help release your physical awareness and increase your spirit awareness. Burn until completed, best—if done on a Monday (emotional support) or Saturday (awareness of spirits).

Recipe: Miss Lydia's Flower Gummies

This recipe can be labor intensive. Feel free to break up the steps over multiple days if needed.

Part One: De-Carbing

❈ ¼ ounce dried flower, finely ground

Place a piece of parchment paper onto a baking tray and place your finely ground flower onto the parchment paper. Bake dried flower at 220° F or 104° C for 20 minutes. Allow to cool completely.

This is a process called decarboxylating or de-carbing the flower. This leads to a greater bioavailability of volatile oils in the active constituents in the flower. Keep in mind that when cannabinoids are ingested, before they can pass the blood/brain barrier, the stomach attaches a fat molecule to the end of the chain so that it can enter the bloodstream. So, it takes a longer time to feel the effects of the cannabis than if it were inhaled.

ENTRY INTO THE BODY

Inhaled THC can take initial effect in 10–20 seconds and attain full effect at 10 minutes. Sublingual (under the tongue) application of THC via tincture (THC extracted via alcohol solution) or glycerite (THC extracted via glycerine solution) can take 30 minutes and last up to three hours. Any amount of the tincture or glycerite that is swallowed rather than absorbed under the tongue will process in the same timing as an edible. Edibles (THC extracted into a fat like ghee, butter, or oil and made into gummies, brownies, cookies, and more) can take up to two hours for initial onset of effect and can last 8–12 hours, depending on dose. So, start low, and go slow. Wait two and a half hours before judging whether or not you've had enough, as invariably the brain will say, "This isn't enough," and try to talk you into an additional dose.

Note: if you have ingested too much and have attained a level of high that no longer feels safe, drink a full glass of water and ingest some potassium (banana is great, or kiwi), as potassium flushes THC from the system, and if you have a CBD-only tincture available, it will down-regulate the THC (counter the effect of the THC already ingested and bring it down to a manageable level).

Part Two: Infusion Process

Once the de-carbed flower is room temperature again, place a small double boiler saucepan on the stove, add water to the bottom compartment, and start over low heat. Add 1 cup of the fat of your choice: butter, ghee, coconut oil, or other edible oils. For this batch we used one part ghee and one part coconut oil. Pick up the parchment paper and brush your ground flower into the double boiler saucepan with the fat. Give the mix a stir and allow the fat to coat the flower. Place a lid on the saucepan to keep the volatile oils in the fat. Allow it to slowly simmer for three hours. Turn off the heat, and allow it to cool; do not take the lid off. When the fat has cooled enough so as not to cause steam burns, strain fat with a fine mesh sieve. Reserve strained plant material for other edible projects like caramels, chocolates, and brownies.

Part Three: Gummy Process

You will need:

- 3 ounces of boxed flavored gelatin of your choice
- 4 ounces infused fat
- ¼ teaspoon corn syrup
- ¼ teaspoon citric acid
- ¼ teaspoon guar gum powder
- ½ teaspoon sunflower lecithin
- 3 packets or ⅓ cup unflavored gelatine
- ¼ cup boiling water

Set up gummy molds on cookie sheets to protect your surface and hands. Spray molds with cooking spray of your choice to allow gummies to release from molds. I found adorable witches, hats, and cauldron molds online; feel free to have fun with it.

With the double boiler still on the stove, but *no* heat yet, take the melted fat and add flavored gelatin, corn syrup, citric acid, guar gum, and sunflower lecithin to pot and stir well.

Pro tip: coat your measuring spoon with a drop of oil so sticky substances slide right off. Stir well.

In a separate glass measuring cup, add your three packets of unflavored gelatin into the boiling hot water to dissolve gelatin. Stir well. Allow to rest.

Turn heat on double boiler to low. Start stirring again. Don't let the mixture burn or the gummies will taste burned. When mixture is *just* hot enough to start to steam, slowly add in unflavored gelatin water mix. Stir constantly. Simmer until texture goes from granular to glassy and smooth. You want the resulting blend to be stringy when you pull the spoon away.

Take a funnel, pot holders or thermal gloves, and a squirt bottle and pour mixture into squirt bottle, the kind used for ketchup and mustard. While wearing thermal gloves, squirt hot gummy paste into prepared molds to desired thickness. Place trays into the refrigerator or freezer to cool.

If you'd like to know how much THC each edible you've created has, type "marijuana dosage calculator" in your favorite search engine.

Check your label, if you have one, to use the calculator. Low quality flower is around 3 percent, and quality flower from a dispensary can be 25–30 percent. Between the gummy mold that I used to make these and the percentage of the THC in the flower that I used, one gummy turned out to be 40 mg of THC. If this was your first experience with gummies, I'd cut a 40 mg gummy into quarters, chew quarter, wait 2½ hours, then estimate your comfort level with your level of high, and record your findings for later.

Common Name: Pau-rosa, Rosewood

Scientific Name: *Aniba rosaeodora*

Botanical Family: Lauraceae

World Origin: Brazil

Plant's Oil: Wood

Scent Description: sweet, woody, soft

Evaporation: Base note

Scent Impact: Empowering, stabilizing, and uplifting depression

MAGICAL CORRESPONDENCES

Application: Not applicable

Element: Water

Day: Sunday

Magical Uses: Balance, breaking bad habits, calm, connection to the divine, emotional stability, good luck, harmony, meditation, psychic protection, restoring libido

Planet: Sun

Astrological Sign: Leo

Suggested Crystal: Selenite—Ruled by Virgo—cleansing aura, gives us direction

Deity/Spirit: Eleos, the Greek personification of compassion

HERBAL LORE/USES

True Brazilian rosewood is an incredible wood, and quite beautiful to look at, as well as smell. This incredible beauty is part of the reason for the downfall of rosewood as well as dozens of other related species in the *Dalbergia* genus (in the *Rosa* family). Because of the robust color and divine scent of the trees in this genus (over three hundred species!), these trees have been made into furniture for thousands of years, and any exotic hardwoods with the same glow have been decimated by poaching, violence, and illegal activities. As a result, the rosewood family as of January 2017 has been under CITES control. All *Dalbergia* rosewood species other than Brazilian rosewood (*Dalbergia nigra*) were regulated under CITES, Appendix II. (Brazilian rosewood is protected by even stricter CITES regulations under Appendix I.) The new rosewood regulations officially took effect on January 2, 2017.

All this is to say that there are essential oils that will be called rosewood, like *Aniba rosaeodora*, that aren't true Brazilian rosewood, but are related closely enough for the magical understanding and aromatic use of the plant. But please don't support questionable sources, as these threatened species are nearing extinction, because of their use for furniture and perfume, even merely for the color of their wood. Please support ethical farming practices whenever possible. The magical associations herein are provided for historical context and use of antique wands, as the author does not support poaching of endangered species.

CREATING SCENT ACTIVATIONS

9

One of the more rewarding relationships with plant allies is the creation of scent activations. What *is* a scent activation? It sounds vaguely like aromatherapy in a sci-fi movie, but we have these embedded programs written into our minds during the course of our entire lives. The smell of bubble bath makes you smile and think of bathtime as a child. The smell of a classic French perfume reminds you of watching old movies with your aunt. The smell of bread baking makes you nostalgic for childhood baking projects.

When scents and memories become linked through repeated exposure, a linked behavior can become automatic.

RELATIONAL MEMORY SAVES THE DAY

The idea for this book came a few years ago during a family funeral. We had lost a great aunt, whom I had not really known. I was attending as a matter of family courtesy. The funeral was being held in the neighborhood Catholic church, as she was Catholic, just as the rest of my mom's family was. I am a Witch. My entire family knows, so for most of the family this is a non-issue. I walked into the church worried that the members of the family who were evangelical would take this opportunity to spew hatred upon me and my choices. I was anxious as I chose a pew to sit in. I was anxious as I pondered whether it would be disrespectful to sing hymns of a religion I was never a part of. I was anxious as the procession started, when the priests and altar boys made their way into the room, leading the casket down the aisle. Then something happened—without pause or conscious thought, my anxiety was gone.

You know when my anxiety evaporated? It was gone faster than a drop of sweat on sunbaked concrete as soon as the procession passed my pew. All of

a sudden, I was ready. I didn't understand why my anxiety suddenly left me. Then, it hit me. The smell of the frankincense and myrrh flipped the switch in my brain that said, "It is time for ritual," and all other thoughts of family problems went out the window. I was ready for the event at hand. I had grounded and centered the moment that incense hit my brain, without any cognizant thought on my part.

I sat respectfully through the proceedings while the gears turned in the back of my mind. My first coven used a lot of frankincense and myrrh because the high priestess was raised Catholic. My brain will always associate that smell with religious ritual because I used it in circle for twenty-two rituals minimum a year for five years. Everyone got dressed in their lovely robes and cords, the incense was lit, and candles alight. The part of my brain that relied on smell for survival didn't know the difference between frankincense and myrrh in a pagan temple, and the same incense used in a Catholic church.

The positive and the negative both exist here: the smell of tequila makes you think of a fight with your best friend that ended in tears. These memories triggered by scent can be difficult to pin down, but when they come on, they can involve whole-body reactions to the memory, as well as flashbacks, but they don't have to be negative. This is the introduction to creating the scent activation. It is possible to overwrite traumatic responses to scent, and I'll be able to go into that further in future work.

The Mechanics of Scent

When we experience a fragrance, whether it be your favorite cologne or fresh tomatoes from the garden, our brains have to process what we're smelling, lightning fast, because our brains need to determine if there is danger involved. In *Homo erectus* and before, a sense of smell was able to tell bitter berries that were potentially poisonous, when food was spoiled, and when lands were lush and fruitful or barren wastelands. Our sense of smell can tell us (a good percentage of us anyway) when rain is coming, when the milk has gone off, and when dinner's ready.

When you're busy trying to place a scent you're unsure of, many things are happening; your brain is scrambling through the list of things you've smelled in your lifetime, in reverse-date order, from the things you've smelled the most recently to the furthest reaches of your lifetime. Our brains store the scents this way to make it the most efficient model, with frequency and recency speeding up the process to cut down on reaction times.

This is why when you smell something that you haven't smelled in years, or even decades, it takes a moment to find the file in your memory marked "circus peanut candy" or "baby shampoo." This also explains why scents are inextricably linked to individual memories.

When we link a smell with a physical action, like in our church story, over time the brain links those behaviors to save time and effort, and instills muscle memory in the unconscious part of the brain. In other experiences, this is why martial artists repeat forms, actions, and reactions over an over: it instills muscle memory. When we're under stress and our thinking brain shuts down for energy efficiency, our muscle memory takes over. In a fight, you don't often have time to stop and think about what to do; action is always faster than reaction. It doesn't happen overnight. In the original example, that link between incense and centering was at least twenty-two times a year for five years.

The number of repetitions and length of time it takes you to create a scent activation will depend on a number of factors. Science has shown us that creating patterns happens differently for people based on a wide variety of factors. The important thing is to work with your brain, body, and experience to create lasting change that can impact your heart, mind, body, and spirit. This is a long-term magical project, but the results are worth it.

This isn't the first time something like this has been suggested. Laurie Cabot put forth a method for activating your psychic senses in *Power of the Witch* (1992) wherein the witch instills an activation by entering a trance state (in which she refers to the alpha brain waves associated with intuition and magic) and adding a prescribed motion, like tapping a finger, to shortcut the route to a trance state. Over time, when the finger is tapped, the brain skips the lead up and jumps to trance state.

This technique works for a variety of personal goals, both magical and mundane.

Part I: Designing the Scent

To create a scent activation, first we have to define a goal. Unlike our traditional magical goals and the process of making them into magical perfumes, we're going to go a step further and look at the grounding or basis for that magical goal, to help understand it further. This will take some inner work on your part, and that's okay. This is a safe place; we'll work through this together. If our goal is prosperity, we're going to have to break it down into significant feelings and related emotions to help tailor the correct oils for your magical perfume to use in aromatic activation. Grab a notepad or journal and at the top of the page, write your goal for your activation.

Factors

- Emotional—Does having your bank balance dip below a certain number elicit a specific emotion for you? Does it feel fearful, threatened, and/or exposed?

- Physical—Does a need for prosperity in your life stem from a fear of homelessness or other risks to your personal safety?

- Spiritual—Can the root of your overspending come from a lack of spiritual understanding of who you are as a person or practitioner?

- Mental—Does your lack of cash flow heighten feelings of depression, frustration, vulnerability?

Once we understand the root cause for the emotion, we can process those feelings in a productive way. Remember, magic is creating change in accordance with your will, so doing a deep dive into your thoughts, feelings, and emotions is magical.

Essential oils have effects on our physical, spiritual, mental, and emotional states, so it's easier to understand each of the needs we are expressing and to form a complete treatment plan when we understand how each of those affects us.

Spiritual Effects

If we only look at the magical or spiritual effects of oils, in this example prosperity oils to create a money blend, we wind up with a list like this: agrimony, allspice, almond, balsam fir, and the like. However, if we look at the elements and planetary associations it becomes: Agrimony, fire, Jupiter. Allspice, earth,

Venus. Almond, air, Venus. When we apply discernment, this provides a lot more information than it does on the surface.

Agrimony provides a fiery ally that burns away attachments and negative associations, and allows Jupiter to slowly expand your prosperity after the surgical removal of negative influences on your financial health. It's a great ally if you are doing prosperity work during the waning part of the month.

MAGICAL TIMING AND TOOLS

Traditional wisdom in witchcraft says you do magic for increase during the waxing part of the month, and banishing during the waning part of the month. But that leaves out the second half of the understanding: you don't have to wait for the right time of the month for your magical working, you have to work the magic around the time you have available to you. We live in a busy society and only have the allotted time that we're available. It's a huge privilege to be able to hire a babysitter because you have a spell you need to cast or magical supplies you want to procure for just the right spell. It's another thing altogether to be able to sit down, look at the materials you have on hand, and write the spell around what you need, when you need it. If you've got a purple birthday candle with the number eight on it, some olive oil, and a pen, you can make it work. This skill is lovingly referred to as "punting."

I once overheard my high priestess joking about offering to bring supplies to a ritual and asking the leader of the next ritual to bring their tools and supplies and making them punt with whatever they had on hand. While it makes for a teachable moment for some, my response was to always carry everything I'd need on hand just in case anyone forgot the items they intended to bring.

It's lovely to plan the perfect aesthetic for a social media post, but magic doesn't wait for the perfect lighting, the perfect moon phase, or the perfect alignment.

DISCERNMENT

Discernment is the skill that is fundamental for witches. Using our judgement and understanding helps us, along with a healthy dose of skepticism, to decide if the fog in a photo is magical, paranormal, or dust in the air. Judgment doesn't have to be negative, even though it can feel that way if we're on the wrong end of it.

If we look at the example, allspice, Earth, Venus, using our discernment, we can extrapolate that in dealing with prosperity magic, allspice is going to ground excess spending and help us understand that spending money isn't always the best expression of love. Sometimes spending time with loved ones and being available with words of comfort or affirmation are even more valuable than buying them something (or ourselves) to make the situation *feel* better.

So, when looking at the correspondences for a plant that we're considering adding to a magical blend, it's important to look at as much of the information as you have access to, before making the leap to include it in your scent activation.

Emotional Effects

If you're concerned your financial woes are due to a lack of gratitude in your current financial situation, you might turn to gratitude oils like bergamot, coriander, or ylang-ylang. Blending these three oils together would yield an interesting blend, but if you look at both the prosperity list and the gratitude list, you'll see that bergamot, pine, cedarwood, and myrrh are on both lists. If your financial woes are due to the fact that you aren't being paid enough, look for oils that boost confidence along with your prosperity. Then go in there and fight for your raise. Magic needs real-world work, too.

If you concentrate on a specific feeling like anxiety that a lack of prosperity causes, incorporating an antianxiety oil will boost your prosperity, even though that oil might not necessarily be aligned with prosperity, traditionally.

Of this list I picked benzoin, because I find the scent not only calming and antianxiety, but also nostalgic and happiness-inspiring. The magic of benzoin includes exorcism, confidence in speech, harmony, love, concentration, and purification. Incorporation of the other attributes of exorcism (to help banish debt) and confidence in speech can increase the efficacy of your prosperity magic.

Physical Effects

It's quite possible to choose an oil for a physical attribute and to utilize the emotional, spiritual, and other correspondences that go with it. Physically benzoin oil can help remedy bacterial or fungal infections of the skin. If you were using it for that purpose and created a chant around confidence in speech so that when you were applying it you encouraged your voice, after a while, just smelling the oil would remind you how confident you can be when interacting with others. The next step in that process would include feeling confident when touching the bottle, even before it was opened, then feeling confident when remembering the bottle or passing a display of roller bottles in a shop. This programming can stay with you for life, the way fond smells make you smile even decades after you've last smelled them. This is why it's important to pick long-term goals for your activation.

Mental Effects

The effects of essential oils on our minds can benefit our magic as they are partnered in our well-being. In this example we can desire the mental capacity to concentrate on the task at hand, such as planning a budget to benefit our cash flow. Essential oils for concentration include basil, bergamot, cedarwood, peppermint, rosemary, peppermint, and vetiver. If we cross-reference the previous lists for prosperity, bergamot is a great oil for prosperity, as well as commanding (great if you have a neurodivergency that can make it difficult to concentrate, like ADHD or attention deficit hyperactivity disorder). Cedarwood can add stability for the long term to your magic. Peppermint grows voraciously, as we'd hope our bank accounts will. Vetiver is a grounding plant and will root our magic in the reality of where we are, instead of apple pie dreams of funds we may never be able to attain.

PUTTING IT ALL TOGETHER

In the process of all this note-taking and personal discovery, it's easy to see how the essential oils put themselves together at this point. The lines of congruity string throughout this exercise and bring us to the understanding of what oils are especially important for this personal programming.

In this example:

1. The fear of poverty drives us to spend money while we have it, because we might not get more.

2. As rational adults we understand that a budget could help alleviate some of the concern by sticking to a plan for where money goes each pay period.

3. A neurodivergency can make it difficult to concentrate, or even fear can cause anxiety around the concept of budgeting, math, or pain of past experiences.

4. Sparks of cash flow excite overspending, leaving you with cash flow, meaning you spend like it's going out of style one day, and are bereft the next, leading to highs and lows in the energetic understanding of money.

All this is to say that once we understand what the origins are, it's easier to execute a plan to make the financials less scary and to support your long-term goals of financial security, because we know there's no way to budget around simply not being paid enough. There is no spiritual influencer or guide that's going to hand us the bucket of cash we'd need to be debt-free for life. Magic works hand in hand with the practical, easy-to-understand ways that we can improve our lives. Magic and the scent activations we're discussing are a way to marry the two ideas.

We are left with a pile of oils. Now's it's time to narrow them down.

ANTIANXIETY

Bergamot (invigorating), Clary sage (lowers stress hormones), Geranium (all twelve varieties), Jasmine, Lavender, Neroli, Patchouli (grounding), Rose, Rosemary, Sweet Orange (uplifting), Tangerine (hospitality), Ylang-ylang

CONCENTRATION

Basil, Bergamot, Cedarwood, Peppermint, Rosemary, Spearmint, Vetiver

GRATITUDE

Bergamot, Cedarwood, Coriander, Frankincense, Myrrh, Rose, Scotch Pine, Ylang-ylang

PROSPERITY

Agrimony, Allspice, Almond, Basil, Bayberry, Benzoin, Cedar, Chamomile, Clary Sage, Clove (brings luck), Galangal (grounding), Ginger (invigorating), Heliotrope, Jasmine, Marjoram, Patchouli

PROTECTION

Agrimony, Angelica, Anise, Bay Laurel, Basil, Benzoin, Cassia, Clove, Copal, Cypress, Eucalyptus, Frankincense, Galangal, Grapefruit, Hyssop, Juniper, Lavender, Marjoram, Myrrh, Pine, Patchouli, Pennyroyal, Rosemary, Sage, Sandalwood, Tangerine, Vetiver

PURIFICATION

Anise, Bay Laurel, Benzoin, Clove, Chamomile, Frankincense, Hyssop, Juniper, Lemon, Peppermint, Rosemary, Sage, Thyme, Verbena

RELEASE

Bay Laurel, Camphor, Menthol, Pennyroyal, Peppermint, Rosemary

SUCCESS

Allspice, Basil, Bergamot, Cassia, Cedarwood, Chamomile, Cinnamon, Frankincense, Galangal, Geranium, Ginger, Lemon Balm, Myrrh, Oak Absolute, Orange Blossom, Patchouli, Sandalwood, Vanilla, Yarrow

WISDOM

Cardamom, Clary sage, Cypress, Sage, Vetiver

When you line up all of the information like this, it's easy to count how many times bergamot comes up, or frankincense for that matter. We can extrapolate from all of our data that these oils are especially beneficial for our prosperity work.

By lining them up we've got a great path to the creation of our scent.

You could choose any one of the oils in the lists above to be broadly associated with prosperity magic, but as these essential oils are single notes, they'll be attuned to their specific energies (see *Blackthorn's Botanical Magic* for more oils to explore) whereas if you create a fragrance of your own, it can be attuned to your specific needs.

We need a principal scent to anchor our scent activation, a scent on which to build our activation fragrance. If we choose bergamot as our anchor point, take a few moments to smell bergamot. It has a sour citrus note to it, as opposed to the sweet citrus of orange or grapefruit. There's also a papery note with a hint of pepper to it. When we look at the anchor point as a whole, the essential oils that will blend well with it start to come to mind. Bergamot is a fiery solar oil, so other citruses are a given. The distilled bergamot essential oil can lack some of the complexity of the other citruses, but the distilled bergamot lacks the phototoxic *bergapten* that can cause burns. Also blending well with bergamot are geranium (all twelve varieties), lavender, lemon, neroli, patchouli, petitgrain, and ylang-ylang. Merely by glancing at the list of prosperity helpers above, we've got ylang-ylang on the lists a few times, as well as patchouli.

Now that we've got some ideas as to what *could* go into the scent, let us look at the magical applications of some of the other oils that blend well with bergamot and the other oils above. Lavender is a Mercurial and Venusian herb, with an airy nature. When looked at under the lens of prosperity support, it could help to uncover hidden expenditures like reoccurring subscription services that you might have missed in your budgetary examination. Lemon also has some business acumen and provides calm, so it'll help the anxiety associated with money issues. Its magic also includes increasing the power of a spell, so it's a fantastic addition to this activation. Neroli can be an expensive oil to work with, so if you can't afford it right now, consider turning to petitgrain. It's derived from the same plant as neroli, *Citrus aurantium* or the bitter orange tree, but neroli is derived from the delicate flowers, and petitgrain is distilled from the leaves and young branches of the tree. It adds a green note that will pair really well with the cool tones of bergamot's aroma. If you pair patchouli and bergamot, you get a note of pepper with both, and it ties the fragrances together, so think of which of the oils on the list of oils blend well with bergamot, and you find ylang-ylang.

Ylang-ylang flowers are in the custard apple family but always remind me of vanilla orchids with their yellow flowers and leggy petals. Ylang-ylang's magic is that of calm, harmony, strength of spirit, love, peace, and relaxing.

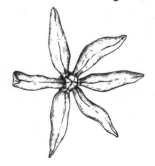

Because the oil is a middle to base note, it stands up against the earthy patchouli in a way most wouldn't expect. This "flower of flowers" not only can really lend a helping hand in raising the energy of the activation, but it also quells anger by lowering blood pressure and taking the wind out of blustery sails. Carefully monitor your drops and keep the number low if you add ylang-ylang to your activation scent, because overuse of this flower can lead to headaches. It'll stand up to those thick, resinous patchouli varieties, especially if you purchase ylang-ylang II or III. (The Roman numerals after the flower name denote that these are products that have been processed multiple times, to create a stronger oil.)

The intermediary step in creating these scents is to take the lids of each essential oil you're considering for the oil and smell them together. It's much easier to rule out an oil with this method than to waste the oils by making and remaking an oil five times because you didn't like one of the components. I place three or four oils' lids onto an index card, a paper plate, or other unscented surface to ensure that oils or lotions on my hands or other surfaces don't color my opinion of the fragrance I'm creating.

Patchouli, ylang-ylang, and bergamot make a great team, with the subtle thread of pepper running through it. There are a base note (patchouli), a middle or heart note (ylang-ylang), and a top note (bergamot) present, and this blend is considered complete, however, you can consider adding a tone or shade as you might with paint to add to or take away from the chord you have created already. In this case, a tone might be vanilla or benzoin for the creamy warmth and sweetness, or black pepper essential oil for tying that peppery note together and bringing it to the forefront.

Keep in mind that any addition to the chord you've created will add its own magical feel to the oil.

- ✳ Bergamot—asking for help, concentration, prosperity, money, banishing problems

- ✳ Ylang-ylang—strength of spirit, raise vibrations, peace, harmony

- ✳ Patchouli—centering, grounding, fairness, hex-breaking, manifestation, money, purification

Possible additions:

- ✳ Benzoin—calm, hex-breaking, purification, wisdom, peace of mind, inspiration

- ✳ Black Pepper—mental alertness, courage, drive away evil, prosperity, justice

- ✳ Vanilla—attraction, focus, calm, passion, luck, increase, comfort, good fortune

In the original equation, bergamot plus ylang-ylang plus patchouli equals an oil that will allow you to pull yourself together enough to ask for help and break hexes. So, this could be used for any emotional issue that robs of us our personal power. If you wanted to tone that collection with vanilla, its papery sweetness would smooth out some of the harshness of the heady floral ylang-ylang, and add the magic of calm focus and good luck. If you decided on a shade of black pepper instead, it could ramp up the aggression in the blend, encouraging you to stand up for yourself after you've pulled yourself back together, and adds the magic of mental acuity. Benzoin would brighten the oil a bit and has a much lower price point than vanilla CO2 (CO2 oils are extracted using carbon dioxide under high pressure). It would add the wisdom of experience to your goals and purification of healing the past, increasing peace of mind.

The next step is to decide how loud you want each oil to be in your blend. The notes we talked about earlier (top, middle or heart, and base designations) are about the volatility of the oils, or how easily they evaporate so that we can smell them. The top notes are the first out the gate, the heart notes bloom second, and the base notes are the last to arrive, always late to the party, but dressed to impress. So, if you can't control the order in which you experience them due to their evaporation, you can have a bit of control in the metaphorical volume you smell them at.

I start blends in 2 ml bottles, so that if it's a total flop and I hate it, I'm not wasting 5 ml or 10 ml worth of expensive materials and the work of several plant spirits. I start with around 25 drops in my head to play with for my budget, but remember that due to the size of diameter in orifice reducers as well as pipettes, your mileage will vary not only from company to company, but also sometimes within brands and even supply companies used by the essential oil manufacturer.

With a budget of 25 drops in mind, I'll allow a bigger chunk of the budget to go to lighter oils that can get lost in heavier, darker scents. I'll also allow for a bigger bit of the budget to go to oils that come from the manufacturer diluted. Since I'm often diluting the oils for my personal use anyway, it can result in our formerly brilliant resin or flower to become lost in the crush of other oils. If I'm using a vanilla CO2 essential oil, it's commonly going to be diluted to 10 or 12 percent to make it usable (it's pretty thick naturally) and affordable. At the time of writing, 1 ml of a quality vanilla CO2 is running around fifty dollars with a 15 percent dilution.

Heavier oils like patchouli and vetiver only need a drop or two in blends because they're going to add a lot of fragrance and we still want to be able to smell the other essential oils alongside them. Heady oils like ylang-ylang will need to keep a low profile as well, so as not to cause a headache after repeated use.

> Discontinue any oil that causes an issue and pursue investigating the root cause, as disregarding it in favor of your magical goal can lead to an allergy or sensitivity, a rash, a burn, or other health complaints. It could be something as simple as irritation from an oxidized oil or rancid carrier oil. Better safe than sorry.

With all these factors in mind, I wound up with:

- 12 drops bergamot essential oil (*Citrus bergamia*) for the ability to ask for help

- 10 drops benzoin oil (*Styrax tonkenesis*) for calm, wisdom, and peace of mind

- 1 drop patchouli essential oil (*Pogostemon cablin*) for centering, grounding, and purification

- 2 drops ylang-ylang essential oil (*Cananga odorata*) for strength of spirit

Now it needs a name. I'm calling this blend *Remember Who You Are* and I hope that it'll help some people gain the courage to be who they're supposed to be, whoever that is.

Make sure to write down your recipe. We are building a relationship that hinges on repetition. If you don't write down the recipe, you won't have it when you need it again. If you think, "I'll remember it," trust me, you won't. As my sensei used to say in black belt class, "a short pencil is better than a long memory."

Part II: How to Use the Oil We Made!
Decide How You're Going to Apply the Oil

The application process is important because we're trying to build a habit, and that can be difficult for a lot of people. So don't beat yourself up if it takes longer than you hope, expect, or desire. Building a habit works best if you can attach it to something that is already habit, like adding a hair mask before shampoo and conditioner, applying moisturizer after brushing your teeth, and so forth.

What this means in terms of an essential oil synergy is to go through your daily routine and find some habits that are already ingrained. If you carry a lip balm in your pocket and reapply during the day, consider carrying a nasal inhaler tube imbued with the synergy you made, to smell at different points throughout the day. They're roughly the same size, shape, and weight. Luckily most nasal inhaler tube brands have a different cap style, so you won't mix them up. If you're someone who applies lotion regularly to maintain your skin's hydration, consider scenting a lotion with your synergy. If your job is the focus of your scent activation, consider diffusing the oil while you work, or scenting salt you can keep on your desk to smell throughout the day. Synergies can be added to a carrier oil and used as a magical perfume to keep you focused on your intention throughout the day. If your goal has to do with sleep or dreams, consider diffusing it ten minutes before bedtime to allow the oil's fragrance to disperse throughout the room so it's ready for you when you walk into the room to prepare for bed.

The frequency with which you can repeat the ritual you're creating for yourself gives you an idea of how quickly you can build the habit. Feel free to add your synergy to a few application methods to add to the variety of places you can utilize the ritual you're building for yourself.

Application Methods

Dilution rate examples

> 1 teaspoon = 5 ml + 1 drop = 1 percent
> 2 teaspoons = 10 ml + 1 drop = 0.5 percent
> 3 teaspoons = 1 tablespoon = 15 ml + 2 drops = 0.5 percent

ANOINTING OIL

This oil has a ritual and magical purpose that aligns with deity, promises, or religious obligation.

Example—Apply to pulse points in an activation seeking the protection of a specific god-form during times of stress. It may have a different dilution rate from a perfume, as it is intended to be used over a smaller portion of the body and less often than perfume. This is a good choice if your scent activation revolves around something like a feeling of safety after escaping an abusive relationship. It could be applied over the center of the forehead to remind the wearer that they are safe and under the protection of their chosen deity. It could be applied to the tops of feet to remember to ground fully at the start of each day.

Suggested dilution rate—1–2 percent

AROMATHERAPY DIFFUSER

Diffusing your essential oils allows you to disperse the oils in the room in which you'll be working or spending some time.

Example—Makes a great choice for using a ritual oil during meditation, active ritual, and religious meetings.

Suggested dilution rate—1 drop of synergy (remember, a synergy is a blend of essential oils, before the addition of carrier oil) in 100 ml of water

AROMATHERAPY "LAVA" JEWELRY

These beaded bracelets feature decorative gemstone beads and (usually) black pumice stones that are marketed to the aromatherapy community. The idea is to scent the pumice with oil to experience the scent all day long. Please use these with caution, and never apply "neat" or undiluted essential oils to the beads, as they leave residue on the skin. Even lavender and tea tree, which have neat or undiluted uses, are not to be used undiluted in jewelry like this as it can cause sensitivities and allergies or chemical burns. Please use these only with diluted oils to prevent burns and irritation.

Example—Black stones are particularly adept at protection magic, so a lava bracelet would be suited to reminding yourself that you're protected, or hiding you from stalkers, thieves, or anyone who wishes to do you harm.

Suggested dilution rate—1 percent

AROMATHERAPY LOCKET

This is a metal locket with an open weave front to allow essential oils and other fragrance oils to waft out with the warmth of your body heat. It allows for all-day fragrance with a small throw—the area around your body where the scent can be perceived by others—so that you can be reminded of your fragrance periodically throughout your day.

Example—A fragrance created to remind yourself that you are prosperous and empowered to create the life you want to live.

Suggested dilution rate—1–2 drops on cotton or wool insert placed inside locket

DIRECT INHALATION

This is smelling the oil directly from the bottle in which the synergy was blended. Not recommended for sensitizing oils or blends heavy in heady aromas like ylang-ylang, as headaches can occur. This is an alternative to inhaler tubes where the blends are top-note heavy, as they evaporate quickly and inhaler tubes can lose the top section of the fragrance more rapidly than the direct inhalation method. Be careful to gently waft the bottle under the nose and move the bottle closer to your nose if needed. Getting essential oils on your nose can irritate skin and mucus membranes.

Example—Waft a blend of lemon-scented essential oils under your nose to raise the energy in your mind in preparation for psychic readings.

Suggested dilution rate—Neat, wafted directly from the bottle

HAND SANITIZER

This alcohol-based medium allows for a quick burst of fragrance that doesn't leave a film on the hands, as with a lotion.

Example—Ideal for applications on the job where a lingering perfume might cause an issue, where lotion could mar paperwork or legal forms, or as a quick fragrance "burn off," meaning you get the aromatic boost without a lingering fragrance that could cause issues with coworkers or allergy-prone friends.

Suggested dilution rate—2.5 percent

HYDROSOLS

Hydrosols are the by-product of making distilled essential oil. They contain .02–.03 percent essential oil dissolved into the solution during the distillation process. They make a good base for skin-safe applications for the face. *Note:* because they are the water by-product of distillation, the smell is closely related to the essential oil, but they won't smell exactly the same.

Example—Create a facial toner using aphrodisiac oils (sacred to Aphrodite) to invoke feelings of self-love or devotion to a goddess of love.

Suggested dilution rate—1 percent

INHALER TUBE

This scent accessory may look like a tube of lip balm, but instead of beeswax and oils, it contains a tube-shaped bit of cotton that gets your synergy added to it for quick bursts of aromatherapy when the need arises, but only upon request. Carry the tube in your pocket and use when the need arises. Take off the lid and place the open end against one nostril and gently inhale, repeating on the other nostril. Then replace the lid tightly so oils don't evaporate.

Example—You've created an aroma trigger to help clear your mind when concentration is needed.

Suggested dilution rate—10–15 drops on the cotton and closed inside the tube.

LOTION

If you're a person with frequently dry hands (or other parts) and find yourself taking a moment out of your day to apply lotions, this is a great choice for your ritual. You already have the built-in habit of looking for and using your lotion; we're just adding the fragrance of your scent activation perfume.

Example—A fragrance created for grounding and centering to deal with stress.

Suggested dilution rate—1.5 percent

MASSAGE OIL

Massage oil is a great way to connect your mind to your body, bond with a partner or partners, or release emotional trauma around touch.

Example—A ritual oil for strength massaged into arms and legs before or after a protest or march.

Suggested dilution rate—2–2.5 percent

ROLLER BOTTLE/PERFUME

This is a very popular option as it is accessible and customizable. There are many varieties due to the popularity of 10 ml roller bottles. There are roller tops available for 5 ml bottles as well. In the realm of 10 ml roller bottles, there are a rainbow of colors, both in colored glass (amber, violet, cobalt blue, emerald green, and more) as well as rainbow tints applied over glass for a number of effects. Instead of submerging crystal chips into your oil and losing volume of your oil (and therefore changing your dilution rate) there are companies

that make roller ball caps for 10 ml roller bottles out of gemstones so you can apply your ritual oils with semiprecious gemstones. Observed roller caps include Moss Agate, Blue Tiger's Eye, Rhodonite, Snowflake Obsidian, Labradorite, Yellow Jade, Hematite, Red Aventurine, Rose Quartz, Clear Quartz, Rainbow Fluorite, and Brecciated Jasper.

Example—An oil created for justice, applied during a marathon letter writing campaign to overturn an unjust law or an unjust conviction, or petitioning for a law not to be passed.

Suggested dilution rate—2 percent

ROOM SPRAYS

These sprays can be created easily with water and essential oils; just don't forget to invite an intermediary to the party. Oil and water don't mix, so you'll need a friend to introduce the two, like salt, rubbing alcohol, or witch hazel.

Example—Create a room spray that is used in high-traffic areas to remind anyone who comes into your home that they are loved, and this is a safe place for them.

Suggested dilution rate—5 percent

SALT DIFFUSER

Adding essential oils to salt is a time-honored method for diffusing fragrance into the air. It's a great alternative to water diffusing, especially near sensitive electronics or in an area where it might be spilled. If the salt gets spilled, it can be swept back into the container it came from. If water spills, it can damage finished wooden surfaces, electronics, or other surfaces.

Example—Make a calming blend to help keep negative emotions from a coworker from impacting your job performance.

Suggested dilution rate—5–7 drops per ½ cup of salt

SCRUB (SALT OR SUGAR)

Scrubs are an effective way to remove dead skin cells, brighten skin's complexion, and increase blood flow. If you're using the scrub on your face, sugar is recommended; as the particles are smaller and smoother, they'll operate delicately on the face. Surfaces that are too large and angular, like ground apricot kernel, cut the skin instead of polishing, causing micro tears and prematurely aging the skin. Salt should be used for the body as the crystals polish for a smoother appearance. Sugar should not be used on the body or in bathwater, as it will encourage the growth of yeast. *Note:* skin cells only live 2.5 days once exposed to air, so if you're exfoliating more frequently than every 2.5 days you are sloughing off healthy, living tissue, which will lead to premature aging of the skin.

Example—A self-love scrub with herbs from the garden and oils that remind you you're worthy.

Suggested dilution rate—5 percent

SOAP

We stop to wash our hands so often, it's practically ingrained, so when adding magic to our habits, soap is a great place to start. If you make your own bar soap, either lye cold process, or melt and pour, it makes a great addition to our practical skills, but even unscented pump soaps can benefit from a bit of aromatic magic.

Example—Create an aromatherapy activation for health and wellness. Each time you wash your hands, you're reinforcing healthy habits, so why not make those habits make room for magical health as well?

Suggested dilution rate—melt and pour 0.5-2.5 percent cold process 3-5 percent (calculate based on weight).

FOR PREGNANT PEOPLE

Suggested dilution rate—0.5–1 percent dilution rate suggested for oils that are safe to use during pregnancy. Some oils to avoid during pregnancy include: basil, birch, cedarwood, clary sage, cypress, geranium, hyssop, jasmine, juniper, marjoram, mugwort, myrrh, nutmeg, peppermint, spearmint, pennyroyal, rosemary, tarragon, and thyme. During the first trimester, when pregnant bodies are more susceptible to changes, avoid chamomile, lavender, and rose. If you have created a scent activation that includes any of these oils, suspend any and all use of oils that can potentially cause a miscarriage. Talk to your medical professionals about resuming your aromatherapy practice after nursing has stopped, so as not to potentially pass along oils during lactation. Essential oils are not recommended for anyone under twelve years of age without the supervision of a clinical aromatherapist or medical doctor. Their livers and kidneys are not equipped to handle the strength of these volatile oils and it can cause organ harm, respiratory failure, and suffocation, among other dangers.

Topical Use Caution

If any of your application methods involve topical application, patch testing is a good place to start. Our bodies are marvelous works of art, but we can develop allergies and sensitivities at any point, even with a positive history of use. I suggest a 0.5 percent dilution rate: 1 drop of essential oil or synergy to 2 teaspoons of carrier oil. Mix and apply to a thinner area of skin such as the inside of the elbow or wrist. Wait twenty-four hours to ensure that there are no reactions. If you're unsure that you'll remember where you applied the mixture, draw a small circle around your experimental spot to ensure you'll have the correct area under observation.

If there is a reaction, discontinue use and investigate immediately. There are a few reasons skin could react, and the easiest to remedy is to make sure your carrier oil isn't rancid. When it goes rancid it can cause a host of irritations, and since it makes up the largest portion of your sample test, it's the easiest to rule out.

Looking to your carrier oil, check the bottle. Are the sides of the bottle pulled in? By how much? As oil ages, it pulls in oxygen, using up the available O_2 in the bottle. (Plastic is not an oxygen barrier, glass is.) The further the sides are pulled in, the more oxygen has been used inside the bottle. Next observe the color. Has the color changed in any discernible way? Does it appear cloudy in some or all of the volume? Even a small portion of cloudy oil can signal the beginning of rancidity. Your first impulse might be to sniff the top of the bottle, but as the oil has theoretically been used before, there could be old, oxygenated oil around the top that could skew your results. Instead place a tablespoon or so of carrier oil into a shallow container like a small, clean bathroom cup, custard cup, or measuring spoon. Smell the oil from this new, clean surface to get an accurate idea of the scent available.

If your carrier oil passes your tests and is deemed useable, it's time to look at our potentially sensitizing oils. Oils such as black pepper, clove, cinnamon, basil, oregano, cassia, lemon myrtle, and lemongrass can be sensitizing to the skin and should be used very sparingly, at 0.5–1 percent dilution only, as sensitivity can result from overuse. Potentially sensitizing oils should be avoided in body massage because you're applying a small amount over a large percentage of your skin. Check your oils for phototoxic effects for similar reasons.

If you have reason to suspect a specific oil, consider patch testing the other oils in the blend one at a time, in a 0.5 percent dilution, to rule them out, rather than exposing yourself again to something you might be allergic to. Remember, some oils can *become* sensitizing if they've aged more than two years; pines and citrus leap to mind, but they aren't the only culprits. Make sure to research your materials as much as possible. It may not be that you're allergic to something new, it could be that the oil that you are working with is old enough to cause sensitization.

TIME

Because we are discussing repeated actions over a period of time, lower dilutions are always encouraged because high volumes and high exposure times can lead even the most gentle lavender to cause issues. Trust your body.

Ritual Actions

It's important, no matter the application method you choose, to employ the same ritual actions so that you can ensure that your brain is understanding the programming you're applying. For instance, if one moment you are thinking about the devotion of Hecate, and the next you're hoping for a winning lottery ticket, you can be giving your subconscious mixed messages. If you have difficulty concentrating for whatever reason, it's best to keep the message short and sweet.

We're looking to pair a reaction; think of it as a physical call and response. You smell your aroma (however you choose to do that), you perform the action.

EXAMPLES

You smell lemon balm, you take a deep breath and embrace calm. Over time, your calming becomes second nature.

You smell calamus, you banish fatigue by drawing energy up from the earth to supplement your own. Soon, you won't need to smell the calamus; you'll think of it and direct your body to draw up that energy. After a while you'll just notice you are tired and draw up that energy automatically, refreshing your mind, body, and spirit.

To start, look at the intention you've set and the method you'd like to employ. It should build your ritual action into the application.

Intention: "I'm not going to let my aggressive coworker get to me."

OILS

- ✜ Neroli for calming, soothing, and stress relief.

- ✜ Ginger for strength and protection.

- ✜ Patchouli for defense and harmony.

It's an invigorating scent because of the ginger, but the brightness of the neroli allows me to not let the coworker get to me personally. The patchouli will ground any nasty words they have for me, like water off of a duck's back. Patchouli is pretty syrupy and dark, so only 1 drop is needed. I don't want to get melancholy. Ginger can be aggressive in return, and I'd rather not get into an argument at work with this person. I'll use 2 drops there. The rest should be neroli to keep to the high road.

METHOD: LOTION

Ritual Action: When I feel my coworker is getting to me, I'll apply my lotion, no more frequently than once every 4 hours. I'll open the container, dot some on each hand, rub it into the skin, hold my hands over my face, and inhale for a moment of grounding. I'll set my magical shields or check to make sure they're operating correctly and go back to the task at hand. The stopping to ground and center when faced with aggression and mean-spiritedness is a healthy way to avoid conflict and escalating the situation.

If the ritual action is helping, but the activation is needed more frequently than application of the lotion is recommended, I'd employ a twofold approach and add the synergy developed above to an unscented lotion and a nasal inhaler tube, so I'm not applying lotion every hour.

After a month or so of this routine, I'd evaluate whether it was helping the situation and adjust my approach if needed. Remember to take careful notes, because if you want to continue the action, or adjust your approach, you'll need to know what you did.

BOTANICAL LISTINGS A TO Z 10

In this volume, as others, you may find conflicting information about the spirit nature of the plants you seek to work with. One volume may list an airy, Mercurial nature while another lists a fiery-natured Mars aspect. Both volumes may be correct. A potential stumbling block could be the nomenclature; the name could be the trickster of the group. Several plants may share the same common name, lending itself to confusion among different practitioners. For example, in my research for bergamot while I was writing *Blackthorn's Botanical Magic*, I had two wildly different sets of associations. I dug through sources for a day and realized they referred to *Citrus bergamia* and *Monarda fistulosa*. The planetary associations could refer to different parts used from the same plant. One plant may have several Latin binomials, such as *Tilia* (Linden) and *Pimenta* (allspice). The best course of action is to do as much research as is feasible at the time to make informed choices in your magical and aromatherapeutic uses.

MAKING A MAGICAL PEN

One of the easiest ways to work with essential oils, especially the ones that are potentially sensitizing, like cinnamon, allspice, black pepper, and others, is to make a magical pen. Add a drop of your essential oil of choice to a 10 ml roller bottle and fill the rest of the way with the carrier oil of choice before placing the roller ball and cap, and rolling the bottle between your hands. Make sure to label the bottle, as unlabeled bottles can be dangerous. If you work with gemstones, there are companies that make roller bottles, where instead of a plastic roller ball, they're made from semiprecious gemstones, so you don't lose volume of oil to gemstone chips.

Carrier Oils

These oils are commonly used in aromatherapy to safely dilute the essential oils to help skin, add magic, and encourage safety for topical application.

Apricot Kernel Oil—Great for sensitive skin, associated with Venus, so useful with spells concerning love, beauty, luxury goods, and Friday. Shelf life: 6–12 months.

Avocado Oil—Anti-inflammatory oil, aligned with prosperity magic and Jupiter. Beneficial on Thursday. Shelf life: 3 months

Coconut Oil—Can lock in moisture in wet skin, acts as a barrier. Aligned with virility magic, goal-oriented magic. Associated with Tuesday. Shelf life 12–24 months.

Evening Primrose Oil—Hydrating for delicate skin like face and under eyes. It is associated with psychic visions and intuition, as well as with boundaries, and good luck and the moon, Mondays. Shelf life: 3–6 months.

Expressed Oil—Solid at room temperature. Great for salves.

Fractionated Oil—Liquid at room temperature. Great for perfume base.

Grape-Seed Oil—Reduces wrinkles, used in lip gloss, and mildly astringent. Magical applications involve fertility, prosperity, banishing sorrow, overcoming self-consciousness, and Mondays. Shelf life: 4–6 months.

Jojoba Oil—Not a true oil, wax in liquid form. Jojoba is highly moisturizing for all skin types. Magically aligned with determination, sheer force of will, and Tuesdays. Shelf life: 24 months.

Meadowsweet Oil—Soothes inflammation, natural source of salicylic acid for clear skin. The magical associations of meadowsweet are Venusian: calming, peace, love, luxury, and Friday. Shelf life: 36 months.

Olive Oil—Heals dry-skin cracks and is easily absorbed. Magical associations of prosperity, good luck, blessings, and Sundays. Shelf life: 18–24 months.

Sunflower Oil—Provides vitamin E, linoleic acid, and antioxidants for all skin types to protect it from external damage. As the name implies, it carries the magic of the sun and is aligned with protection, prosperity, and Sundays. Shelf life: 12 months.

Sweet Almond Oil—A light texture, and makes for a good slip massage oil. Magically it is a forgiving oil to work with, aligned with prosperity, alertness of the mind, protection of children, beauty, and prophecy. Because of the high vitamin E content, it has a shelf stability to benefit its lower price point. Shelf life: 9–12 months.

For an in-depth study of these carrier oils and more look in *Blackthorn's Botanical Magic*.

Dilution of Essential Oils

When looking at the oils used as a carrier and their volumes, we are using the sensitive dilution rate of 1 percent that is generally used on sensitive areas or with potentially sensitizing oils like black pepper. This dilution is the general guideline or GRAS (generally regarded as safe) dilution rate. When dealing with potentially sensitizing essential oils, less is more. If you're using the oils for aromatherapeutic or emotional benefit, 1.5 percent dilution is recommended.

How Long Do Herbs Last? How Much Do I Use?

As long as this herb is something I use in my cooking, my rule is one to two years in the spice cupboard, and then it gets moved to the magical supply cabinet, until it goes to the compost. How do I know it goes into the compost? When it has lost all its color, flavor, and scent. For this reason, I don't suggest going to your local witchy shop and buying one of everything you can afford, no matter how much your little heart desires, because if you don't know that plant yet, you likely aren't going to reach for it in a spell. Wait until you have a specific use for it and buy an ounce or two. Buy the smallest amount that seems reasonable because the magical Law of Contagion tells us that the spell only needs a pinch. Spells aren't more effective just because we include a huge amount. Just like our spells don't need the biggest crystal either.

What if I Have Allergies?

If you are unfamiliar with an essential oil from a specific plant, and don't know how you'll react to it topically, there are a few steps you can take to ensure a safe experience. If you know you're allergic to a listed essential oil, seek out a safe substitution; no spell is worth a trip to the emergency room.

1. Grab your notebook where you take down recipes and test oils for quality. Remove the lid of the oil, and place the oil about a hand's width away from your nose. With the opposite hand, gently waft the aroma towards your nose. We use the wafting technique in chemistry to catch aromas without getting close enough to cause airway damage. Record any memories you might have, emotions that come up, or thoughts you have, as they play an important role in warning us of any danger. Even if you don't have a topical allergy to an essential oil, you can have traumatic associations with that aroma, and it's a good idea to examine those at a later time, potentially with a licensed therapist.

2. If no traumatic feelings or physical reactions occur, you can move to gently smelling the bottle for a slightly more concentrated dose. Again, record any findings.

3. In the event that you have no issues, take a 10 ml roll-on bottle, place 1 drop of the essential oil into it, and fill it with a carrier oil that you *know* you aren't allergic to. One drop in 10 ml of carrier oil is a 1 percent dilution rate and listed for sensitive applications. Place a drop of oil from your diluted magical pen on the inside of the wrist or elbow, where it won't be exposed to direct sunlight in case it's a phototoxic essential oil such as angelica, lemon verbena, some of the citruses, bergamot, opoponax, or marigold (tagetes). Circle the drop of oil with a pen and observe.

> If redness, irritation, pain, burning, hives, or other reactions occur, flush with carrier oil and then gently wash with soap. Carefully pat dry. Record any findings.

Candle Magic

Here are some answers to frequently asked questions about the candle spells.

What do I do if I don't have the candle color listed in the spell?

There is no harm in substituting another candle color, especially if the color correspondence provided doesn't fit with your culture or experience, as you are the one doing the magic. Your thoughts, feelings, and experiences are valid. My suggestions are only that. You have to feel empowered to make the magical choices for your own highest good. I'm just here to facilitate that. You know your needs best.

Candle Carving: How do I do that?

The words described in the spells below can very easily be carved with a ballpoint pen into the candles being used. Candles aren't made of steel or other hard metals. That being said, ritual theater can be important to some practitioners. If you'd like to use a specific candle scribe, there are some really incredible artisans that make dedicated ritual tools like that. If you're handy, you may want to make or dedicate one yourself. They can be as simple as a nail from a hardware store or as complicated as your crafty heart desires. I like the look of masonry nails. They have flat, rectangular heads and an antique look. Some suggestions: a polymer clay pencil shape with a nail embedded in the tip. You can easily incorporate color magic with polymer clay. If you are a woodworker you'll find every wood has its own magical associations. Design a wand shape that appeals to you and drill out narrow end tip to add a nail for a carving tip. The only limit is your own imagination.

Fire safety: Make sure to have a fire extinguisher in any room where candle magic is being performed. Safety first.

The Magical Uses of Bayberry Candles

A traditional Yuletide charm for prosperity in the new year goes like this: *A bayberry candle burned to the socket/Brings luck into the home/And gold in your pocket.* So burning a bayberry taper candle made from the wax of boiling bayberry fruit to remove the waxy coating is not only a nod to traditional New England practice honoring the tradition of the fruit, but also a powerful magical ally year round.

Attraction—To attract a sexual partner, anoint with sweet almond oil (unconditional love) and burn on a Friday (love). Burn until complete.

Blessings—To petition for monetary blessings, anoint with grape-seed oil (prosperity) on a Sunday (success). Burn until complete.

Clarity—To bring clarity to a situation, anoint the candle with evening primrose oil (clear sight) and burn on a Wednesday (communication). Burn until complete.

Control of a situation—Anoint a candle with mineral oil (control) and burn on a Tuesday (victory). Burn until complete.

Defense—To defend yourself in court, anoint the candle with grape-seed oil (protection) on a Thursday (justice). Burn until complete.

Energy—To see an increase in your energy, anoint the candle with fractionated coconut oil (goal oriented) and burn on a Sunday (success). Burn until complete.

Fortunes, good—To ensure your continued good fortune, anoint a bayberry taper with sunflower oil (long-term blessings of the sun) on a Sunday (personal empowerment). Burn until complete.

Happiness—Anoint the candle with avocado oil (joy) and burn on a Monday (emotional security). Burn until complete.

Harmony—Anoint the candle with avocado oil (fertility). Best if done on a Monday (emotional security). Burn until complete.

Hex-breaking—Anoint the candle with jojoba oil (overcoming obstacles) on a Tuesday (victory). Burn until complete.

Influence, protect from—Anoint the candle with evening primrose (clear intuitive vision) on a Thursday (protection). Burn until complete.

Jealousy, to ease—Anoint the candle with grape-seed oil (love) on a Friday (love). Burn until complete.

Justice—Anoint the candle with fractionated coconut oil (goal oriented) on a Thursday (protection). Burn until complete.

Luck—Anoint the candle with olive oil (prosperity) on a Sunday (success). Burn until complete.

Money—Anoint the candle with olive oil (prosperity) on a Tuesday (victory). Burn until complete.

Peace—Anoint the candle with grape-seed oil (emotional peace) on a Monday (emotional security). Burn until complete.

Prosperity—Anoint the candle with olive oil (money) on a Sunday (luck). Burn until complete.

Protection—Anoint the candle with sweet almond oil (protection of nature spirits) on a Thursday (power). Burn until complete.

Purification—Anoint the candle with sunflower oil (long-term goals) on a Saturday (banishing). Burn until complete.

Stimulation—Anoint the candle with avocado oil (proliferation) on a Sunday (beginnings). Burn until complete.

Success—Anoint the candle with sunflower oil (speedy magic) on a Sunday (success). Burn until complete.

Tranquility—Anoint the candle with sweet almond oil (nourishing) on a Monday (emotional well-being). Burn until complete.

Wealth—Anoint the candle with olive oil (prosperity) on a Wednesday (change). Burn until complete.

Well-being—Anoint the candle with sweet almond oil (nurturing) on a Monday (emotional well-being). Burn until complete.

Wishes—Anoint the candle with grape-seed oil (divine requests) on a Thursday (power). Burn until complete.

ALLSPICE

Scientific Name: *Pimenta officinalis, P. dioica, P. vulgaris,* et al.

Botanical Family: Myrtaceae

World Origin: India

Plant's Oil: Berries and leaves

Scent Description: Fiery, spicy, warm

Evaporation: Middle note

Scent Impact: Antidepressant, energizing

Magical Correspondences

Application: Diffuse or dilute heavily

Element: Fire

Day: Tuesday

Magical Uses: Love and lust, protection, banishing, prosperity, gambling luck

Planet: Mars

Astrological Sign: Aries

Suggested Crystal: Fire Agate—Ruled by Aries: burns away fear

Deity/Spirit: Andarta—Brythonic goddess of victory

> ### WARNING
> Do not use this essential oil if you have a history of blood clots; if you are on anticoagulants, aspirin, or Warfarin; or forty-eight hours before any surgical procedure. Keep away from mucus membranes.

Herbal Lore/Uses

It is such a widely utilized plant that it has fourteen synonyms in the Latin binomial that all correspond to allspice, so named because it tastes like a blend of so many spices, like clove, cinnamon, ginger, and more. In common usage today, allspice is a part of a particularly popular fall mélange, pumpkin pie spice (a mix of cinnamon, ginger, nutmeg, allspice, and cloves) used to flavor everything from American pumpkin pie to traditional sweet breads and more. It's a historic blend that comes into seasonal enjoyment as soon as the weather turns chilly.

Spells

Attraction, physical—Place a drop of amber paste (perfumed paste made from amber resin) on one wrist and gently massage with the opposite wrist to spread the fragrance. Add a drop of diluted allspice oil to a scent locket and visualize being seen as attractive—in a healthy way—to the people around you before leaving the house for the day.

Compassion—During times of stress, with a chance of compassion fatigue, carry three small allspice berries in a small handkerchief in a pocket on your nondominant side. Smell the small packet when additional reserves of compassion are needed.

Confidence—Anoint a small piece of paper or cloth with a drop of allspice essential oil and place it inside the shoe you wear on your dominant foot. Let the essence of allspice carry your confidence through the day.

Consecration—In a sturdy mortar add 2 ounces of a carrier oil of choice and add an allspice berry. With the pestle, break up the berry and grind it in a counterclockwise motion, visualizing any impurities being driven out. Use this anointing oil for ritual tools, altar spaces, and sacred journals as appropriate.

Courage—Grab an orange candle and write the word "courage" on it with a ballpoint pen or candle scribe and then anoint with diluted allspice essential oil. Burn on a Tuesday.

Determination—Place 1.5–2 teaspoons of black tea in an infuser, and add one allspice berry. Pour water at 212° F (100° C) and allow the tea to steep for 5 minutes. Remove infuser; add sweetener if desired. Drink while thinking about the situation that requires boldness and see it resolving.

Energy, physical—Place a drop of allspice essential oil on a tissue and place it in the pocket of your nondominant side to energize the spirit of your "incoming" energy. When you need a boost throughout the day, give it a sniff, in through the nose and out through the mouth. Ground and center yourself, and see yourself connected to the earth for times when your energy needs some sustainability.

Fear, to overcome—Place one allspice berry in your mortar and cover with a tablespoon of your carrier oil of choice. Crush the berry with the pestle and grind finely. Massage into the soles of your feet to ground you in the real, the here and now. Remind yourself of your strength and see yourself without the fear.

Friendship—Grab a yellow candle (joy) and inscribe "friendship" on it. Anoint with diluted allspice essential oil and view your life filled with the happiness of rich friendships and alliances. Burn on a Sunday (joy, attraction, happiness).

Good Luck—Place a small amount of pumpkin pie spice on burning incense charcoal in a fireproof container like a censer, and smoke cleanse the exterior of a home or business to attract luck. (Burn potentially irritating herbs only in well-ventilated areas.)

Healing—Place a teaspoon of whole allspice berries in a blue pouch and anoint it with consecrated water. Give it to the one in need of healing and let them know you are thinking of them until they are well again.

Kindness, to receive—In a well-ventilated space, burn a small frankincense tear with a small pinch of ground allspice, while envisioning yourself wrapped in a cloud of kindness, support, and comfort.

Money—Anoint the smallest note in your currency, a dollar bill, with diluted allspice essential oil, either at the corners or with a symbol of prosperity. Fold neatly and tuck it into a rarely used part of the wallet so that you don't spend it. Allow it to attract more prosperity to your wallet. Best on a Sunday (luck).

Pain, to relieve (stomach)—Sit in a comfortable position, and place a single drop of allspice essential oil on a tissue. Allow your mind to relax, and take three soft breaths, in and out. Relax each muscle, from the toes up to the top of your head, taking special care to breathe through your belly. Take note, if abdominal massage feels appropriate for relief of gas or constipation, always work in a clockwise manner to follow the path of the intestines. Counterclockwise motions can exacerbate the issue of constipation.

Power, to increase—Grind an allspice berry in a mortar and pestle with a clockwise motion to increase the power grounded in this powder. Once at a fine texture, sprinkle inside the shoes (if you go without socks, consider placing the powder under any insole present to keep from potential irritants), and see yourself grounded in your power. Consider doing this before asking for a raise, having a difficult conversation with loved ones, or when feeling insecure.

Protection—To protect families, warm apple cider on the stove with allspice berries, cinnamon sticks, and freshly sliced ginger coins and serve on chilly nights.

Spirituality—Place a drop of allspice essential oil in a scented locket on a piece of cotton or wool and feel connected to your ancestors, prominent deities, spirits, or the Universe. Take slow, measured breaths, in through the nose and out through the mouth, while concentrating on that connection.

Lava bead aromatherapy jewelry allows undiluted essential oils to come in contact with skin and can cause sensitivities or contact dermatitis. Please be aware.

Strength/willpower—Draw a stick figure of yourself on a piece of paper. Outline it with diluted allspice oil from your magical pen, or anoint the paper. Fold toward you three times and place it under a candleholder or fireproof dish and burn a candle in the holder (tea light preferred). Burn on a Sunday (protection) for best results.

Success—Take a yellow (success) piece of paper and write out the situation that requires perseverance. Anoint the paper with diluted allspice essential oil and fold four times. Place it in the shoe of your dominant foot. Keep in your shoe until either you wear a hole in the paper or your situation resolves.

Recipe: First Date Jitters

This spicy first date perfume oil has the magic of lust and beauty, for your first date jitters, or meeting your crush. It has the magic of strength and joy if you're rekindling romance.

- 10 drops allspice essential oil (*Pimenta officinalis*) for physical attraction, sex, lust, friendship, determination, overcoming fear

- 2 drops patchouli essential oil (Pogostemon cablin) for sexual energy, strengthening the body, harmony

- 15 drops tangerine essential oil (Citrus reticulata) to awaken joy, inspire hospitality, defend your boundaries, power your magic

Blend the synergy in a 2 ml bottle. For dates at home, diffuse 1 drop in 100 ml of water 10 minutes before your date arrives. Alternately, place 1 ounce of rubbing alcohol in a 2-ounce spray bottle, add the 2 ml bottle to the 2-ounce spray bottle, and top off with water. Spray in the air as a room refresher, to inspire spice, warmth, and arousal. To wear as a perfume, add 5 drops of synergy to a 10 ml bottle, and top with the carrier of your choice. Add the roller ball and lid, then label. Best if made on a Friday.

BALSAM FIR

Scientific Name: *Abies spp.*

Botanical Family: Abietaceae

World Origin: Idaho, USA

Plant's Oil: Oleoresin

Scent Description: Resinous, sweet, deep, sharp

Evaporation: Middle note

Scent Impact: Emotional calm, improved sleep, antianxiety

Magical Correspondences

Application: Diffuse, dilute

Element: Fire, Water, Air

Day: Thursday, Sunday, Saturday, Friday

Magical Uses: Exorcism of baneful spirits, health, purification, restorative

Planet: Jupiter, Sun, Saturn, Venus, Mercury

Astrological Sign: Capricorn (Earthy Saturn), Sagittarius (Fiery Jupiter)

Suggested Crystal: Fergusonite—Ruled by Aquarius and Virgo: enhances self-esteem, inner strength

Deity/Spirit: Snoqualm—God of the Moon from the Snoqualmie people of the Pacific Northwest, called The People of the Moon

---

WARNING
Use 0.5-1 percent dilution, as irritation may occur.

Herbal Lore/Uses

There are over fifty species of fir trees that have a history of botanical use going back thousands of years. Because of the wide variety of species and botanical ranges in habitat and environment, each species has adapted to its own harsh clime and thus has a different chemical makeup. This variety in herbal actions is largely responsible for the large variety of planetary rulerships noted above. The variety in medical applications of nearly every part of these majestic trees, useful in herbal medicine, is astounding. The trees themselves are also known to survivalists, foragers, and hikers due to their wide range of benefits. People who otherwise wouldn't know a quaking aspen from an oak tree know they can make botanical Band-Aids from the sap if they fall while hiking, or make a tea with the needles for their laxative properties. The gold rush had frontier doctors prescribing fir resin for cold, wet coughs as a warming herbal action, hence the solar magic denoted above.

These trees were so important to native populations that there was much mythology surrounding them. Lumberjacks would refuse to fell fir trees, lest they offend or hurt the spirit of the woman inside the tree. The Chippewa have used fir or *a'ninandak'* for headaches since before their recorded history.

The story of how fir trees came to the Cascade Mountains is the contribution of the Snoqualmie people of the same region. They named themselves after Snoqualm, the god of the moon. They are the People of the Moon, and the god that gave them their name, Snoqualm, features prominently in the story. Once, there were no spruce, cedar, pine, and fir trees on earth. It was said that Snoqualm/Moon kept these trees in the Sky Land for himself. He kept the sun in a box, and the earth was dark. Snoqualm grew curious about the shadowy realm below and asked Spider to weave him a rope down to the mountaintops so that he could view the world below his. Spider agreed and wove the long, sturdy rope for him.

Blue Jay and Fox saw Moon using his rope to view the earth, so they climbed the rope up to the bottom of the sky, where Blue Jay poked a hole in the clouds for them to enter Sky Land. As they scrambled up into the new land, they viewed trees they'd never seen and Fox was in awe. Blue Jay decided to investigate the trees, while Fox wandered to Moon's home. Outside the home Fox spotted a beaver trap, disguised himself, and hopped into the trap. When Moon returned from his visit below he was happy his trap had borne fruit in the form of Fox disguised as a beaver. He butchered the pretend beaver and went to sleep.

When night fell, Fox came back to life, took back his skin, and ran back to Blue Jay. Here is where two sources diverge. In one version of the story Fox stole the tools to make fire, because the world was dark and cold. In the second, Fox grabbed as many trees he could carry under his arms on his way back to Blue Jay. Moon woke up and saw his beaver pelt missing and beaver tracks leading into the woods. In the Sun version, he grabbed the box containing the Sun to keep anyone from stealing it.

When Fox returned to the hole in the sky, he used his beaver disguise to chew most of the way through the rope Spider had woven. Fox and Blue Jay started climbing down the rope to escape before Moon caught them. As Moon was climbing down the rope after them, he realized too late that the rope was frayed and beginning to unravel under his weight. He slipped and had to let the box containing the sun fall open to keep himself upright. As soon as Fox and Blue Jay were safely on the ground, the rope finally snapped, leaving Moon with nothing to hold onto. He crashed into Mount Si and became a part of the mountain, and that's why when you look at the mountain, you can still see the face of Moon.

Fox and Blue Jay planted all the trees they collected to they could be enjoyed by everyone.

Spells

Assistance, divination/psychic—If you are psychically blocked, light an incense charcoal tablet and burn a pinch of fir needles or fir resin over the charcoal. Inhale the smoke gently and allow your mind to relax and accept the connection to the other realms provided by fir.

Awareness, spiritual—To extend your awareness outside of your body, diffuse 1 drop of fir essential oil in 100 ml of water. Sit or lie comfortably and center your awareness on your body. Feel the energetic body that overlays your physical one and imagine it getting much larger, and then much, much smaller. Play to the extent you feel comfortable exploring the limits of your spiritual form, as it will help increase your spiritual awareness of your physical form as well.

Blessings (mother and baby)—At such a time as is appropriate, gather water for the mother and baby, as well as a fresh fir stem if possible. If impossible, a handful of dried fir needles placed into cool water will suffice. Ask the water to be blessed in whatever manner is appropriate for your tradition. Sprinkle the foreheads of mother and baby with the fresh fir branch, and ask for their growth, closeness, understanding, and compassion.

Calm/clarity—Use if you have questions about your situation, or need to center yourself after a stressful time and need to understand why you are facing these times. Add 1 drop of fir essential oil to a 10 ml roll-on bottle and fill the rest of the way with carrier oil. Cap with a roller ball and lid before gently rolling it between your hands to blend the oils together. Once your oils have blended, draw a question mark "?" over your heart and gently massage in, with clockwise circles, feeling your calmness increase and clarity come to you. Alternatively, carve a question mark into a chime candle that feels right for your situation, anoint the candle with your magical pen, and burn on a Monday for emotional clarity and calm support.

Clearing/cleansing—To clear a space of negativity, burn fir needles or resin over charcoal, seeing any evil spirits or negative energy being driven out by the force of the smoke.

Comfort—In times of emotional duress, anoint a wool or cotton pad small enough for essential oil jewelry with a drop or two of fir essential oil. Wear all day, and allow the vapor of the fragrant oil to remind you throughout your day that you are loved, you are worthy, and you are safe. You won't smell the oil every minute of your day, so when you notice it, take a moment to center yourself and repeat those words aloud or silently and believe them.

Creation/inspiration—For the creatives among us, if you are creating a new project, fir is the best ally. When we create, whether it is a painting, a song, a book, or even just a slide deck for work, fir can spark that communication through its connection to Mercury and Air. Allow some air into your workspace if possible. If you're working in a scent-free environment, add 7–10 drops of fir essential oil onto the cotton of a nasal inhaler (they are about the size of a tube of lip balm), and when indulging in creative endeavors, take a slow, deep breath in through one nostril, and then the other. You'll begin to feel the connection to Mercury and your creative drive in no time. This is especially helpful during Mercury retrograde!

Defense—To protect you, your home, or your space, grab an ounce of dried fir needles (fresh may be sticky!) and sprinkle them in the four corners of your space, whether it be bedroom, dorm room, apartment, or cubicle. See or feel the space seal itself against all comers.

Digestive problems—If you're experiencing digestive upset, irritable bowel syndrome (IBS), gastroparesis, or other digestive tract issues, take a fir magical pen (see above) and trace the digestive tract on your belly. Gently massage the oil into your belly in a clockwise direction (never use counterclockwise massage motions on the lower abdomen as it can cause constipation) and feel the soothing magic of your spirit.

Emotional expression—When in times of overwhelm, the weight of our feelings can get trapped in our hearts, like a bottle of soda in a hot car, just waiting for a chance to blow up under the slightest provocation. Instead, build yourself a relief valve by allowing those feelings to escape as needed. To one cup of salt, add 15–20 drops of fir essential oil; stir to incorporate. Leave those to the side while you draw a warm bath. When the tub is half full, sprinkle in as much or as little salt as you'd like. Salt is physically and emotionally nourishing. Epsom salts are perfectly fine to use, as they contain magnesium that can be absorbed into the skin to aid your rest and recovery. Sadness, depression, and grief all take a physical toll on the body that is discounted by popular culture because in their minds, depression or sadness happen in the mind. Our bodies also keep track of what's going on, and also need nourishment. Take your time in the bathtub, as our bodies need time to get to know each other again before the feelings can be processed.

Energy, increase—If you've been feeling under the weather, sluggish, or tired, add 7–10 drops of fir essential oil to a nasal inhaler, stopper the end, and allow to absorb for 10 minutes. When the oil has had time to disperse, unscrew the cap and gently inhale in through one nostril, and out through the mouth, repeating on the opposite side.

Forest Spirits—To connect with the tree spirits of the forest, add 7–10 drops of fir essential oil to a cup of Epsom salts and stir thoroughly. Allow them to rest while you draw a bath, calling to the energies of the trees you seek to commune with. The water that once nourished their roots now flows through your water tap, through the magic of the water cycle. Once the tub is half full, begin adding salts to the warm bathwater until you reach the desired fragrance. Remember the law of contagion: as little as a pinch is perfectly fine and magical if you're concerned about an overwhelming fragrance or potential sensitization.

Grounding—To aid in removing excess disparate energies, diffuse 1 drop in 100 ml of water in the space where you will be grounding yourself, 10 minutes before your practice is to start, to allow the scent to dissipate throughout the room. Sit or lie comfortably and practice breathing in through the nose and out through the mouth. Once you are connected with your breath, feel or see the scattered excess energies in your arms and legs come into the center of your body and then feel/picture it going deeply into the ground where the earth can use it far better than we can. If you can't picture things in your head (many can't) it feels to me that it has the texture of TV static.

Happiness/hope—To restore joy in your heart, grab your fir magical pen, and draw a heart, smiley face, or other symbols that represent joy on your chest. Massage the oil into your skin in a clockwise fashion to increase those feelings.

Harmony—To restore harmony to a space, light an incense charcoal tablet and place a pinch or two of fir needles on the glowing red coal. *Please note:* conifer needles have significantly less moisture in them than their herbal counterparts and fresh needles can be used, but they may not burn as quickly or easily. If you have access to fir trees, instead of cutting live branches, scoop dead needles into a brown paper bag and allow them to continue to dry in case of rain or atmospheric moisture that could mold your new harvest.

Inflammation—Fir has been used in magic and herbal medicine for its anti-inflammatory action for hundreds of years. Choose the joints or tendons that are inflamed and draw a counterclockwise spiral over the inflamed area. (Keep the oil away from openings in the skin as it could cause discomfort.) Massage into the skin in a counterclockwise motion to banish the pain, heat, and stiffness.

Insight—If you need insight into a specific problem, light an incense charcoal disk and place in a fireproof dish. When it is burning well, add a pinch or two of fir needles. Bathe yourself in the smoke and watch the patterns made by the smoke. Allow your mind to wander, unobstructed. Softly focus your eyes as you watch the patterns made by the smoke and allow the insight you need to come to you.

Blackthorn's Book of Sacred Plant Magic

Past lives/reincarnation—Sit or lie in a comfortable position. With your fir magical pen, draw clockwise spirals on your wrists, the tops of your feet, and your forehead. Massage the symbols into the skin and gently inhale the aroma. Visualize or feel yourself getting younger and younger. Journeying back through the womb and into the void of the "Before," think of your last life before this one, and allow the images to come to you. How do you know the difference between a genuine experience and a projection? The element of surprise. If it feels like a fairy tale or storybook, it's likely a projection. If the experience surprises you and has you look at your life in a new way, it's likely a genuine experience.

Peace—To experience peace, add 1 to 2 drops of fir essential oil to an aromatherapy locket and feel the warmth and peace that come with true understanding. Allow the aroma to accompany you all day. *Note:* because of the safety mechanisms of the nose, you'll go nose-blind to it after a few minutes, and you'll only catch the occasional whiff of the scent during moments of your day. When you notice the scent, stop and take a moment to appreciate the peace it brings you.

Prosperity—Take a dollar bill of your choosing and anoint the four corners of the bill with diluted fir essential oil. Next, fold the bill in half towards you, in half again, and in half again, always towards you to bring in prosperity. Once folded, place into a seldom-used area of your wallet or change purse, to keep from spending it outside of an emergency. Of course, if an emergency arises, spend it and consecrate a new one as soon as possible. The great thing about doing prosperity work with trees is that they think in terms of lifetimes, rather than minutes, so your prosperity will be rooted in stability and longevity, rather than quick alternating bursts of famine and luxury.

Protection—Let's make a protection amulet. Into a small bottle (if you are near a craft store, they sell bottles small enough) place fir needles or a small bit of tissue with a drop of fir essential oil. Alternatively feel free to use salt (purification) and 2 drops of fir essential oil. If you're using an especially tiny bottle, feel free to cut the fir needles down to confetti size. Bless the new amulet for protection in whatever tradition is close to your heart, tie a cord around the neck of the bottle, and wear. Consider charging it under a full moon occasionally to remove any harmful buildup of negativity.

Seeing the big picture—In English there's an idiom that says, "you can't see the forest for the trees." What this means is that you have spent so much energy looking for a specific thing, that you can't see what's right in front of you. To see the bigger picture, grab a small piece of paper (think sticky note sized) and draw a simple fir or pine tree. It doesn't have to be fancy. Feel free to elaborate with trees, picnic tables, whatever you like. Anoint the four corners of your picture with diluted fir essential oil. Next take a chime-sized candle and anoint with fir oil. The color of the candle should reflect your theme of the bigger picture you're attempting to understand. Burn it on a Thursday for expansion, Wednesday for communication, or Sunday for protection.

Recipe: From beneath You

Supreme grounding blend, or to process grief. Give it to the Earth; she can handle it.

- 7 drops balsam fir essential oil (*Abies spp*) for spiritual awareness, comfort, peace

- 6 drops parsley seed essential oil (*Petroselinum crispum*) to conquer grief, encourage honor, increase memory

- 2 drops patchouli essential oil (*Pogostemon cablin*) for peace of mind, harmony, grounding

- 10 drops Vanilla CO2 (*Vanilla planifolia*) for restoration, peace, inspiration, comfort

Diffuse this synergy, 1 drop in 100 ml water, to ground excess energy and anxiety. For grounding on the go, add 7–10 drops to a nasal inhaler tube cotton. Avoid parsley during pregnancy.

BENZOIN

Also Known As: Gum benzoin

Scientific Name: *Styrax tonkinensis, S. benzoin*, et al.

Botanical Family: Styracaceae

World Origin: Thailand, Indonesia

Plant's Oil: Bark

Scent Description: Creamy, sweet

Evaporation: Base note

Scent Impact: Ease of grief

Magical Correspondences

Application: Diluted for topical uses, direct inhalation on a limited basis

Element: Air

Day: Sunday

Magical Uses: Calming, purification, concentration, prosperity, inspiration

Planet: Sun, Mars

Astrological Sign: Sagittarius

Suggested Crystal: Spirit Quartz—Aligned with Pisces: brings freedom from fear.

Deity/Spirit: Ran—Norse goddess of the sea

WARNING
Limit direct inhalation as lightheadedness, headache, nausea, or vomiting may result.

Herbal Lore/Uses

The history of this ally goes back thousands of years with a long history of topical, religious/spiritual use, as a perfume, and as a medicinal plant. Because of the thick, resinous nature of the oil, both the resin and the oil have been used for bronchitis, colds, and coughs. The aromatherapeutic value of benzoin also eases grief and encourages communication. The magically airy nature of this plant is evident even before you take into account its history as an incense and its popularity as the base for many incense blends. Though not commonly mentioned alongside frankincense and myrrh, benzoin is commonly found in western Catholic, as well as Russian Orthodox, incense blends and burned over charcoal as Hindu temple incense. The sweet resins are also included in incenses in China, India, and Japan, as well as incense used in Arabic countries.

These same sweetly resinous qualities that are popular in incense make it a highly sought after ingredient in perfumes to slow the evaporation rate of the scent. If you are blending benzoin in perfumes, Australian sandalwood (*Santalum spicatum*), juniper (*Juniperus communis*), lavender (*Lavandula angustifolia*), myrrh (*Commiphora myrrha*), and benzoin work well together.

Benzoin is part of the Styrax family with 134 members of the genus, not to be confused with Storax, a related resin. *Styrax tonkinensis*, which is suitable for prosperity magic and can be found all across Thailand and Vietnam, is the source of benzoin Siam. *Styrax benzoin* is used to make Sumatran benzoin, which also includes cinnamic acid and lends itself to cleansing and purification magic. The food and fragrance sectors use *Styrax tonkinensis*. Due to the solvent extraction method used for creating this vanilla-rich oil, it isn't a true essential oil, as it can still contain a larger percentage of the alcohol used to extract the oil from the bark it is processed from.

Spells

Astral projection—Place a tear of benzoin on a lit charcoal disk, in a firesafe container. Waft the smoke over your body, starting at your head and grounding any disparate energies from the various parts of your body as you go. When you reach your feet, visualize a third eye, in the center of your forehead, opening and allowing your consciousness to leave your body to travel to other realms. Don't forget to leave an etheric light on inside your body, so it looks like someone is home. Breath evenly, in through your nose and out through your mouth, for the duration of your spirit journey.

Calming—Anoint a tissue or cloth with a drop of benzoin oil and waft it gently in front of your nose as you visualize the source of fear, excitement, or anger moving farther and farther away from you, looking smaller and smaller in the distance, until you know in your heart it is gone. Carry the tissue in your pocket on your nondominant side for the rest of the day.

Concentration—Take 1/2 cup of the salt of your choice and place it into a glass dish. Add 5–7 drops of benzoin oil to the salt and mix thoroughly. Place the dish near your workspace to aid focus on the task at hand. If the smell is overwhelming, move farther away from your nose until it is an afterthought, rather than all-consuming.

Confidence (to speak)—Write out the situation that you need to bring to light. This airy incense plant will be happy to lift your burden. Anoint a yellow (communication) candle with diluted benzoin oil, and burn on a Sunday (protection), Wednesday (communication), or Thursday (expansion).

Exorcism—To banish evil from your home, burn benzoin tears in the home, starting at the top of the home and working downstairs to the bottom, where a window is opened to allow any evil spirits out. If there is only one level, start in the north near an open window, and move counterclockwise around the home driving evil spirits out, returning to the open window to drive out those spirits. If there are children in the home, let them join in the spirit, make it a laughter-filled, joyous occasion; and it'll be easier for the children to understand any negativity is gone if they helped expel it from the home. Having them banging pots together, ringing bells, or even banging on an empty cereal box will add plenty of extra joy, mirth, and energy to the working.

Harmony—Diffuse 1 drop of benzoin oil per 100 ml of water in any areas of the home that have become discordant, clogged, or argumentative. If conflict is anticipated, diffuse benzoin in the space at least thirty minutes prior to arrival of conflict, if possible. It's never too late!

Hex Breaking—Dilute 1 to 2 drops of benzoin oil in 10 ml of carrier oil in a roller-ball bottle to create a magical pen. *Optional:* add 1 to 2 drops of lavender (*Lavandula angustifolia*) to the bottle to reveal secrets of those sending hexes your way, so you know who your enemies, false friends, and jealous rivals are.

Inspiration—Burn one benzoin tear with three clove buds (good luck) to inspire you to create the masterpiece you've had in mind for a while. Your inspiration knows no bounds with benzoin in your corner.

Knowledge—Diffuse benzoin while studying to help retain the knowledge you've worked so hard for. If there is a test, presentation, or other deadline for your work, add a drop of benzoin to a scent locket to wear on the day of your spotlight. If you don't have a scent locket handy, grab a tissue, anoint it with a drop of oil, and carry it on your dominant side all day. Consider using your benzoin magical pen as perfume/cologne for the day. Draw magical signs, symbols, or sigils on your skin before gently massaging the oil into your skin.

Love—To show the universe you are ready to receive a new love interest, write the word "acceptance" on a pink (innocent love) candle and burn on a Friday (Venus/love) or on a full moon.

Meditation—Anoint your wrists with a drop of diluted benzoin oil and sit or lie down in a comfortable space. Practice breathing slowly and evenly, in through your nose and out through your mouth, if you need help focusing on your breath.

Memory—To preserve memories, diffuse 1 drop of benzoin oil per 100 ml of water while taking a trip down memory lane. Consider building a memory box filled with trinkets, photos, and ephemera. Add three benzoin tears to the box to continue to preserve the memories that comfort us.

Peace of mind—To calm fears and restore faith in the outcome, write out the fear plaguing your mind on a piece of paper, or if you're artistically inclined, consider drawing it. Fold it up and place it under a candleholder. Inside the candleholder place a black candle (banishing) with the word "fear" engraved on it with a pen. Anoint with benzoin and jojoba oil (overcome obstacles) and burn on a Saturday or during the waning moon.

Prosperity—To draw prosperity towards you, anoint a bill or coin in your local currency with a drop of benzoin oil, fold it towards you twice, and place it in a seldom used pocket in your wallet where you are unlikely to spend it outside of an emergency (in case of emergency, of course spend it; let's be practical, you can always bless another one later).

Psychic Power, to increase—To a 10 ml roller bottle, add 1 to 2 drops of benzoin oil, and jojoba (remove obstacles) carrier oil to the brim. Cap and roll gently between your hands. On a Monday (intuition) anoint the center of your forehead with benzoin. This is where the pineal gland resides, thought to be the seat of all psychic power. See a small circle opening to allow extrasensory information to come to you. You might consider placing a filter over that open circle to filter out things you don't want, like negativity from strangers. Simply envision a filter over that spot on your face. If you can't see in your mind's eye (reports say nearly 20 percent of people have no internal monologue and similar numbers for those who can't visualize inside their heads at all) you can draw the filter over your forehead with your magical pen to block out anything harmful to your psyche. Remember, your intuition is supposed to help you; if it isn't helpful, or is overwhelming, you can always close that circle in increments until you get it dialed in just the way you want it. Your filters may not be the same as other friends, and that is okay; your boundaries are your own, and yours to control. If you'd rather receive intuitive information in your dreams, rather than waking hours, you can build that information into your personal filters.

Purification—In a fireproof bowl or cauldron, light incense charcoal (not briquettes for the grill) and let it fizzle until burning evenly. If you are unsure if the burning is bright and even yet, sprinkle powdered lavender (purification) or clove (luck) onto the coals and see if it smokes. If it doesn't, consider attempting to relight the charcoal (using tongs). If the charcoal has been exposed to humid air, it can denature the saltpeter that allows it to burn evenly, and you may need either a new disk or a windproof lighter (they put out a higher-temperature flame). Place a benzoin incense tear on the charcoal. Once it is burning well, scoop the smoke over the areas of the body or object you'd like to cleanse. If you'd like to add protective qualities, consider following up with burning dragon's blood resin.

Recipe: Transforming Trauma

This oil is designed for the step after Grief Support (see page 168). Once the initial shock has worn off and the supportive friends have gone home, but the trauma remains, this blend offers the grounding support to help you put one foot in front of the other, until you're able to navigate the new normal on your own, or during painful anniversaries of trauma.

- ❋ 20 drops benzoin essential oil (*Styrax tonkinesis*) for calm, love, memory, and peace

- ❋ 5 drops myrtle essential oil (*Myrtus communis*) for magical charms, resolving heartbreak, releasing sorrow

- ❋ 5 drops petitgrain essential oil (*Citrus aurantium*) for grounding traumatic flashbacks, transforming sorrow, banishing depression

Blend this synergy in a 2 ml bottle, place the reducer cap, lid, and label. Diffuse during traumatic anniversaries. Place in an aromatherapy locket for emotional support during trying times. In the aftermath of recent trauma, place 20 drops in a nasal inhaler tube and carry on your person for more frequent grounding help.

CALAMUS ROOT

Also Known As: Sweet flag

Scientific name: *Acorus calamus*

Botanical Family: Acoraceae

World Origin: India, Asia, Russia, Siberia, Nepal, and the United States

Plant's Oil: Root/rhizome

Scent Description: Musky, dark, strong, earthy

Evaporation: Base note

Scent Impact: Tranquilizing effect, release stressors enough to fall asleep

Magical Correspondences

Application: Diffuse, dilute

Element: Earth

Day: Sunday, Monday, Wednesday, Friday, Saturday

Magical Uses: Binding, healing, joy, knowledge, prosperity

Planet: Sun, Moon, Mercury, Venus, Saturn

Astrological Sign: Leo, Cancer, Gemini, Virgo, Libra, Capricorn

Suggested Crystal: Sunstone—Ruled by Leo, Libra: removes energy drains

Deity/Spirit: Apollo, Sun god and god of prophecy (Delphi).

> **WARNING**
> Avoid during pregnancy.

Herbal Lore/Uses

Calamus is a plant that has been written about, utilized, and praised for four thousand years, since ancient Sumerian and Egyptian writings as well as in Ayurvedic medicine and traditional Chinese medicine. In traditional Chinese medicine, calamus was used to treat bronchitis, relieve asthma symptoms, and chewed to cure a toothache as it would numb the area for a time. During the Great Depression that numbing action was useful as people chewed small pieces to banish nicotine cravings. The words abound for this delightful ally, so much so that Walt Whitman wrote thirty-nine poems to sweet flag in his work, *Leaves of Grass*.

This marshy monocot can't flower unless it is growing directly in water, the muddier the better. It looks like a relative of the cattail, as they are often found in similar areas. Each plant grows vertically out of a horizontal rhizome. This moisture-loving flower has been used for everything from remedying coughs and scenting perfumes to magical dominion and magic for joy. Because its flower is a spadix, it is covered with tiny yellow flowers and has a triangular stem. If pollinated successfully, it produces a berry. Due to its toxicity it has been banned in the United States in internal applications for humans as it causes prolonged nausea and vomiting, and has been instead utilized in the pest-management field. Though both plants are monocots (grasslike flowering plants), it is easily differentiated from its look-alike the Bearded Iris by the ruffled edges of the leaves and calamus's signature sweet smell.

In perfume the mentions go back just as far. Calamus was mentioned in Exodus 30:20–25 as a key ingredient in Moses's anointing oil. That is, if the calamus we mention (*A. calamus*) is in fact the one mentioned, because as we know, common names can muddy the waters (pun absolutely intended). It's possible the calamus mentioned in the Bible was a type of sedge (*Cyperus spp.*), as they have a similarly heady smell.

Exodus Chapter 30, Verses 22–25 (King James Version)

22 Moreover the LORD spake unto Moses, saying, 23 Take thou also unto thee principal spices, of pure myrrh five hundred shekels, and of sweet cinnamon half so much, even two hundred and fifty shekels, and of sweet calamus (*kaneh bosm) two hundred and fifty shekels, 24 And of cassia five hundred shekels, after the shekel

of the sanctuary, and of oil olive an hin: 25 And thou shalt make it an oil of holy ointment, an ointment compound after the art of the apothecary: it shall be an holy anointing oil.

If you wish to create perfume with this heady, earthy aroma that aligns with base notes, the fleshy root is best harvested and tinctured immediately rather than dried, as much of the aromatic qualities are inherent in the moisture of the rhizome. Start with the highest-proof vodka you can procure in your area, as the water content in the root will enter the solution and lower the percentage on its own. If you are able to tincture the root, the magical applications below can be used readily. Once the chopped rhizome has macerated in vodka for a minimum of eight weeks, it can be used in magic and perfumery. It is a strong base note, so will add fixative properties to your perfume blends. Do not feel as though you need to strain the root from the ensuing tincture as it will take a *long* time to break down the woody texture of this material. If you're only using a few drops at a time, you can replace the lost volume of vodka with more vodka as it ages. The root will continue to break down over time. To this tincture, you can add the essential oil for magical perfumery, for both depth of scent and budgetary concerns. In magic, if you don't have a tincture, you can make a calamus spray: take a 1-ounce glass bottle and fill it halfway with rubbing alcohol. To this add 10 drops of calamus essential oil and cap. Give the bottle a shake to incorporate the oil into the alcohol solution. Uncap and fill the bottle the rest of the way with water, distilled if available. Mix to incorporate and label.

Spells

Animals—The sweet smell of calamus lends itself to sweet disposition of animals. If you work with animals and hope to gain their favor, anoint behind the ears with calamus tincture or spray.

Appetite—To stimulate appetite diffuse 2 drops of calamus essential oil in 100 ml of water 30 minutes before mealtime. Repeat as needed.

Asthma, bronchitis (to soothe)—The inflamed bronchial tubes are quite sensitive, so proceed slowly. Diffuse 1 drop of calamus essential oil in 100 ml of water in the same room as the patient, but start it on the opposite end of the room as the patient, so the moist air can be introduced slowly so as not to inspire a coughing fit. If this strength is too much for inflamed tissues, reduce the strength by half, by adding another 100 ml of water before transferring some of the diluted oil/water mixture to the diffuser. Repeat daily until inflammation reduces.

Balance—To restore emotional balance, take a nasal inhaler tube and add 5–7 drops of calamus root essential oil. Place the plug into the bottom and ensure the cap is secured tightly. Allow to rest on its side for 10 minutes before opening. Once open, take two deep breaths, in through the nose and out through the mouth. The grounding action of this earth-aligned root will ground any excess energies and allow the imbalance to correct itself.

Binding—For anyone who has intent to harm you or yours, take a small piece of calamus root, a piece of paper with the threat's name written on it, and black yarn to your worktable. Wrap the paper with the target's name on it (include birthdate or any biographical data you have, like sun sign) around the small piece of calamus root. If you don't have access to the root, place a drop of diluted calamus essential oil on the named paper. Take the black yarn or thread and wrap it around the paper until it is no longer visible. When you have a solid black ball of fiber, place it into a small bag and put them in the freezer. They will no longer be a problem. Once the threat has passed, journey to the nearest big-box store or busy commercial area and throw it away in their trash can. These modern crossroads will carry them far away from you, and no threat will return. Don't look back.

Domination—Your will is iron. To exert dominion over another, write their name on a small piece of paper. Anoint the paper with diluted calamus essential oil or spray. Place in the heel of your shoe worn on your dominant foot. If you're right-handed, likely your dominant foot is right. Keep the paper there until you've worn a hole in it. Once it has a hole in it, burn it to seal the intent. If the aim is to change abusive behavior, for example, leave your target a "get out of jail free" clause. In this example, if someone changes their behavior and attends therapy, the need for domination will end.

Exorcism—To banish evil spirits from your space, you can burn calamus root over incense charcoal tablets, or spray your home with the calamus spray outlined above. Monthly cleansing of your space is recommended.

Fatigue—To banish fatigue, add a single drop of calamus essential oil to the aromatherapy locket of your choice. Due to the strong earthy smell, you may consider adding another essential oil to boost the energizing energy of your locket; consider citruses as they contain top notes associated with joy and energetic feelings.

Healing—Into a blue bag (healing) place a small piece of calamus root, or a cotton ball anointed with a drop of calamus root essential oil. The healing work of calamus is especially useful in magic for healing of airway-related issues like asthma, bronchitis, and COVID. Have the patient wear or carry it at all times until they are healed. Due to the strong, sweet smell, consider adding a drop of lavender (*Lavandula angustifolia*) to add centering and peaceful energy as well as a pleasant smell.

Joy—If in need of the magical energy of joy and happiness, take a purple (ambition) candle and carve the word "joy" onto the surface with a ballpoint pen. Anoint with sunflower oil (happiness and protection) and place into a candleholder. Light the candle and burn until complete.

Knowledge—During study, diffuse a drop of calamus essential oil in 100 ml of water. Allow the scent to ground you in the subject matter and if there is an associated test, wear a drop of the oil in a scent locket on the day of the test to remind you of all you have studied.

Love—To signal to the universe that you're ready for a new loving relationship, take a pink candle for romantic love and carve the word "love" onto the surface with a ballpoint pen. Anoint with olive oil for proliferation. Place into a candleholder and burn until complete. Best if done on a Friday (Venus). We aren't using anyone's name on the candle here because we're attracting your ideal partner, and we never know who the universe has in mind for us. Consent is paramount.

Luck, bad (remedying)—Turn your bad luck around with the grounding energy of the earth. Place a drop of calamus essential oil onto a piece of cotton and place it into a gold- (fast luck) or orange- (success) colored bag. Empower it according to your practice and carry it with you until your luck changes for the better. Best if done on a Thursday (luck).

Money—Take a gold (fast luck) or brown (stable finances) candle and carve the word "money" into the surface of the candle with a ballpoint pen. Anoint the candle with calamus oil diluted in olive oil for good money luck and place it into a candleholder Light the candle and burn until completed. Best if done on a Sunday (blessings) or Thursday (luck).

Oracular work—This moving meditation involves water, and it will be good to have a towel handy. Take two glasses of similar size and fill one halfway with water. Add a drop of calamus essential oil. Breathe deeply until you enter a trance state. With half-closed eyes, place the towel over your lap and begin pouring the water from one glass to the other. The moving meditation is part of keeping the trance state. This is water scrying: you are watching the reflected light over the meeting of water between two glasses. Allow messages to come through your consciousness as you repeat the outpouring of water from one glass to the other. Speak aloud your visions so that your waking mind will remember the wisdom you have received. When you're done, wash the glasses thoroughly. Record any observations for future contemplation.

Peace, tranquility—Sit or lie comfortably while you diffuse 1 drop of calamus essential oil in 100 ml of water. Breathe gently in through the nose and out through the mouth as you visualize or feel each muscle group relaxing independently of each other, from your toes, working your way up to the top of your head. Repeat as needed. If you fall asleep, even better.

Protection—To protect your home, take a piece of paper and draw a figure of your home, whether an A-frame, a stick for a stand-alone house, a rectangle for an apartment or condo, or the like. Add your address to the *back* of the paper. Place a diffuser on top of the paper and fill with 100 ml water and 1 drop of calamus essential oil. Turn on the diffuser and let the protection diffuse throughout the property. In the event that a person is under threat, use their name or a photo instead of the home address.

Reverie (sensual daydreams)—The Venusian energies of calamus lend themselves to the magic of reverie, daydream, and pondering. The luxury of daydreaming should never be confused with dissociation, when our brains need to go offline for a moment or two. Both are natural by-products of being born into these bodies, but one is a conscious effort that employs an experience of the senses in a controlled environment, and the other is unscheduled, uncontrolled, necessary downtime. To enjoy the reverie of the senses, diffuse 1 drop of calamus essential oil in 100 ml of water. If you have it, feel free to add a drop of any other Venus-aligned essential oil, including rose or lemon verbena.

Situation, control—To control a situation that's gotten out of hand, find a small box, matchboxes are great, or if you have a small coffin-shaped box from your Halloween crafts, even better. Outline the situation at hand on a small piece of paper. If you're concerned your box may be found, use symbols instead of words. Fold it up until it fits in the box you have. Take a cotton ball (or as many as you need to fill the box) and place it on top of the situation report. Fill it enough that you can still close the box but there's not even room for air. Place a drop of calamus essential oil onto the cotton ball and close the box tightly. Empower the box to help you maintain control of the situation for as long as is needed. If it won't be disturbed, you can keep it in the freezer to keep your control. If the freezer isn't secure, place it in a safe place. Once the situation has resolved you can take your box to the crossroads or your nearest big-box store parking lot and throw it in the trash there, without looking back. If you work with gods, a polite "thank you" to Hecate won't go amiss.

Recipe: To Bed with Old Ghosts

Sometimes we need to put the past behind us before moving on to the next adventure.

- 3 drops calamus essential oil (*Acorus calamus*) for binding, soothing, protection, and to remedy bad luck

- 13 drops frankincense essential oil (*Boswellia sacra*) for removing blocks to justice

- 13 drops lavender essential oil (*Lavandula angustifolia*) for balance, centering, gentleness

- 1 drop vetiver essential oil (*Vetiveria zizanioides*) for banishing, grief, and grounding

Blend the oils in a 2 ml bottle. Cap and roll between your palms to mix. Then remove the lid and with a pipette or eyedropper, place 3 drops of the synergy you just created into a 10 ml bottle, and fill the rest of the way with the carrier of your choice. Place the roller ball and cap, then label. You can wear this as a perfume, anoint ritual candles, and empower petitions. Diffuse 1 drop in 100 ml of water.

CYPRESS

Also Known As: Blue Cypress, Mediterranean Cypress

Scientific Name: *Cupressus sempervirens*

Botanical Family: Cupressaceae

World Origin: Spain, France, Germany

Plant's Oil: Branches, twigs, and needles

Scent Description: Balsamic, piney, sticky, sweet

Evaporation: Middle–base note depending on extraction

Scent Impact: Eases feelings of loss and grief, increases sense of security

Magical Correspondences

Application: Diffuse, dilute, massage, bath

Element: Earth

Day: Saturday

Magical Uses: Death, grief, divination, protection, harmony

Planet: Saturn, Pluto

Astrological Sign: Capricorn, Aquarius

Suggested Crystal: Lepidolite—Ruled by Libra: transforms grief into hope, releases suffering

Deity/Spirit: Crom Cruach, Irish god of fertility and death

Herbal Lore/Uses

Cypress is the name of the game. It has twenty-five taxa (the plural of taxon, or a grouping of class, family, or species) and Mediterranean cypress has been studied for a wide variety of applications. While the studies are scientifically aimed at health applications of this plant material, it has a long historical use for everything from Egyptian coffins to historical use in China to stop bleeding gums. Perhaps owing to its history in ancient Egypt, it's no surprise to see that cypress is associated with grief, loss, death, and chthonic (underworld) deities. Cypress trees were often planted in cemeteries to support those in grief.

Though the plant is sometimes called blue cypress, due to the gray-blue hue of the leaves, if the oil that you've purchased is truly blue like blue chamomile, or blue yarrow, it has been dyed, and therefore the quality of the oil is suspect and should be investigated further.

> The leaves and cones of *C. sempervirens* have been used as folk remedies in different parts of the world for antiseptic, antipyretic, anthelminthic, astringent, antirheumatic, antihemorrhoidal, antidiarrhoeic, and vasoconstrictive purposes . . . (Orhan, Tumen, 2015).

Spells

Accept loss—Diffuse cypress essential oil in the home of those suffering a loss to comfort them through the denial stage of loss, through to acceptance. This isn't to say that it'll be an easy trip, or one they'll only take once. When we talk about the stages of grief in a therapeutic setting, those stages were developed in relation to hospice patients, rather than the ones being left behind. Instead of steps, they feel more like shingles flying in a tornado; any one shingle is likely to hit you at any time, for any reason. One moment you feel like you're having a decent day and can handle a few light errands, and then you're crying in the produce aisle because your loved one will never eat another mango again. Everyone deals with loss in their own way, at their own time, and they owe no one an explanation as to what they're feeling, or how long they're feeling it. If you feel you've been impacted by grief to a greater extent than you'd expect, consider a grief support group or one-on-one therapy to help you move with your feelings, rather than against them.

Anxiety, to calm—Anxiety can be difficult to deal with due to its taking over entire systems within the body, perpetuating the cycle. To surround yourself with woody, supportive care, look to cypress. Add 1–2 drops of cypress essential oil to a scent locket of your choice. Beneficial features to look for are a cotton or wool pad to place your oil of choice on, and a chain that is short enough to waft the oil to your nose, but not so short that you don't want to wear it.

Assertiveness—When it's time to speak up for yourself, ground yourself through the roots of the cypress tree by anointing your pulse points with diluted cypress essential oil. Add 1 drop of cypress essential oil to a 10 ml roller bottle and fill the rest of the way with jojoba (overcoming). Add the rollerball cap and topper. Roll the bottle gently between your hands to mix the oils. Allow the bottle to rest a few moments and apply the diluted oil, seeing (or feeling) the strength of cypress rooting you in your own power. Speak up, speak out, and may your voice be heard.

Awareness of ancestors—Light an incense charcoal tablet and add a pinch of dried cypress when it is glowing red. Arrange photos, drawings, and other depictions of ancestors, including grave photos, rubbings, and other mementos. Call to your ancestors by name if you know them. Even if you don't know the names of your ancestors, whether due to adoption or other circumstances, we don't always know our lineage, but they are still there for you. (For more information, check out *Badass Ancestors: Finding Your Power with Ancestral Guides* by Patti Wigington.)

Banishing—To banish someone for good, take an orange (success) or black (banishing) candle on a Saturday (banishing) and carve "Just GO" onto the candle and anoint with diluted cypress oil. Place the candle into a candleholder or a fireproof container. If you have a printed photo of the target, place it under the candle. If you don't have a photo, write their full name (and birthdate if you have it) on a square of toilet paper and place it under the candle. Burn the candle until it has burned out (never leave a burning candle unattended). When the candle has finished, burn the photo and flush the ashes. If you have toilet paper, use it, and then flush it. They'll leave in a hurry.

Binding—To keep someone from harming you, you'll need a length of ribbon and a photo, as well as diluted cypress essential oil. Best if done on a Saturday (binding). You'll need enough ribbon to circle the photo you have chosen a few times. Choose a color that feels appropriate to your situation. Anoint the ribbon with diluted cypress essential oil and rub it into the fabric. Starting at one end tie a knot in the ribbon, "by knot of one, the spell's begun." Grab the opposite end, of the ribbon and tie another knot, "by knot of two, (name of target) is through." Fold the ribbon in half to find the middle and tie another knot, "by knot of three, (name) will leave me be." Find the middle of the point between one and three to place knot number four, "by knot of four hear my roar." Place the next knot between three and two, "by knot of five, I will thrive." Tie the next knot between one and four, "by knot of six, your will, I'll eclipse." Find the space between knot four and three to tie another knot, "by knot of seven you'll have no question." Between knots three and five, place your pen-ultimate knot, "by knot of eight, get it straight." Place the last knot between five and two, "by knot of nine, this is my design." The final pattern should look like this: 1–6–4–7–3–8–5–9–2. Wrap the knotted ribbon around a photo of the target of the binding action to keep the magic intact. Store the wrapped bundle in a safe place in case further action is required.

Bitterness, to release—Emotions like bitterness are difficult to release, as we may be reminded multiple times of the causal factors that led to the feelings that nurture bitterness, like betrayal, anger, and the like. To combat bitterness, cypress helps us resolve the grief that lies behind those feelings. However, even that magic isn't instantaneous. On a Monday (emotional security), find an aromatherapy scent locket that appeals to your taste, as well as your bottle of cypress essential oil and any materials you use for blessing and charging magical components (incense, water, salt, or more). Bless the scent locket and the bottle of cypress essential oil in whatever method is close to your heart. Consecrate the locket to your purpose, releasing bitterness, resolving grief, and so forth. Add 2 drops of cypress essential oil to your locket's cotton or wool pad. (If it came with a lava bead, I'd replace it with a fabric insert for safety.) If you don't have a method of consecration yet, just tell the locket what you need it to do. Talk to it as you would a dear friend. Be as specific as you would with a dear friend when asking them for their help. Talk about the backstory; lead on with the intricacies of the plot. No matter how long your friendship with cypress has taken, whether this is the first meeting or you've been friends for decades, it's up to the level of communication you've developed. Allow them to utilize their own spirit in your aid. Once you start to wear the locket, you'll notice the scent a lot at first, and the cypress will be able to work diligently to help you resolve your feelings. After ten minutes or so, your nose will have discounted the scent as no threat so you'll start to ignore the scent with your conscious mind, but the cypress is still there, doing its job: healing your trauma, helping you resolve the past, and releasing the bitterness that has plagued your heart and spirit. As you notice the scent at different times during the day, turn your mind to the act of releasing those feelings as you work in concert with cypress.

Blessings—If you have access to cypress branches, a freshly cut branch makes a lovely asperging (sprinkling) tool. Pour some clean, cool water into a bowl, and use the energy of the freshly cut cypress branches to sprinkle charged water onto people, places, and objects. If fresh cypress is unavailable, place a pinch or two of dried cypress into clean, cool water and bless as normal. Sprinkle the water with clean hands as normal.

Calm/centering—Diffuse 1 drop of cypress essential oil in 100 ml of water for 10 minutes before coming to breathe slowly and evenly to release tension, anger, or other destructive emotions.

Clarity—In order to gain clarity on a subject, state your question out loud or in writing. Clearly stating the issue will make it much easier for you to interpret the answer given, if it is clear at the start. Next, light an incense charcoal tablet and add a pinch of dried cypress to it, once it is burning readily. Softly focus your eyes and allow the patterns in the smoke to become fuzzy. If you wear glasses, simply remove them. Follow the patterns of the smoke and allow them to bring you the answers you seek.

Comfort—If you have access to fresh cypress branches, take an old pot and fill it with cool water. Place it onto the stove; if you have a woodstove or fireplace, even better. The heat from the fire will help the water release the sap trapped in the branches and the volatile oils in the needles. You also can obtain the comfort of cypress by diluting the essential oil, 1 drop in 100 ml water.

Concentration—It can been very frustrating to need to accomplish a task, especially if there is a deadline looming. If you are having trouble meeting the deadline and want to concentrate, add 7–10 drops of cypress essential oil to the cotton insert inside a nasal inhaler tube, place the stopper in the end, and make sure the cap is tightly secured. Allow it to rest for 10 minutes or so, so that the oil can soak into the cotton and disperse. Once it has rested, remove the cap, place the open end under one nostril, and inhale gently, in through the nose and out through the mouth. Repeat on the opposite side. Refocus on the task at hand, and repeat if needed.

Confidence—On a Sunday (personal empowerment) take a peach (strength) or orange (success) candle and carve the word "confidence" into it. Anoint it with diluted cypress oil and place into a candleholder. *Optional:* place a photo of yourself under the candleholder, you will have a bit of extra oomph if it's a photo from a more confident time. Light the candle and allow it to burn completely.

Court—To win in court, place the name of the court case or your opponent on a piece of paper, anoint it with diluted cypress essential oil, and place it in the shoe of your dominant foot. Works well for confidence on the day of court, or start as soon as possible to get the case thrown out before it makes it to the day of.

Dead, to remember—Find an appropriate photo of the deceased, if possible. On a green (healing the past) or pink (honor) candle carve "remember" on the candle. If you have a framed photo, set up the candle in front of the photo, so that the candle's flame will be reflected in the pane of glass in front of the photo. If unframed, simply place it under the candleholder. If no photo is available, write their full name, craft name, or chosen moniker on a piece of paper, including their date of birth, if known. Anoint the candle with diluted cypress oil and empower the candle as you see fit. Talk to the spirit on the other side of the veil and let them know you remember them. Let them know that they are still in your heart, in your thoughts, and if appropriate that they are in your prayers. Light the candle and allow to burn until completed.

Defense—To defend your home against magical harm or physical threat, take a 2-ounce spray bottle (glass or #1 plastic is best) and place 2 tablespoons of witch hazel inside. Add to the witch hazel 10 drops of cypress essential oil. Give the solution a swirl to incorporate before filling the bottle the rest of the way with water. Spray around the interior walls of your home (taking care with fabrics in case of dyed cypress essential oil), and envision (or feel) the cypress drops connecting into a net or a network of vines to keep ill-intentioned magic and people from your home. As plastic is not an oxygen barrier, try to use up the spray rather than leaving it sit in the bottle for later.

Divination—Light an incense charcoal tablet and apply a pinch or two of dried cypress to the charcoal once it is burning well. Allow your focus to soften and your thoughts to wander as you observe the patterns made in the smoke of the cypress. Allow thoughts to pass you by, as you contemplate the question before you. Allow the answers to come from within as you divine meaning from the smoke.

Fatigue—To overcome fatigue, gently inhale directly from the cypress essential oil bottle (careful, don't get it on your nose; if this happens wash immediately, as undiluted oils can cause skin reactions). If you need a longer-term solution, especially near sensitive electronics that could be damaged by diffusing water, grab a votive candleholder, and a tissue or two. Place 2–3 drops of cypress essential oil onto the tissue after placing it inside the decorative holder. It'll diffuse gently over several hours, and without a large throw, just in case your office has a low-scent policy. When your brain notices the cypress, it'll reinforce the wakefulness intention you set when you poured the drops initially.

Forgetfulness—Take a nasal inhaler tube and insert the cotton into the tube. Add 10 drops of cypress essential oil to the tube and place the stopper in the end. Ensure that the cap is carefully in place. Allow to rest for 10 minutes to absorb the oil into the cotton. Once the oil has been absorbed, take the cap off of the tube, place the open end against one nostril, and inhale gently in through the nose and out through the mouth. Repeat on the opposite nostril. When your mind wanders away from the remembered tasks, the smell of cypress will bring you back around to the thing you've forgotten.

Grief, to protect against—If you work with those in grief, protect yourself against the emotional overwhelm of the clients: anoint your heart, the backs of hands, and the tops of feet with diluted cypress essential oil. Symbols like plus signs (+), also known as an equal-armed cross, thought to balance the energies in the body, mind, and spirit, are beneficial. Massage into the skin with clockwise spirals to increase the protection against grief. As an added bonus, cypress helps those in grief accept their loss and make peace with it.

Habits, to overcome, bad—Habits don't get that way overnight and they are hard to break; it's not just you. The first step in breaking any habit is to talk about the impact that it is having on your life and admitting that it isn't good for you. Diffuse 1 drop in 100 ml of water and sit down with a notepad, stapler, and other writing supplies. Breathe in the scent of the cypress oil while concentrating your focus on the center of your body and bringing your energy to your heart. Look inward and start to make a list of the negative ways your bad habit has impacted your life, and if possible, how it can or has affected your family or friends. Next, create a list of ways your life could be improved, should you break your bad habit. Remove both sheets from the notepad and staple the benefits list on top of the consequences list. If you don't have a staple, folding will work just fine. Anoint the four corners of the paper with diluted cypress oil to cement the victory of the benefits over consequences. On top of this list, place a candleholder or fireproof container. Take a black (endings) or green (healing the past) candle and write "end" or "break the habit" on the candle, depending on space. Anoint it with the diluted cypress essential oil that you anointed the paper with. Light the candle and burn until complete.

Happiness—To overcome thoughts that rob you of your own joy, take a peach (quiet joy) or orange (thoughtfulness) candle and carve "happiness" into it. On a Sunday (personal empowerment) or a Monday (emotional security) anoint the candle with diluted cypress essential oil and place into a candleholder or fireproof container. Burn until complete.

Harmony—To work in concert with the people, spirits, or land around you, diffuse 1 drop of cypress essential oil in 100 ml of water, allowing the water vapor to carry your wish for harmony throughout your space. To add an air of stability to the newly harmonious vibrations of your space, take a brown (stability) candle and carve "harmony" onto it. Anoint with diluted cypress essential oil and place into a fireproof container. Burn until complete.

Healing—To speed healing, find a light-blue pouch (healing), and place 2 pinches of dried cypress needles inside. If you don't have access to dried cypress, place 2 cotton balls into the pouch, add 2 drops of cypress essential oil, and close. Bless the bag in the way that feels appropriate to you, and if possible, allow it to sit in the moonlight for a night. Present to the person in need of healing.

Influence, to protect against—To protect against outside influence, find an aromatherapy locket of your choice, and add 2 drops of cypress essential oil to the cotton or wool included in the locket. Consecrate with the four elements and ask for it to protect its wearer against harmful influences. Present to the intended. They'll smell the oil strongly at first, and as the cypress protection is needed less and less, they'll notice it less often. If protection is still needed, refresh the cypress oil after a lunar cycle (twenty-eight days).

Inspiration—The need for inspiration is just as sudden as the ideas inspired by that spark. If you're stuck for an idea, diffuse 1 drop of cypress essential oil in 100 ml water while breathing in through your nose and out through your mouth, softly. Don't try to think of anything specifically, just let your mind wander where it will. If it tries to remind you of the important things like groceries, and bills, and dinner, and so forth, just allow those thoughts to pass by, without lingering. Gently redirect your attention to the idea of inspiration. If you have difficulty concentrating on an empty mind like I do, try doing something like putting a puzzle together, and allow your mind to work on the issue in the background.

Justice—To find justice, if it is safe to do so, find a local courthouse. I like to grab an apple and a bottle of water in a brown paper bag for a picnic. I'll sit near the landscaping of the courthouse and eat my apple and drink my bottle of water, so that security knows I'm not a threat. (Avoid the side entrance where prisoners are brought in, for safety, as these bushes are often where contraband is discarded before entering the courthouse.) When you are finished with your picnic, grab a handful of the landscaping dressing, soil, gravel, or mulch. This material has been on the grounds of the courthouse, so it carries the energy of justice. On a Thursday (justice) or Friday (just judge) take a candleholder and place a pinch of soil in the bottom. If you have landscaping gravel, it likely won't fit into the candleholder, so arrange it in a circle around the base of the candleholder. Take a red (bravery), magenta (immediate action), or orange (success) candle and carve the word "justice" onto it. Anoint the candle with diluted cypress essential oil and place it into the candleholder. Light and allow to burn safely until complete.

Learning—To help increase understanding during the learning process, add 2 drops of cypress essential oil to an aromatherapy locket's cotton pad, place inside the locket, and close. Empower the locket to aid you in learning, and place it around your neck or give it to a loved one. The initial fragrance will fade from notice after about ten minutes, but the magic of cypress will stay with them. If needed, refresh fragrance after a lunar cycle (twenty-eight days).

Lost items, to return—On a Wednesday (messengers) take a small piece of paper, and write the name of the object that you've lost on the paper. On a blue (knowledge of location), white (magical aims), or gold (fast luck) candle, carve the word "return" along the length of the candle. Anoint with diluted cypress essential oil and place into a candleholder or fireproof dish. Burn until completed. Either the object or the truth of what happened will come to you.

Peace, to give—Granting peace to someone is not our job, but a selfless act nonetheless. To give them peace, grab a silver (resolve inner conflict) candle on a Monday (emotional security) and carve "peace" onto the candle. Anoint the candle with diluted cypress essential oil and place it into a candleholder. Burn until complete.

Protection, to increase security—Cypress's action for protection is unlike other planetary actions. Unlike the Sun, whose solar protection burns away evils before they can befall you, cypress is an agent of Saturn and Pluto, so the protection that comes from these planets is supportive. Saturn rules mastery, so here's to becoming a master at your craft. Saturn is also the ruler of time itself, so feel that time expanding and giving you all of the time in the world to respond to a threat, especially if the offender has broken the law (another Saturnian area). To increase the protection around you or a loved one, take a small piece of paper and draw a stick figure to represent the protectee. No need to be artistic about it, if it isn't your strong suit. We just need to represent them. Then draw a bubble around them an inch or so away from their stick. This represents the protective bubble cypress is going to empower. It'll look like a gingerbread figure when your bubble is complete. Make sure to name the stick with full name, date, time, and place of birth, if you have them. We want the protection magic to have the best chance possible of finding its target. Make a cypress magical pen if you haven't yet. Take a 10 ml roller bottle and place 1 drop of cypress essential oil inside. Fill the bottle the rest of the way with the carrier of your choice. I like jojoba because of its long shelf life and magically it is attuned to overcoming impossible odds. Place the roller ball and cap onto the bottle and roll gently between your palms. Allow to sit for ten minutes to allow oil to blend. With your magical pen, draw the magical border of your target to show cypress where to concentrate their focus. On top of the paper, place a candleholder. Take a red (concurring fear), peach (strength), or white (cancel magical aims) candle on a Sunday (personal empowerment) and carve the word "protection" into it. Anoint the candle with your magical pen and place into the candleholder. Burn until complete. Save the paper representation of your target in case they need more specific help later.

Release—To release people, feelings, or emotions, take an incense charcoal tablet and light it. Place into a fireproof container. Sprinkle 2 pinches of dried cypress needles onto the burning charcoal and name aloud that which you are releasing. Feel the weight lifting as you allow this hardship to leave your life forever. Know it is done, and well done.

Sorrow, to ease—The weight of sorrow needs oxygen to lift. Allowing cypress to bring some air into the room will allow the sorrows to be processed more fully so that they can lessen. The loss of a loved one doesn't go away; however our hearts grow to accommodate the loss as a part of us. Cypress can grow up to 115 feet (almost forty meters!) and ten feet wide. That's a lot of air to support your breath as you learn to move through grief to establish your new normal. Diffuse 1 drop of cypress essential oil in 100 ml of water. You'll notice the scent strongly at first, until your nose becomes used to the smell, then you will catch whiffs of it here and there as it is needed. This will help your heart grow around the sorrow and allow it to lessen the pain you are experiencing. To continue the work, consider getting an aromatherapy locket to carry the oil of cypress with you to ease that sorrow when it arises for the first lunar cycle.

Strength—The strength of oak is legendary, but that Jupiterian influence is a physical boon, whereas the strength of Saturn is more in the realm of the inner landscape. An iron will, tempered with the air of cypress branches, brings the strength of concentration, ambition, and tenacity. To increase your internal fortitude take a yellow candle (success) and carve the word "strength" into the surface. Anoint the candle with diluted cypress essential oil and place it in a candleholder. Light and allow to burn until complete.

Tranquility, stress, to relieve—To relieve stress and promote tranquility, diffuse 1 drop of cypress essential oil in 100 ml of water. Breathe deeply, in through the nose and out through the mouth. Feel the stress leaving each muscle group individually, starting at the toes and working up to the top of the head. Once you have relaxed every muscle from the feet up, start from the top down, infusing the now-relaxed muscles with tranquility. Know that you are safe and protected.

Truth, to discover—To discover the truth of a matter, take a peach (truth) or blue (wisdom) candle and carve the word "truth" into it. Anoint with diluted cypress oil. *Optional:* add a drop of diluted benzoin to reveal treachery. Best if done on a Tuesday (victory) or Thursday (justice).

Willpower, to increase—If you have experienced too many hardships in too short a period, it can be difficult to find the resolution to complete goals ahead of you. In order to shore up your resolve, take a yellow (will), orange (encouragement), or peach (strength) candle on a Sunday (empowerment) or Saturday (responsibilities), and carve the word "will" into the surface. Anoint the candle with diluted cypress essential oil. If the willpower includes endings like relationships or friendships, add a drop of myrrh oil to the dilute to promote safety. Place the candle in a fireproof container. Light and allow to burn until complete.

Recipe: Grief Support

Physical and emotional support for those in grief.

- 5 drops cypress essential oil (*Cupressus sempervirens*) for acceptance of loss, awareness of ancestors, comfort

- 20 drops lemon balm essential oil (*Melissa officinalis*) for soothing emotional wounds

- 10 drops frankincense essential oil (*Boswellia carteri*) for spiritual support and antidepressant

- 5 drops May Chang essential oil (*Litsea subeba*) for prayer, uplifting, and strength

Add all essential oils to a 2 ml bottle to create a synergy. Diffuse 1 drop in 100 ml of water in home of grieving family, or add 1 ml to nasal inhaler tube cotton, place bottom, and ensure cap is tightly secured. Inhale once per nostril every 4 hours as needed.

DAVANA

Scientific Name: *Artemisia pallens*

Botanical Family: Asteraceae

World Origin: India, England, United States

Plant's Oil: Whole plant

Scent Description: Herbal, fruity, hint of vanilla and blackberry

Evaporation: Middle note

Scent Impact: Meditative, aphrodisiac, improved self-image

Magical Correspondences

Application: Diffuse, dilute for topical applications

Element: Water

Day: Monday

Magical Uses: Sleep, divination, love

Planet: Moon

Astrological Sign: Cancer

Suggested Crystal: Red Jasper—Ruled by Taurus: calms anxiety for restful sleep

Deity/Spirit: Shiva—God of Transformation

WARNING

Davana is abortifacient and an emmenagogue, which brings on menses. Do not use if pregnant or nursing. Avoid with a history of seizures. Can increase menstrual flow; use with caution. Do not use on people under twelve years of age, or those in fragile health.

Herbal Lore/Uses

Though davana is a member of the *Artemisia* genus and many people consume it multiple times a day, most modern consumers have never heard of davana—because its a flavoring for cola. This is another example of the fact that just because something is commonly found in our lives, doesn't mean it can't be magical. The religious uses of davana include garlands, wreathes, and offerings to the Hindu god Shiva, especially in southern India where it originates.

The history of this herb goes back to ancient times, with included written history as recent as the 1800s. It has been used to make perfume, as well as flavoring for foods like baked goods. The davana oil is highly prized with perfumers for its chameleon-like habit of changing its scent profile from wearer to wearer.

Its medicinal history lists that it has anti-inflammatory and antimicrobial effects that have made it popular in topical applications. It has a history of lowering blood sugar and as a vermifuge (like its other artemisia siblings) for alleviating intestinal worms.

Spells

Anger, to resolve—Diffuse 1 drop of davana essential oil in 100 ml of water. Sit with the diffuser as you breathe gently in through the nose, out through the mouth. Place your dominant hand over your breastbone and apply gentle pressure; include a weighted blanket or other tools as needed to regulate the nervous system. Feel your anger resolving; say it out loud and include your own name. Speaking in the third person can feel odd, but we are programmed from a young age to react well to the sound of our names. "Amy's anger is resolving." "Amy's feelings are understandable, and she is processing them well." Take a deep breath between affirmations.

Animal communication—The animal in question does *not* need to be present for this; remember animals have different sensitivities to plants than humans do. Diffuse 1 drop of davana essential oil in 100 ml of water 10 minutes before starting to allow fragrance to dissipate in the room. With a notebook and your favorite writing utensil, write a letter to the animal you are hoping to communicate with. Though animals don't think in words, the way people do, we are adept at the image language used by our animal compatriots. Once your letter is finished, write a letter back to yourself from the animal with whom you are communicating. It can feel silly, however we are opening a dialogue in our brains that allows us to be open to receiving the instruction from our animals that they are hoping for. Practice this once a day for a month to connect and cement the psychic bond with your fair companion. Remember, just because you connect with your pet doesn't make them a familiar spirit unless they specifically agree to that working relationship. Not all pets are familiars, nor should they be.

Banish misfortune—Light an incense charcoal tablet and place it into a fireproof dish. Place a pinch of dried davana herb on the burning charcoal and as the smoke rises, feel any harm, ill luck or misfortune be chased from your space. Consider following that up with something protective to keep the misfortune from returning. I suggest dragon's blood or frankincense tears.

Binding—To keep someone from harming you, grab a black candle (banishing) and write the name of the person worthy of binding along the side of the candle. Then anoint the candle with diluted davana essential oil and place into a candleholder. Burn until completed. Best if done on a Saturday (binding).

Bitterness, to resolve—This uses a favorite magical tool of mine, flash paper. It's tissue paper impregnated with saltpeter, the same substance that helps incense charcoal burn evenly. Flash paper combusts in an instant and is used by stage magicians to create a puff of fire that leaves no smoke, ash, or burns. Write on a piece of flash paper (1" x 2" is fine) the source of your bitterness. On a light-blue candle, write "resolution" and anoint with diluted davana essential oil. Burn on a Saturday (banishing) or Monday (emotional security).

Counter enemy attack—Davana is a lovely decorative herb in the same genus as sweet annie (*Artemisia annua*) and makes beautiful decorative wreathes. Take a wire form, a spool of floral wire (it doesn't have to be a heavy-gauge wire, as davana is a soft-stemmed plant), and your davana. You can order it fresh from specialty plant shops as it is cut as a floral green. Wire a 2-inch bunch to the wire frame in the center position. Keeping the wire in touch with the form, tuck the next handful of davana at the top position and wire it in place. Switch to the bottom or outside rung of the wire frame and place the next bundle, containing around the wire frame as you go. It will radiate out in a wreath shape, and it will add fullness as you alternate inside, middle, outside. When you return to your starting point, tuck the last bunch under the first and don't forget to create a wire loop with which to hang it. While you work, envision your home being wrapped in a network of davana branches that create an impenetrable net that keeps all enemy attacks from your home. Feel that net tighten as you finish the wreath. Hang the wreath on your front door or just inside the front door to cement its place in your protection network.

Courage—Diffuse 1 drop of davana essential oil in 100 ml of water. List all of the things that make you feel courageous, while you take slow, even breaths in through your nose and out through your mouth. After 10 minutes, leave the room and leave your fears behind. Refer to the list when you have doubts.

Death, peaceful—To open the way for the peaceful passing of a loved one, write their name on a white candle (purity of intent) and anoint with diluted davana essential oil. Take an index card or similar piece of paper and fold it in half, lengthwise. Draw a circle for a doorknob on the front of the card, and inside, shade the interior black to represent the void in between worlds. Set up your magical doorway near the rear of the candle, but not so close as to be a fire hazard. Safety first. Write the name of your loved one on the front of the door in bold. If they have loved ones that have gone before, feel free to list them below the subject's name to call them to await your subject on the other side.

Defensive magic—Take a handful of dried davana and add it to a mop bucket filled with steaming hot water. Add a capful of ammonia (ownership) to the water and allow it to steep for 10 minutes. If you don't have the herb, use 7–10 drops of davana essential oil and skip the steeping step. Take the mop bucket out to the front porch (only use half if you also have a back porch), pour the bucket of water onto the porch, and give it a good scrub. If you live in an apartment, use the water and a clean cloth to wash the outside of the front door. Feel or see a heavy steel door closing and locking behind you so no harmful magic can enter behind you.

Disharmony, resolve—In an 8-ounce spray bottle, add a tablespoon of witch hazel or rubbing alcohol and a teaspoon of salt. Add 7–10 drops of davana essential oil. *Optional:* add 2 drops of lavender (*Lavandula angustifolia*) for harmony. Fill the bottle the rest of the way with water and seal. As you walk through your space, spray the air in the room that has the disharmony, seeing or feeling the energy of the room shifting. If visualizations are helpful, see the sun's rays chasing away any harmful energy.

Displeasure, to cause/hex—To return harm someone caused you, especially from narcissism, gather a small mirror (a compact is perfect) and a peach (truth) or red (fast action) candle on a Tuesday (Victory) and anoint it with diluted davana essential oil. Add a drop of jasmine absolute (justice) to the candle oil. Set up the candleholder in front of the mirror to return the harm they caused. Burn in a fireproof container until finished. *Optional:* write out the harm they caused to expel the poison and speed the spell.

Divination with spirits of the dead—Light an incense charcoal tablet and sprinkle a pinch of dried davana over the burning charcoal. Call out to the spirit you wish to speak to or commune with. Close your eyes and breathe slowly, in through your nose and out through your mouth, picturing the spirit you wish to talk to or hear from. Invite them into your space. If this is a person with a history of abuse, consider casting a circle for your protection, so you can make sure they've been banished when you've finished your conversation.

Dreams, peaceful—Diffuse 1 drop of davana essential oil in 100 ml of water 15 minutes before retiring to bed. Allow the fruity vanilla scent to guide you to the land of peaceful dreams. Rest well knowing you are protected here.

Elemental magic—To invoke elementals, burn a pinch of davana over an incense charcoal tablet while calling to the elementals: gnomes in the north, sylphs in the east, salamanders in the south, undines in the west. Replace as your tradition defines.

Endurance—To increase your endurance, add 1 drop of davana essential oil in a 10 ml roller bottle. Fill the rest of the way with a carrier oil of your choice. Place the roller cap and external cap and roll gently between your hands. Allow to rest for 10 minutes. Anoint hands, feet, and heart each with a drop of diluted davana essential oil and massage into the body in clockwise (increase) circles. Feel yourself fill with the tingling warmth that signals a renewed energy. Know it is done, and done well.

Find helping spirits—To call your helping spirits to you, burn a pinch of dried davana over an incense charcoal tablet while calling to the universe to send your helping spirits. If you know any of their names, call them now. If you don't, ask for the aid of beneficial spirits now. Thank the universe or other appropriate gods or spirits.

Freedom—To increase personal freedom, diffuse 1 drop of davana essential oil in 100 ml of water while outlining (either in your head or in a journal) the ways in which your freedom can and will improve. On a peach (strength) candle write the word "freedom" and place into a candleholder. Best if done on a Tuesday (victory).

Happiness—On a gold or yellow candle (protection of joy) write the word "bliss." Anoint with diluted davana oil, and burn on a Sunday.

Healing—If you or someone you love is in need of healing magic, place a fresh or dried vase of davana by their bedside. If it is unattainable, diffuse 1 drop of davana essential oil in 100 ml of water. The healing spirits of the plant will bring wellness to the infirm.

Initiation—To bless an initiate before ritual, take a bunch of fresh davana and dip it into charged, fresh, cool water, and sprinkle over the initiate. If fresh davana isn't available, add a teaspoon of witch hazel or rubbing alcohol to a bowl. Add 3 drops of davana essential oil to the witch hazel, top with cold water, and bless according to your tradition. Use your fingers to sprinkle the charged davana water over the initiate.

Lust—To inspire lust in yourself, find a red (lust, passion) or magenta (immediate action) candle. Carve the word "desire" on the candle, and anoint with diluted davana essential oil. Place into a candleholder or other fireproof container and burn until completed. Best if done on a Friday.

Protection from accidents—Into a white bag (serenity) place a handful of dried davana, or a cotton pad with 3 drops of davana essential oil on it. Close the bag, then cleanse and consecrate the bag by passing it over a candle and saying "protect us (anyone riding in the car) from accidents"; continue to pass the bag over or through each element and repeat "protect us from accidents." Once it is blessed, place the bag in the glove box or other out-of-the-way part of the interior of the vehicle where it won't be disturbed. Empower it annually by adding a frankincense tear and a drop of davana oil. When you buy a different vehicle, open the pouch and compost the herbs or cotton and make a new bag.

Psychic power—To increase psychic power, practice your preferred form of divination while diffusing 1 drop of davana essential oil in 100 ml of water. Read tarot, practice automatic writing, scry in the pattern of the water droplets created by the aromatherapy diffuser, or employ your talents as best fits your abilities. Practice makes habit.

Purification—Light an incense charcoal tablet and place a pinch of dried davana on the burning disk, allowing the smoke to permeate the space and purify it from evil spirits, negativity, and more. For added purification, add a frankincense tear. Follow up with dragon's blood resin for protection from the energies' return.

Release resentment—Diffuse 1 drop of davana in 100 ml of water. While the fragrance permeates your space, on a piece of paper (or flash paper) write a list of resentments, or detail what caused a single resentment. Take as much time as you need to process the root of this resentment. In a fireproof dish, place a handful of salt (purification), crumple the paper on which you've been writing into a ball (but not too tightly, it still needs air to burn!), and carefully light. Best if performed on a Saturday (banishing).

Settle overthinking—Racing thoughts, repeated thoughts, or overthinking can be exhausting. If you're having trouble breaking the loop yourself, take a nasal inhaler and place the included cotton inside the tube. Add 7–10 drops of davana essential oil to the cotton, place the stopper in the end, and allow to sit for 10 minutes and absorb. Once it has rested, uncap, rest the open end against one nostril, and gently inhale. Allow the sweet herbal fragrance to wash over you and get you out of your spiral. Gently inhale through the nose, and exhale through the mouth. Align the inhaler along the opposite nostril and repeat. If possible, change your body's position to cement the change in subject in your mind.

Uncrossing—Gather a gray (confusing your enemies) or black (banishing) candle on a Saturday (banishing) or during the dark moon. Write "uncrossing" on the candle. Into a small bowl add 2 cups of salt and 10 drops of davana essential oil. Mix thoroughly and set aside. In the bathroom start a warm bath. Once the water is half filled, add as little or as much salt to the bath as you'd like. In a fireproof dish, light the uncrossing candle. When the bath is ready, climb in. Rinse yourself head to toe in the davana water, taking special care with the eyes. Rest and feel yourself unburdened from any hexes, curses, jinxes, or bad luck. Allow the candle to burn out (never leave a burning candle unattended). Know your spell is done and well done.

Visions—To inspire visions, light an incense charcoal tablet and sprinkle 1 to 2 pinches of dried davana onto the surface. Allow the smoke to transport you to your inner landscape where you can readily receive visions from your subconscious mind and retain the information received therein. Breathe slowly, in through your nose and out through your mouth. *If you have trouble concentrating:* add 1 benzoin tear (psychic power) to the charcoal as well. Instead of closing your eyes, softly focus your eyes on the rising smoke patterns and allow your mind to wander. If subjects aside from the current focus come up, just allow them to pass by as they float on down the river of your consciousness. You can acknowledge them without focusing on them too readily. When your visions have ended, write a summary of your experience in your journal or book of shadows so you can refer to it later.

Recipe: Fiery Sword

The ultimate apotropaic; no evil can stand against this oil.

- 3 drops davana essential oil (*Artemisia pallens*) for self-defense, countering attacks, banishing misfortune, purification, uncrossing

- 1 drop angelica (*Angelica archangelica*) to invoke the sword of the Archangel Michael

- 17 drops frankincense essential oil (*Boswellia sacra*) for purification, removing blockages

- 3 drops galbanum essential oil (*Ferula dummosa*) for apotropaic, spirit summoning, exorcism, sacred

- 5 drops may chang essential oil (*Litsea cubeba*) for strength, banishing, new beginning, renewal

Blend essential oils in a 2 ml bottle, place the reducer cap, and label. Diffuse 1 drop of synergy in 100 ml of water to cleanse the house of evil spirits, negativity, and/or miasma. Regular spiritual cleansing is recommended on a twenty-eight-day cycle if possible. To cleanse people, places, and objects, add 3 drops to a 10 ml roller bottle and fill with carrier oil of your choice. Meadowfoam oil is suggested for further sanctifying powers.

Apply the roller and cap, then label. Be careful applying any oil to wooden surfaces as oil can damage wooden finishes.

DILL

Scientific Name: *Aethum graveolens*

Botanical Family: Apiaceae

World Origin: Hungary

Plant's Oil: Whole plant

Scent Description: Herbaceous

Scent Factor: Astringent

Evaporation: Middle note

Scent Impact: Calm autonomic nervous system—this pairs well with Roman chamomile (*Anthemis nobilis*) for Attention Deficit Hyperactivity Disorder (ADHD, previously ADD)

Magical Correspondences

Application: Dilute over stomach for digestive upset, diffuse for inhalation

Element: Air

Day: Wednesday

Magical Uses: Love, protection, banishing, communication

Planet: Mercury

Astrological Sign: Gemini

Suggested Crystal: Bruneau Jasper—Ruled by Gemini: shows the web connecting all life

Deity/Spirit: Neith—Egyptian goddess of wisdom

WARNING

Do not use dill essential oil during pregnancy.

Herbal Lore/Uses

The reach of dill goes as far back as medical texts in Ancient Egypt, around 3000 BCE. The mention of dill in the Papyrus of Ebers (1550 BCE) led to the expansion of the reputation of this herb. The Egyptians prized it so heavily that Roman gladiators would rub the seeds over their bodies before matches. The terpene content of dill includes carvone (30–45 percent) and limonene (15–25 percent) meant that the muscle fibers could operate more smoothly and they are both powerful anti-inflammatory and anti-arthritic chemicals naturally present in the volatile oil. After this the Roman Empire started to spread the seeds far and wide to grow it as a symbol of good luck, to ward off harmful magic against the Empire and inspire love. These magical uses persist to this day.

After dill's mention in Dioscorides' De Materia Medica (78 CE) and Hildegard of Bingen's (1098–1179) work, dill continued to appear in the minds of people continuing for hundreds of years after Bingen's death and subsequent canonization. This communication herb is warm and inspires friendship in many forms, from its reputation for treating bad breath to helping adherents stay awake in church during the Colonial era. It was so helpful in its role for staving off hunger, and relieving halitosis and gas, that they would chew the seeds and called it "Meeting House seed."

Its reputation extended to all types of digestive upset, where seeds were steeped in warm water to relieve gas, cramping, bloating, and colic in babies.

Spells

Aggression, avert—To turn away aggressors, place 1 drop of dill essential oil in a 10 ml roller bottle and fill with the carrier oil of your choice. Anoint pulse points at wrist, neck, and behind the knees. Envision (if you can) a steel bubble surrounding you, impenetrable to aggression, hate, or malice. If you can't use your mind's eye to see that bubble, you can physically draw one around you. If you're concerned about onlookers, simply act like you're stretching; in all honesty, most people are too concerned with their own lives to wonder about a random person stretching their back.

Assistance—Place a drop of dill oil on petitions asking for the assistance of air elementals, ancestors, principal deities, and spirits.

Awaken magic—Add 1 drop of dill essential oil to a 10 ml roller bottle and fill the rest of the way with the carrier oil of choice before anointing your body to awaken your magic.

Banish lawsuits; protection, business—To protect your business from frivolous or fraudulent lawsuits take a copy of foundational documents for your company or related documents like business licenses, place a drop of dill essential oil or a teaspoon of dried dill, fold the herb inside the documents, and seal inside an envelope. Decorate the exterior of the envelope with protective symbols, signs, or sigils from your practice and keep in a safe place.

Defensive magic—While wards and shields are an important part of any witch's tool bag, defensive magic cannot be overvalued. (For more specifics, check out *Blackthorn's Protection Magic* and *Psychic Witch* by Mat Auryn.) Head to the farmer's market, grocery store, inexpensive market, or independent witch shop, and find your dill. It can be from the spice aisle in the Dollar Store (or your local version) or your own kitchen, since we will be sprinkling it instead of eating it. Stand in the north quadrant of your yard if you have one (if you don't have one, see the second version), and sprinkle dill around the perimeter of your space—walking clockwise—envisioning a wrought-iron fence, painted black and eight feet high, surrounding your property. Those decorative yet functional spikes keep all manner of evil from your doorstep. Ghosts and related spirits aren't fond of iron, either. If you live in an apartment, townhome, or other configuration, where you don't have access to a yard, finely grind your dill into a powder, and, starting while facing north, walk clockwise through your space, leaving pinches of dill powder in the corners of the rooms you pass through on your way back to your starting point. Envision a steel sheeting surrounding your space so no malice can penetrate. Know your space is sealed and protected. So mote it be.

Hexing/Uncrossing—More often than not, if a plant is listed as hex breaking, it will also be quite adept at creating hexes. If someone has harmed you, abused your trust or someone you love, take a piece of paper, and draw an equal-armed cross (+) in the center of the paper. Name the cross with the name of your target. Add their date of birth if you know it. Around the outside of the cross draw a circular arrow counterclockwise at the edge of the cross so that it is unwinding the beneficial luck and blessings that have been bestowed upon your target. Draw over the circular arrow with your diluted dill oil, showing the energies how you wish them to unravel the life built by your target. If your target is someone you were close with, consider petitioning their helping spirits to allow your magic to teach them. Leave your target an "out" clause, such as, "if you get therapy and stop abusing your loved ones, the effects will cease." Conversely, if you feel you or someone you love has been cursed/hexed/jinxed (for the difference between them, please reference *Blackthorn's Protection Magic*), follow the above steps with a clockwise arrow. Reinforce the clockwise arrow with your dill oil and ask your helping spirits to remove any curses or ill intent directed towards you.

Home, protection—With a large fireproof container such as a cauldron that contains sand or gravel, place lit charcoal inside. (Keeping tongs handy for safety is a great idea.) On the full moon, place a goodly amount of dried dill herb on the burning charcoal and walk clockwise around your property to bless and protect all inside from evil. If you live in an apartment or do not have access to the perimeter of the building, you need much less herb for the smoke. First, start in the north and continue clockwise around the home to instill protection. Consider adding dragon's blood to the charcoal to boost the protective qualities of the dill you are burning. It has a musky sweet scent to it, so it will uplift the herbal fragrance of the burning dill.

Knowledge, oracular—Burn dried dill herb over incense charcoal while divining the answer you see in the smoke. If unable to burn incense, diffuse 1 drop of dill essential oil in 100 ml of water while practicing your breathing techniques. Allow your mind to wander and problem solve while you maintain your breath. The answers will come.

Magical skills—To help bolster your magical skills, diffuse a drop of dill essential oil in 100 ml of water while engaging in magical studies, meditation, visualization, or energy work.

Recipe: Guard Dog Love

✤ 5 drops dill essential oil (*Aethum graveolens*) for protection, to awaken magic

✤ 10 drops Mandarin essential oil (*Citrus reticulata*) for calm defense, soothing tension, protection

✤ 10 drops pine essential oil (*Pinus sylvestris*) for friendship in adversity, divine protection, aid

Diffuse this synergy to inspire divine guardians. Add 5 drops to a 10 ml roller bottle and fill with jojoba for protection magic anointing.

ELEMI

Scientific Name: *Canarium luzonicum*

Botanical Family: Burseraceae

World Origin: Philippines

Plant's Oil: Gum

Scent Description: Resinous, deep, woody, hint of citrus

Evaporation: Middle-to-base note

Scent Impact: Meditative

Magical Correspondences

Application: Topical anti-inflammatory, diffuse, dilute

Element: Air

Day: Wednesday

Magical Uses: Centering, divination, grief, and magical skills

Planet: Mercury

Astrological Sign: Gemini

Suggested Crystal: Serpentine—Ruled by Gemini: enhanced meditative state

Deity/Spirit: Asclepius—Greek God of Healing

> ### WARNING
> When oxidized, can cause skin irritation; shelf life of two years unrefrigerated, three with refrigeration.

Herbal Lore/Uses

Elemi has a history of use dating back to ancient Egypt where a poor man's frankincense was used as a part of the embalming process. This lesser known member of the Burseraceae family has a scent similar to frankincense, including its signature hint of citrus on the back. The name *elemi* is derived from the Arabic word that means, "as above, so below," one of the axioms that form the foundation for both European and Islamic alchemy.

Elemi resin is a supremely sticky resin that has been used since the 1700s to help doctors on battlefields close wounds and keep infection at bay. It also banishes bacteria, fungi, and viruses. Its pain-relieving qualities were appreciated by those injured in the line of fire. The bandage is also antiemetic, which, given battlefield conditions from the 1700s to today, was greatly needed. Elemi is so durable as a bandage that industrial applications include it being added to varnish. As an added bonus, it is an expectorant, so chest colds didn't stand a chance.

Spells

Centering—To aid in centering your focus, take a nasal inhaler tube and place the cotton inside. Add 7–10 drops of elemi essential oil to the cotton, and place the stopper in the bottom. Make sure the lid is tightly capped and allow to rest for 10 minutes. Once the oil has been absorbed , uncap the top, place the open end of the inhaler against one nostril, and gently inhale through the nose and exhale through the mouth. Repeat on the opposite side. Feel your scattered energies come to the center of your body, and send them down into the earth where they can more readily be utilized by the earth, without harm.

Compassion—To help give yourself compassion, take a light-blue (spiritual healing) pouch and place 3 tissues or cotton balls inside. Add to the bag 2 to 3 drops of elemi essential oil and tie closed. Bless the bag as appropriate for your practice. Remind yourself that we are all human and deserving of care, compassion, rest, and nourishment. Carry in your pocket during times of increased stress. Every time you brush up against the bag, you'll remind yourself to walk with compassion for yourself.

Grief—Grief is a tough emotion, because each time we think we have mastered it, it roars back to life, reminding us that each day is a new version of normal until we make peace with the feelings of grief. The loss won't go away, and your love won't either. We are simply making a cooperative agreement with grief to get along as best we can. Elemi can help us forge that working arrangement by keeping the lines of communication open. Take the cotton or wool pad from a scent locket and add 1–2 drops of Elemi essential oil. Tuck the fabric into the locket, bless the necklace with the four elements, and ask that Elemi provide you with the grief support that you seek, cooling the raging fires of grief's anger with the element of air. Wear it for a lunar cycle (twenty-eight days) before renewing the oil in the locket if needed.

Grounding—Grounding is the working partner of centering as discussed above. If you cannot visualize the energies in your body needing a calming influence, try this instead. Excess energy in the body always felt like sharp static running along my arms and legs, and grounding is the act of giving that excess energy back to the earth from which it came. Diffuse 1 drop of elemi essential oil in 100 ml of water. Breathe slowly in through your nose and out through your mouth while feeling the static in your body pooling in your feet, and when your feet overflow with that energy, it spills onto the hungry ground to be soaked up by the earth, who can use it to nourish all the plants growing right now. Repeat as needed.

Healing—Healing magic is multivalent and can be many things to many people. Whether you need physical, spiritual, emotional, or mental healing, elemi is here to assist your healing journey. Take a peach (physical strength), purple (spiritual healing), blue (emotional healing), or silver (resolve inner conflict) candle and carve "healing" into the surface with a pen. Anoint the candle with diluted elemi essential oil and burn on a Sunday (personal empowerment).

Magical skills, to increase—Ignite an incense charcoal tablet and place into a fireproof container. When it is burning well, place a small tear onto the hot charcoal. Bathe in the smoke as you ready yourself for magical practice.

Peace—Add 1 drop of elemi essential oil to a 10 ml roller bottle and fill the rest of the way with the carrier oil of your choice. Draw a symbol you associate with peace in the center of your chest and allow the feeling to soak into your heart as you massage the oil into the skin in clockwise circles. Allow yourself to accept the calm being offered.

Psychic development—Diffuse 1 drop of elemi essential oil in 100 ml of water as you breathe slowly and evenly, allowing any thoughts to slowly drift on, without direct action or inner comment. Breathe deeply in through the nose and out through the mouth. Close your eyes and practice the divinatory skills you seek to acquire, whether tarot, scrying, remote viewing, or others.

Recipe: Endless Summer

Revel in the feel of summer sun just a little longer.

- 10 drops elemi essential oil (*Canarium luzonicum*) for centering, grounding

- 15 drops benzoin essential oil (*Styrax tonkinensis*) for inspiration, wisdom

- 4 drops clove bud essential oil (*Eugenia caryophyllata*) for dispelling negativity, protection

- 8 drops petitgrain essential oil (*Citrus aurantium*) for release negative emotions, defend against psychic attack

- 3 drops rose essential oil (*Rosa centifolia*) for compassion, peace, gentleness

Blend synergy in a 2 ml bottle. Diffuse 1 drop in 100 ml of water to banish symptoms of fall blues. To wear as an uplifting perfume add 5 drops of synergy to a 10 ml roller bottle, fill the rest of the way with the carrier of your choice, cap, and roll between your palms to blend.

FENNEL

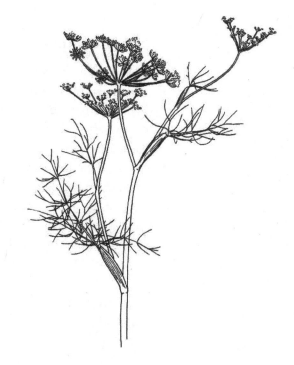

Scientific Name: *Foeniculum vulgare*

Botanical Family: Apiaceae

World Origin: Australia, Spain

Plant's Oil: Seeds

Scent Description: Herbal, sweet, astringent

Scent Factor: Mild

Evaporation: Middle note

Scent Impact: Increases feelings of well-being, antianxiety

Magical Correspondences

Application: Diffuse, dilute, direct inhalation

Element: Fire

Day: Wednesday

Magical Uses: Protection, purification, divination, health, eliminating stress

Planet: Mercury

Astrological Sign: Gemini, Aquarius

Suggested Crystal: Diamond (black preferred)— Ruled by Aries, Leo, Taurus: avert devils, prosperity

Deity/Spirit: Dionysus

WARNING
Avoid in history of epilepsy; use with caution during pregnancy.

Herbal Lore/Uses

Fennel's history in botanical medicine is vast and wide. It has been used in infusions for conjunctivitis, regulating menstruation, and relieving gas. Today it is often added to cookies given to increase breast milk production. In the history of herbal medicine, fennel was noted as one of the five great appetite-stimulating roots, along with celery, parsley, and others. The Greeks, Egyptians, Chinese, and Romans all used fennel. The plant itself conveyed courage, sharp eyesight, and daring.

The stalks of dried fennel were burned as torches used to invoke Dionysus during his ecstatic rites. Dionysus carried a stalk of fennel as a staff (as both a priapic wand, [invoking the magic of the phallus], and a weapon) so the priestesses of Dionysus carried staffs—called a thyrsus—made of the dried stalks of fennel wrapped in ivy to symbolize their station.

The essential oil can be diluted and used as a toner to balance oily or dry skin and added to moisturizer for protecting mature skin. The aromatic use of fennel will also contribute to emotional wellness in conveying a sense of comfort and well-being.

For perfumers, fennel adds a spicy aroma that pairs well with orange and citruses, lavender, rose, sandalwood, and geranium.

Spells

Aura purification—In a well-ventilated space, add 1–3 teaspoons of dried fennel seed to a burning incense charcoal disk. Waft the smoke over the entire body, both top to bottom and front and back. Intrusions can hide in sneaky places like the back side of the heart, so make sure the smoke touches everything it can to purify the aura, especially after traumatic events, after contact with unknown spirits, or under uncontrollable circumstances.

Avert psychic attack—Starting at the highest point of your home, place a pinch of dried fennel in each corner of the home or apartment, sealing the home against intrusion.

Blessing children—Place one teaspoon of crushed fennel seeds in a 2-ounce glass bottle and fill with carrier oil of choice. Allow to sit in a dark cabinet for a minimum of two weeks; one lunar cycle is preferred. Once the oil is infused, take a drop and bless the child in whatever tradition you prefer, while anointing forehead, heart, hands, and feet. If the child is old enough to understand the blessing, explain what you are doing and why and then allow them to participate by placing a drop on each hand and having them place it where it feels appropriate to do so. This is a great lesson in bodily autonomy and consent.

Courage—During tough times it can be difficult to take the time you need to ground and center yourself. Diffuse 1 drop of fennel essential oil in 100 ml of water before difficult tasks, or place a drop on a piece of wool or cotton inside an aromatherapy necklace to stick with you all day. You won't notice after a few moments, but rather you'll catch a whiff of it during times of stress when your body and brain need it the most. It will remind you of your inherent courage.

Eloquence—Before public speaking, presentations at work or other times when smooth speech is required, place 7–10 drops of fennel essential oil onto a cotton insert in a nasal inhaler, place the stopper in the bottom, and allow the cotton to rest for a few moments to absorb the oil. Before speaking, take a moment to ground and center your excess energies while breathing gently in through your nose and out through your mouth. Feel the excess nervousness trickle down into the earth, leaving you feeling grounded and calm. Repeat as needed.

Energy—When an energetic boost is called for, crush a teaspoon of fennel seeds in a mortar with a pestle if you have one, or between two tablespoons if you don't. Place in a mug, pour 8 ounces of boiling water over the seeds, and allow them to steep for 5 minutes. Feel the warmth and vibrancy of the sun infusing the tisane. Sip the fennel water while allowing the warmth to spread to your body and reminding your corporeal self that you have everything you need.

Fertility—Place 1 drop of fennel essential oil in 10 ml of carrier oil (roller bottle recommended for follow-up applications). Draw symbols of fertility on your lower stomach (never place essential oils onto the genitals) and massage in clockwise circles for increase in fertility. Repeat as needed.

Healing—Place a teaspoon of fennel seed (lightly crushed) or a cotton ball with a drop of fennel essential oil on it into a pale-blue drawstring bag. Charge the bag for healing the intended recipient of the bag by telling the charm exactly whom it is for and what they need healing from.

Money—Grab a pinch of fennel seed from the spice cabinet and place it into your wallet. Whisper, "Money grow, mound like snow," nine times to cement its job. Replace annually.

Pain Relief—Add 2 drops of fennel essential oil to a 10 ml roll-on bottle and fill it with the carrier of your choice. Two percent is a gentle therapeutic dilution rate. Cap and roll the bottle gently between your hands. If you have time, let it sit for one hour to ensure proper dispersal. Draw symbols of pain relief on your back, for magic to relieve your back pain. Draw symbols of dispersal on the stomach to relive pain from gas or bloating, and massage into the skin.

Power (to amplify)—Light a charcoal disk in a fireproof dish; use tongs to hold if available. Once the disk is hot enough, lightly crush fennel seeds and add them to the smoking charcoal. Bathe in the smoke of the burning fennel seeds to amplify the power of your magic before casting a spell or performing a ritual to ensure your aim is true.

Protection—Place a few tablespoons of fennel seed into a bottle of cheap eighty-proof vodka, or, if you are sober the highest purity rubbing alcohol you can find at the pharmacy. Allow to sit for 6–8 weeks in a cool, dark space, like a cabinet. Once the fennel has fully infused, use the resulting alcohol to create a barrier of protection around your home, if it is a free-standing structure, feel free to pour right from the bottle. If it's an apartment or condo, add the solution to a spray bottle to spray in the four cardinal directions of the space. Make sure to avoid wooden surfaces or lightly colored fabrics in case of staining.

Purification—Varying your purification routine is incredibly valuable for making sure the space stays energetically vibrant. You can anoint doors and windows with diluted fennel oil to seal them against evil intrusion. A pinch of fennel over the front door jamb will purify anyone coming in the front door.

Sacred, the—To invoke the sacred beings of your tradition, burn fennel seeds on charcoal to purify and empower your space, and invite gods, spirits, and ancestors to your space.

Sight, magical (to improve)—Gather evening primrose gel caps, a pin, and fennel seed. Crush a teaspoon of fennel seeds in a mortar with a pestle, or between two tablespoons. Once the fragrant oils have been released, place them into a shot glass or other similar vessel. From the jar of evening primrose oil capsules, extract three. Prick the gel cap (careful with that pin!) and squeeze the oil onto the crushed fennel seeds. Give them a light stir and let them sit for an hour. When you come back, the oil will have started smelling like fennel seed. Anoint the heel of your hand (the side opposite your thumb) on both hands (this is the mound of the moon, and the moon is associated with intuition) and gently massage it around the temples and the third eye. Don't get it into your eyes or it can cause irritation. Evening primrose carries the magic of psychic sight, as does fennel. Repeat on the dark moon for greatest insights.

Stress, relieve/tension release—Taking a 10 ml roll-on bottle, add 1–2 drops of fennel essential oil, fill to the top with the carrier oil of your choice, and place the cap. Roll gently between your palms to blend. When blended, use the roller ball to apply the diluted oil to your neck and shoulders and massage in. Breathe in gently through the nose and out through the mouth. Stress will dissipate. Repeat as needed.

Victory—In order to overcome any battle before you, grab a red candle (Mars) (chime candles work great for this), a pen, a candleholder, and your fennel magical pen. Onto the red candle, draw three lines creating an upward pointing arrow. (↑) This is the rune Tiwaz, and it confers victory in battle. Anoint the rune with your diluted fennel oil to reinforce the victory. Burn on a Tuesday (Mars).

Recipe: The Reckoning

This oil is the beginning and the end. Use this oil to reveal secrets and lies, ensure victory, and Reclaim. Your. Power. Nothing can stand against you with the oil at your back.

- ❋ 5 drops fennel essential oil (Foeniculum vulgare) for averting harm, destroying obstacles, and ensuring victory

- 1 drop frankincense essential oil (*Boswellia sacra*) to maintain philanthropic goals
- 10 drops lavender essential oil (*Lavandula angustifolia*) for revealing secrets, strength, and intuition in battle
- 10 drops orange essential oil (*Citrus sinensis*) for persuasion, to reclaim your power

I came up with this blend during my clinical aromatherapist practicals for a client who was presenting with gastroparesis. The client in question is also a Witch and in her feedback she noted that using it also increased the magical aim for removing obstacles to her goals in magic, as well as her gastric distress. I love it when the clinical aromatherapy and magical aromatherapy come together in one powerhouse.

JUNIPER

Scientific Name: *Juniperus communis,*
J. osteosperma, J. scopulorum

Botanical Family: Cupressaceae

World Origin: Utah, (United States); Europe; Asia

Plant's Oil: Berries, branches, twigs

Scent Description: Piney, sharp, warm

Evaporation: Middle note

Scent Impact: Inspires feelings of connection, love, and peace

Magical Correspondences

Application: Diffuse, dilute

Element: Fire

Day: Sunday

Magical Uses: Abilities, protection from harm, aura cleansing

Planet: Sun

Astrological Sign: Aries

Suggested Crystal: Tiger Iron—focused intent, will, courage

Deity/Spirit: Athena, Greek goddess of wisdom and warfare

WARNING
Avoid if pregnant or nursing.

HERBAL LORE/USES

Juniper is the ultimate apotropaic plant. It has a history of warding homes against malefic magic, evil witches, thieves, ghosts, and accidents. This heavy hitter should be on the list of every practitioner's "go bag" for magical emergencies. This reputation was so strong that even French hospitals burned it inside the hospital to protect patients from diseased air. The practice has been largely replaced with lavandin essential oil (*Lavandula x intermedia*) based cleansers due to the high concentration of antimicrobial chemicals naturally occurring in higher percentages than lavender (*Lavandula angustifolia*).

Juniper is so adept at protection and cleansing that it was added to funeral pyres in ancient Greece and Rome to protect the grieving and allow the spirit of the deceased to move on to the next life. It is sacred to Hecate and burned in rites to Circe, Hades, Artemis and Persephone as well.

Spells

Abilities/talents—To remind yourself that you are capable and magical, diffuse 1 drop of juniper essential oil in 100 ml of water during study or learning.

Accidents, protection from—Place 1 drop of juniper essential oil in a 10 ml roller bottle and fill the rest of the way with the carrier oil of your choice. (Remember to label!) Anoint your car, bike, skateboard, sneakers, and the like with your magical pen. Feel free to use symbols of protection. If you're unsure of how oil will interact with your chosen material, remember to choose an obscure place to test color fastness.

Action, enable—When you're feeling stuck and need to spring into action, take a sprig of juniper, or a handful of juniper berries, an incense dish, charcoal, tongs, and a windproof lighter to your ritual space. With the tongs, pick up the charcoal and light it. Add the juniper to the burning charcoal and bathe in the smoke as it cleanses you of your inhibitions and fears.

Anger, protection from—To quell anger, diffuse 1 drop of juniper essential oil in 100 ml of water, while breathing gently, in through the nose and out through the mouth. On each inhale, count to four, hold for four, exhale for four, and rest for four. Repeat until anger passes.

Animal health, protection—To protect the health of your animals, anoint a cloth 2" x 2" with a drop of juniper essential oil and place it with a photo or representation of your pet(s) on your altar, or near a special place for them. (Essential oils containing 1,8-Cineole like rosemary and tea tree can be harmful to pets, but juniper does not contain 1,8-Cineole. Still, use caution with any essential oil around your pets, especially birds, as they are very sensitive to the chemicals that occur naturally in many essential oils.)

Aura cleansing—Take a cup of Epsom salts and add 10 drops of juniper essential oil. Stir well to incorporate. Draw a warm bath and sprinkle the bath salts into the tub as the tub fills. Allow salt to dissolve before getting into the tub. Center yourself once immersed in the water and see any negativity, curses, hexes, or miasma dissipate as the warmth soothes your spirit. Exit the bath and pat dry. Picture your aura sealed and renewed against any attack.

Awareness of past lives—Place 1 drop of juniper essential oil into a 10 ml roller bottle. Fill the rest of the way with jojoba oil (overcoming obstacles). Insert the roller ball and cap. Roll gently between the palms to mix so as not to introduce more air to the oil than necessary. Lie comfortably where you're unlikely to be disturbed. Anoint the center of your forehead with the roller ball in a spiral that goes clockwise from the inside out, thus opening your pineal gland, thought to be the seat of psychic power. Breathe slowly in through the nose and out through the mouth to enter a relaxed state. Allow your mind to wander into the past and see what images greet you.

Banishing—Banishing room spray ingredients: a 2-ounce bottle made of glass or #1 plastic, juniper essential oil, witch hazel or rubbing alcohol, water. Add 2 tablespoons of alcohol or witch hazel to the bottle. Add 10 drops of juniper essential oil to the bottle and swirl to incorporate. (Remember, oil and water don't mix, so you need a friend to introduce them to each other.) Once incorporated, fill the rest of the way with water. Spray into the air to banish negativity from a space. To banish a person, write their name on a piece of paper in black ink (banishing) and spray liberally with the juniper spray. Burn a black candle (banishing) over the name to speed the magic.

Depression, transformation—To transform symptoms of depression (magic isn't a cure for depression; don't stop taking your medications without consulting your healthcare professionals!) take an aromatherapy locket, place 1–2 drops onto the included cotton or wool, and place inside the locket. Remember, I do *not* endorse "lava bead" jewelry or anything that allows undiluted oils to contact skin directly; this can cause severe chemical burns and allergic reactions. Summon the disparate energies in your body and bring them to the center of your being until you feel tingly and warm in the center of your body. Send the excess energies into the earth and bring up fresh energies from the earth to send into the locket you've created. Empower the locket to lessen symptoms of depression and empower the energy you need to function. Remember, whether or not you have been diagnosed with depression, never use your own energies to empower objects and spells. We are low energy enough when battling depression symptoms; using your own energy rather than that of the earth can lead to tiredness, nausea, worsening depression, dissociation, and other symptoms. Wear the locket all day. You won't notice the scent every minute, as your nose will discount or forget you're wearing it so it doesn't distract you during the day; you will simply smell small wafts of it at varying points during the day, reminding you of your magic.

Dreams—Diffuse 1 drop of juniper essential oil in 100 ml of water for 10 minutes before retiring to bed for the evening. This will allow the scent to permeate the room and get to work as soon as you enter your space. As you drift to sleep, breathe in through the nose and out through the mouth, slowly and evenly. Relaxing into your body as you drift off to sleep will allow the juniper to remind you of health, love, and spiritual awareness. Juniper also increases circulation through the kidneys and promotes nerve regeneration, so sleep is the perfect time to work with this incredible ally. It takes juniper berries (they're a true cone, not actually a berry) eighteen months to mature, so set your goals for the long term when working with this coniferous shrub.

Evil, protection from—Hang bundles of juniper over doorways to sweep away any lingering malefic magic from entering your home on the back of someone who comes into your home: friends, family, service workers, and others.

Fertility—Place a handful of dried juniper berries in a forest green (fertility) or light-blue (calm encouragement) bag and place them under the mattress before intercourse. They're dried, so it isn't a problem to leave them there until a fertilized egg has settled.

Ghosts, protection from—With a mortar and pestle, grind a handful of juniper leaves with ½ cup of your salt of choice. (*Optional:* add steel wool by cutting into a steel wool pad with scissors. Iron is apotropaic and repels ghosts.) If your home has multiple levels, go to the lowest level, as close to the ground as you can get. Sprinkle the mixture inside the home along the exterior walls of the building to create a fence to keep ghosts out. If you'd like to do this around the exterior of the home instead, grind juniper leaves and steel wool, without the salt, as salt will kill plants. Consider wearing gloves when working with steel wool, as the tiny fibers can become embedded in the skin and cause irritation.

Happiness—To inspire joy, take a 10 ml bottle and add a drop or two of juniper essential oil. Fill the rest of the way with the carrier of your choice. I suggest fractionated coconut if possible for its direct, singular focus in magic. Anoint pulse points and envision your favorite color radiating out of every pore, empowering your happiness.

Harmony—To banish contention in the home, diffuse 1 drop of juniper essential oil in 100 ml of water. Open windows if possible to refresh the space.

Healing—For healing magic, take a blue candle (healing) and anoint with diluted juniper essential oil. Place 1 drop of juniper essential oil into a 10 ml roller bottle. Fill the rest of the way with jojoba oil (overcoming obstacles). Insert the roller ball and cap. Roll gently between the palms to mix so as not to introduce more air to the oil than necessary. Don't forget to label! Anoint the candle starting in the center and working your way out, pushing any impurities, negativity, or obstructions out of the candle and filling it with your intention for healing. Place in a candleholder. On a small piece of paper, write the name of your target for healing ("John Smith") and any biographical data you have (date, time, place of birth, screen names, email address, and so forth), place the paper underneath the candle to make sure the healing goes to the correct John Smith. Light the candle and make sure to stay in the room with it while it burns for fire safety.

Hexes, to avert—To keep hexes from your home, burn juniper-based incense to enforce a bubble of protection around your home at all times. Juniper is an evergreen shrub, just as we want your home's protection to be evergreen. Make sure to have a routine of cleansing your home with magic, every lunar cycle if possible. Varying the botanical ally and the method of cleansing is a best practice. This month you might diffuse juniper essential oil throughout the house. Next month you might scrub the floors with a pine essential oil floor wash and burn dragon's blood incense. Not every nasty thing will respond to every method of cleansing; by varying your routine, you ensure that your home is properly clean, and you ensure that no one knows what you'll be cleaning with before you get to work. Friendships come and go, and we don't want today's friend to have ammo to use against you tomorrow if the relationship crumbles.

Honors—To receive the honors you are owed, tie a red thread (attracting magic) around a gold candle (success), and anoint with diluted juniper essential oil. Place into a candleholder and burn on a Sunday (success). (Make sure to be nearby keeping an eye on the candle as the thread catches fire.)

Invisibility/to avert detection—True invisibility is the stuff of movies and television; however, the best invisibility is to pass unseen. (See "The S.E.P. Field" in *Blackthorn's Protection Magic*.) To ensure you're able to pass unseen, start with a diluted juniper spray. Juniper spray ingredients: a 2-ounce bottle, (glass or #1 plastic) juniper essential oil, witch hazel or rubbing alcohol, and water. Add ¼ cup of rubbing alcohol or witch hazel to the bottle. Add 10 drops of juniper essential oil to the bottle and swirl to incorporate. (Remember, oil and water don't mix, so you need a friend to introduce them to each other.) Once incorporated, fill the rest of the way with water. Spray your arms and legs (if you have a history of sensitivity to conifers, place a drop of the spray on the inside of your wrist to test for irritation) and imagine your image of yourself being erased. When moving so as not to be detected, make sure to move evenly and as normally as possible. If you actively try to sneak, it puts a big neon sign on your aura that says, "I'm up to something."

Libido—To increase personal sexual desire, diffuse juniper in areas where you spend the most time, to slowly increase your desire over time. To increase site-specific arousal, place ¼ cup of salt in a glass bowl and add 3–5 drops of juniper essential oil. Place the bowl near the space where you hope to inspire arousal, for example, next to a bed. This will inspire a stronger response as it is a more concentrated volatility.

Light the way—The protective aspects of juniper inspire driving away of negative forces, and lighting the way for helpful spirits and entities, including family and ancestors. To ask for the aid of your family, both blood and chosen, light an incense charcoal tablet and place juniper leaves on the charcoal. The leaves seem to burn more efficiently on charcoal than the berries (cones) do. Notice the slight blue tinge to the smoke, and understand that this is a flag waving to your friends, loved ones, and family that have crossed the veil. If remembering them at Samhain-tide, consider leaving out coffee, favorite foods, and drinks to welcome them to your home.

Love—To signal to the universe that you are ready for a new loving relationship in your life, gather diluted juniper essential oil, a red (love) candle, and a candleholder. Place 1 drop of juniper essential oil into a 10 ml roller bottle. Fill the rest of the way with jojoba oil (overcoming obstacles). Insert the roller ball and cap. Roll gently between the palms to mix so as not to introduce more air to the oil than necessary. Don't forget to label! Carve your own name on the candle, as you are the one seeking the loving relationship. Anoint with the diluted juniper essential oil. Place the candle into the candleholder and burn on a Friday (love) or Sunday (success).

Negativity, to banish—Diffuse a drop of juniper essential oil in 100 ml of water to banish negativity in the home and allow in positivity.

Prosperity—Find a bill with the highest denomination you can afford. Anoint the four corners of the bill with diluted juniper essential oil. (Fours in magic are for stability.) Place it on your work surface. Next take a green candle (fast money), gold candle (success), or brown candle (financial stability) and carve your name or initials into the surface with "prosperity" or a $ sign, depending on space. Place into candleholder and burn on a Sunday (success).

Protection from harm—To protect a loved one from harm, place three juniper berries into a small pouch and empower either by your own tradition or by bringing up energy from the earth and pouring it into the charm. Tell the charm what you are looking for: "Protect John Doe from evil spirits," or "Protect Suzy from hexes, curses, and jinxes." Let the person know that it is a protective talisman and to keep it with them whenever possible, in a pocket, purse, wallet, or even their shoe if needed.

Protection from theft—To protect small specific items, like jewelry, consider protecting the jewelry box they are kept in, rather than anointing the jewelry itself, as carrier oils can mar the finish on some items. *Note:* oils can also dissolve stains and glosses that protect wood, so if you're anointing a wooden box, dilute the oil in rubbing alcohol or witch hazel instead of carrier oil. Anoint the wooden box in an inconspicuous place so if there is any staining or issues, it won't detract from the beauty of the item itself. The same goes for any wooden surface, for instance if you're anointing a television stand to protect the television from theft.

Purification—Burn juniper-based incense to purify your home or other space. Remember to burn something afterwards so as not to leave a vacuum in the space for negativity to come back. *Suggestions:* dragon's blood for protection, benzoin for confidence and harmony, cypress to calm anxiety, or cardamom for courage.

Spiritual transformation—For those undergoing spiritual transformation, self-dedication, initiation, or other transformations, light the way with juniper incense. It blesses and protects the person or people who pass through the arches of knowledge and eases the growing pains of change.

Wishes, for loved ones—Grab a pink candle (loved ones), diluted juniper oil, and a candleholder. Place 1 drop of juniper essential oil into a 10 ml roller bottle. Fill the rest of the way with jojoba oil (overcoming obstacles). Insert the roller ball and cap. Roll gently between the palms to mix so as not to introduce more air to the oil than necessary. Make sure to label! Carve the word "wish" and your loved one's name onto the candle and anoint with the diluted juniper essential oil, pushing out any lingering negativity. Burn on a Friday for loved ones, or Sunday for success.

Recipe: Walk Tall

Use this blend to increase confidence in mannerisms, speech, and business dealings.

- ❁ 20 drops juniper (*Juniperus communis*) essential oil for purification and protection

- ❁ 5 drops black pepper (*Piper nigrum*) essential oil for confident speech

- ❁ 5 drops cardamom (*Elettaria cardamomum*) for confidence, antianxiety

Diffuse in places where confidence is needed, 1 drop in 100 ml water. Add 3–5 drops to ¼ cup of salt to diffuse near electronics, as in a cubicle. Alternately, add 1–2 drops to a scent locket worn around the neck to empower communication for speeches, presentations, and proposals.

LIME

Scientific Name: *Citrus x aurantifolia, C. medica, C. x latifolia, C. acida var.*

Botanical Family: Rutaceae

World Origin: South Asia, Iran

Plant's Oil: Peel

Scent Description: Sweet, citrusy, fruity

Evaporation: Top note

Scent Impact: Uplifting for the spirit

Magical Correspondences

Application: Diffuse, dilute

Element: Water, Fire

Day: Friday, Sunday

Magical Uses: Antidepressant, love, luck, focus

Planet: Venus, Sun

Astrological Sign: Taurus, Leo

Suggested Crystal: Honey Calcite—Ruled by Cancer: mental clarity

Deity/Spirit: Hestia, goddess of the hearth fire

WARNING

Lime as well as many citrus essential oils can be phototoxic on the skin for up to 48 hours, due to the presence of bergapten and other furanocoumarins. Citrus and pine oils over 2 years of age are also phototoxic due to oxidation. Avoid UV light after application. Lime oil if distilled is non-phototoxic, but expressed lime essential oil does contain bergapten. Expressed lime oil will have a slight green color to it, but be aware that unethical companies may dye their oils. Always test for yourself at home. If you don't know the brand that you have is distilled rather than expressed, act accordingly.

Herbal Lore/Uses

It is the fruit that saved the Royal Navy, from scurvy, that is. Yes, scurvy is a disease, not just a pejorative used in old pirate movies. Scurvy causes the breakdown of collagen in the body, leading to bleeding gums, bruising, and reopening of previously healed scars. Collagen is used in every part of the body, from blood vessels to hair and skin. So, all of the tropes surrounding piracy in the 1800s are due to a lack of proper vitamin C absorption. The British Royal Navy was able to correct this oversight when citruses arrived from South Asia and they started sending ships out to sea with plenty of vitamin C-containing citruses.

Lime oil has been used in aromatherapy to support those with respiratory weakness and low immune system function. Limonene is a terpene, or a key chemical component of lime essential oil, that has anti-inflammatory properties, as well as antirheumatic (relieves swelling), antibacterial, antioxidant, and antiviral properties. It also helps improve circulation topically.

Spells

Antidepressant—The high limonene content (50–60 percent) in lime essential oil is uplifting for those experiencing a depressive episode and in need of a bit of levity. To boost feelings of well-being, diffuse 1 drop in 100 ml of water. Though lime is stimulating, the relief of the veil of depression may cause feelings of tiredness that are physical, rather than emotional. As with any depression symptoms, treat yourself gently and speak to healthcare professionals if symptoms persist.

Fidelity—For magical aid in staying true to your relationship agreements, place 1 drop of lime essential oil into a 10 ml roller bottle. Fill the bottle the rest of the way with the carrier oil of your choice. I recommend jojoba as it has a long shelf life and a low instance of allergy. Cap and roll the bottle between your hands. Allow to rest for a few moments before applying. Take a pale-blue (spiritual healing) candle and carve "fidelity" into the candle with a ballpoint pen, if safe to do so. Your safety is paramount. Anoint the candle and place it into a candleholder. Light and allow to burn completely. Best if done on a Friday.

Focus—To maintain focus during your day, add a drop of lime essential oil to the cotton pad of an aromatherapy locket. Wear or carry that locket all day to keep you in the moment throughout the day. If jewelry isn't your style, you can make a nasal inhaler. (See below.)

Friendship—For magic to bring new friendships, take a pink (friendship) candle and write "beginnings" on the surface with a ballpoint pen. Anoint the candle with diluted lime essential oil and place into a candleholder. Light and burn until complete. Best if done on a Sunday (personal empowerment/luck).

Healing—To promote healing, especially for a weakened immune system or respiratory ailment, diffuse 1 drop of lime essential oil in 100 ml of water in the recovery room. If 1 drop is too much, reduce by half by adding to a bowl with an additional 100 ml of water and move the diffuser to the other side of the room.

Higher self—To connect with your higher self, place 1 drop of lime essential oil into a 10 ml roller bottle. Fill the bottle the rest of the way with the carrier oil of your choice. Cap and roll the bottle between your hands. Allow to rest for a few moments before applying. Apply to your heart center and the top of your head to connect your thinking heart with your higher self. Massage the oil in, in clockwise circles to increase connection. Feel the two spaces connect energetically, like plugging into an electrical socket. Allow the lime essential oil to raise the vibration of your energy to your highest good. I do this visualization with lime essential oil before seeing my tarot clients to make sure I've connected with my highest self for my client's well-being. To ground afterwards, I smell patchouli or vetiver essential oil.

Love—To signal to the universe that you're ready for a new romantic partner, take a gold (fast luck) or pink (innocent love) candle and write "new love" on it with a ballpoint pen. Anoint the candle with diluted lime essential oil and place into a candleholder. Light and allow to burn until complete. Best if done on a Friday (Venus, love) or a Sunday (success).

Loyalty—To inspire loyalty in others, add a drop of lime essential oil to an aromatherapy locket. Since lime is a top note, pair it with a drop of another watery Venus oil, vanilla. When you're shopping for vanilla, go with the

Vanilla CO2 to be sure you're getting a true vanilla. It'll smell like a decaying library. Vanilla is attraction, calming aggression, and happiness. It'll tell potential followers that you're worthy of their loyalty.

Luck—Take a gold (success, fast luck) candle and inscribe "luck" on the surface of the candle with a ballpoint pen. Anoint with diluted lime oil and place into a candleholder. Burn until complete. Best if done on a Sunday.

Overcome powerlessness—To encourage feelings of emotional strength, we are going to make an aromatherapy inhaler. Simply ensure the inhaler tube's cap is tightly screwed onto the base, and insert the cotton into the tube. Then add 7–10 drops of lime essential oil to the nasal inhaler tube, place the stopper in the bottom and allow it to rest on its side for a minimum of 10 minutes before attempting to use, as oil can leak if not absorbed fully before opening. When you feel your emotions shifting, simply uncap the tube, inhale once with the left nostril and once with the right while breathing carefully in through the nose and out through the mouth.

Sexual desire—To inspire sexual feelings and banish anxiety, anoint the heart center (under clothing to avoid phototoxic burns) in the shape of a heart. Massage into the skin in clockwise direction while imagining scenes that inspire lust and sexual desire. Feel the energy of the earth come up from under your feet, filling you with warmth, life, and energy.

Stimulant—Place a drop of lime oil on a tissue and carry it in your nondominant side pocket. When you find yourself lagging behind, smell the tissue and reset yourself.

Strength—Place 5 drops of lime essential oil into ½ cup of the salt of your choice. Place it where you work for the strength you need.

Recipe: The Muses

To befriend your Muse and inspire creativity.

- ❈ 5 drops lime essential oil (*Citrus latifollia*) to inspire friendship

- ❈ 20 drops cardamom essential oil (*Elettaria cardamomum*) for protection, fearlessness

- ❈ 10 drops frankincense essential oil (*Boswellia carteri*) purification

- ❈ 20 drops tangerine essential oil (*Citrus reticulata*) for calm, clarity, inspiration

This synergy is the one to turn to if you're standing in your own way, creatively. Diffuse 1 drop in 100 ml of water or add two drops to a 10 ml roller bottle and fill the rest of the way with carrier oil of your choice.

LINDEN

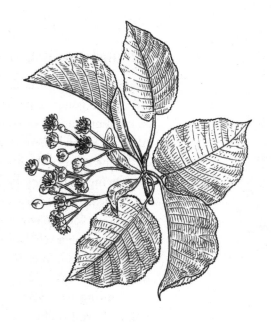

Scientific Name: *Tilia spp.*

Botanical Family: Malvaceae (subfamily Tiliaceae)

World Origin: Europe, North America

Plant's Oil: Flowers

Scent Description: Honey, blousy, amber, musky, and floral

Evaporation: Top note

Scent Impact: Sedative, nervine, provides emotional support and comfort

Magical Correspondences

Application: Diffuse, direct inhalation

Element: Air

Day: Thursday, Friday, Monday

Magical Uses: Good luck, attraction, protection from baneful spells, strength, honesty

Planet: Jupiter, Venus, Moon

Astrological Sign: Sagittarius, Libra, Cancer

Suggested Crystal: Rhondite, astrological sign of Taurus, balances energies, empowers users to calm in the face of chaos

Deity/Spirit: Hermes, Greek messenger god, connect to your inner messenger, use your voice

Herbal Lore/Uses

Linden, or, lime tree, is one of the oldest tree species on the planet with botanical records going back seventy million years. For scale, there are fossil records of small marsupials existing seventy million years ago alongside dinosaurs in Alaska. Linden blossoms are so delightfully floral that their honey is considered to be some of the finest honey known.

Owing to its long history, the lore around linden is vast. The tree, featuring heart-shaped leaves, is associated with Freyja, goddess of truth, war, and seiðr (Norse magic of communion with the spirits). This association with truth was so ingrained in the beliefs surrounding the tree that trials were held underneath its branches, because it was believed that no one could tell a lie standing there. Weddings, first dates, and other social gatherings, as well as law-drafting, were also scheduled around linden trees because of its association with truth-telling. The aura of goodness was so pervasive that linden was planted in cemeteries to keep them free of evil spirits.

Woodworkers among us are often familiar with linden under a different common name, bass wood. This wood is a blanched white and nearly featureless. It is soft enough for intricate chip carving but strong enough to last for generations, so much so that musical instruments are also a popular use for bass wood, from drums to electric guitars.

The species name Linden gives us even more background on the plant. The word "lind" is a 16th century Middle English word for kind, or gentle. Don't confuse the common name "lime tree" with the citrus fruit however, as the only thing they have in common is the color green for their fruit. In contrast, the fruit of the linden tree is barely bigger than the head of a pin. The scent isn't citrusy at all, as the blousy flowers of this titan (reaching heights of forty meters) are floral and high in volatile oils, so if you're making a linden tea, make sure to put a lid on it, so you don't lose all of those gorgeous oils to the atmosphere while they are steeping. They are so full of life, in the form of volatile oils, that linden oils (a common perfume base) are distilled from the dried flower material rather than the fresh, as is normally done. However, don't let the bees fool you; parking your car under a linden tree can coat it in a sticky "honey" resin that can destroy your car's paint.

You've likely smelled linden or even tasted it, without even knowing. The glycerite of this flower (flowers are steeped in glycerin to extract the volatile oils and chemical constituents rather than alcohol, which would produce a tincture) carries a heady black cherry flavor, as linden is used in foods as natural cherry flavor or in perfumes, room sprays, and even incenses. The first time I tasted a linden glycerite, I was immediately transported to the local mall of my teen years where a popular mall goth store carried their own store-branded incense labeled "Vampire," which provided a heady cherry aroma.

Spells

Act respectfully—If someone has been behaving disrespectfully towards you, grab a black chime candle (banishing), a candleholder, and linden extract. If you can't find the extract, grab a pinch of the dried flowers to put in the bottom of the candleholder where it won't be a fire hazard. Carve "disrespect'" onto the candle and anoint with a drop of linden extract. (If the person is especially harmful, consider replacing "disrespect" with the target's name [and birthdate if you have it] to banish the perpetrator rather than the behavior.) Banishing work is best done on a Saturday, or during the waning to dark moon, but don't let that stop you from ensuring your safety. See *Blackthorn's Protection Magic* for more information.

Apotropaic—To turn away evil spirits add 3 drops of linden extract to a damp cloth, and wipe down the interior door jambs of the doors that lead to the outside of your house: front door, back door, garage door, and more. I like to work counterclockwise (banishing), both on the door itself and among the doors I have to do. Say, sing, or chant "thrice around the circle's bound/evil sink into the ground."

Assistance with communication—The airy nature of linden will aid in smoothing communication. If you are having a miscommunication with a friend, invite them over for linden tea (always check to ensure they're healthy enough for herbal teas) to discuss the issue. Linden is the truth-teller, but also associated with love, so get it all out into the open and see if it's worth continuing the relationship. Sometimes we outgrow relationships, and that's okay, too. No one has to be the bad guy for one or both of you to decide this friendship no longer works.

Attraction, customers—If you anticipate a stressful day in the shop, consider brewing a cup of linden tea for yourself and anointing the doorway of the business with linden to attract customers that are kind and appreciate what you have to offer.

Attraction, friends—Add a small handful of linden to a bucket of hot water and allow to steep for 10 minutes, or until the water is cool enough to submerge your hand without injury. Grab a clean cloth or two and wipe down the exterior of your home's doorways to attract friends to your home.

Attraction, love—Into the base of a candleholder, add a drop of linden extract or a pinch of the dried flowers.

Beauty—Gently wash your face as normal. Pour a small handful of dried linden into a reusable tea bag or other steeping aid. Add it to a large mixing bowl and cover with 4–6 cups of boiling water. Allow the herbs to steep for about 5 minutes. Lean over the bowl of steaming water, and carefully tent a towel over your head and the bowl to create a steam facial. Allow the steam to penetrate your pores for about 10 minutes, unless dizziness or irritation from the heat begins to bother you. The steam from the linden has strong antioxidant properties and it will hydrate your skin for a fresh, glowing look. Gently swipe a clean cotton pad over your skin to absorb excess water, as the linden balances sebum production in the skin. This balancing act is helpful to both oily and dry skin. Once the water is cool enough to no longer burn the skin, bottle 8 ounces in a spray bottle to use as toner for up to seven days. Store in the refrigerator to inhibit bacteria/mold growth. Discard after seven days. Pour the remainder of the infusion over your hair to soothe an itchy or irritated scalp.

Calm—Place 4 tablespoons of dried linden herb into a pint glass jar. Fill with 12 ounces of sunflower oil (protection, peace) and allow to steep in the sun on a warm day, or in a dark cabinet for two weeks. Sunflower oil has a year shelf life; if you're allergic, try to substitute with a similarly long-lasting neutral oil. When calm is needed, anoint specific body parts that denote the need for calm. For instance, if the heart needs support, massage the oil into the chest;

if thoughts are rushing around your mind, rub your temples; and if your spirit needs peace, massage your shoulders.

Divination—Light an incense charcoal tablet and place a pinch of linden (flower, leaves, or wood) on the burning charcoal. Softly unfocus your eyes as you stare into the incense smoke; feel yourself relax. *Optional:* add a frankincense tear for spiritual abilities to increase the strength of the visions. Allow the patterns of the smoke to help you relate to your question or situation. Breathe slowly, in through the nose and out through the mouth.

Dreams—To increase beneficial dreams, especially of a divinatory nature, place 1 drop of linden glycerite under the tongue up to 30 minutes before bed. As you close your eyes, breathe softly and consider the answers you hope to receive in your sleep. Consider placing a journal or notepad on your bedside table with a pen to record upon waking, as dream insights are often fleeting.

Emotional warmth—Place a handful of linden in a muslin bag, a stocking, or other mesh material. Run a warm bath and place the large tea bag you've made into the water to steep. Linden is nourishing for the emotional heart center and will increase your ability to listen to your heart, and to show gentleness for yourself and your present needs. Best if done on a Friday.

Encouragement—We all need a little encouragement sometimes! Grab a yellow candle (thought) and write "I can do it" on the side of the candle. Place a drop of linden extract in the bottom of the candleholder before placing the candle on top of it. Burn until completely gone, observing fire safety rules. Best if done on a Sunday (energizing).

Fidelity—With your partner(s) on a Friday (Venus/love), gather together to discuss vows of fidelity and discuss what constitutes fidelity in your relationship structure. Talk about specific examples of what breaking that fidelity might look like. Everyone's relationship boundaries are different. What you assume might be the same in everyone's minds may be completely unrealistic in their minds. Communication is key, and linden has it in spades. Once everyone has been heard, place a drop of linden glycerite under the tongue and kiss the other participants.

Good luck—On a Sunday (solar protection, luck, joy) anoint the tops of the feet, hands, heart, and head with a drop of linden extract to be blessed with luck all month long. *Optional:* Give thanks for all you have. Gratitude is always joyful.

Justice—To ensure you have the justice you seek, place a handful of linden in a large muslin bag and place it into a mop bucket of hot water. *Optional:* add other justice allies like jasmine (justice), frankincense (divine justice), or patchouli (just judge). Allow to steep for 5 minutes before mopping the floor to bring justice into your home. If legal paperwork is needed, make copies of the documents, and anoint them with linden, jasmine, frankincense, or patchouli. If you know you are the wronged party, consider adding a pinch of dirt from your local courthouse to an envelope before adding your legal paperwork. Keep this copy in a safe place for any magical follow-up that may be needed.

Love—To draw love to you, grab a red (lust) or pink (romantic love) candle and write "draw love to me" or similar wording along the side of the candle. Anoint with a drop of linden extract imagining or feeling love draw closer to you. *Optional:* place a pinch of dried basil from the spice rack in the bottom of the candleholder before placing the candle inside. Basil is love and faithfulness (and eases grief). Best if done on a Friday (Venus/love).

Marriage—If you're hoping your partner(s) will propose marriage, find a white (purity of intent) or pink (romantic love) candle and write "marriage" along the side of it. Anoint the candle with a drop of linden extract. *Optional:* let the universe know why you want to marry your intended. Best if done on a Friday (Venus/love).

Protection, home—Add a pinch of linden (flower, leaf, or wood) to a burning incense charcoal disk. Envision or feel the home filling with the protective light of the sun, burning away any negativity or harm that would come to residents of your home. Best if done on a Sunday (protection).

Relationships—To strengthen currently existing relationships, take two white candles (purity of intent) and write your name on one, and the name(s) of the others involved on the other. Once named, anoint candles with diluted linden oil or glycerite. Place them in candleholders for safety, and place the candles as close together as they can get. No need for string to bind them; your magic will do that for you, and we don't need a fire hazard. Burn the candles together/at the same time to allow linden to strengthen the bonds you share. Best if done on a Monday (emotional support).

Recipe: Linden's Respectful Response Drops

For magic involving strength, loving communication, protection, and justice.

- 1/3 cup plus 1 tablespoon cut and sifted linden flower and leaf
- 1 tablespoon honey
- 1 tablespoon powdered orange peel plus a little for dusting
- 1 teaspoon lavender or ginger syrup

Tip: you can find a recipe for flavored syrups in *Blackthorn's Botanical Brews*, page 185.

Place your linden into a food processor. Grind the linden into a fine powder and sift into your mixing bowl to catch any large pieces. Sift in orange peel powder. (Feel free to substitute other powdered peel like lime for a lime/black cherry combo.)

In a custard cup, place your teaspoon of liquid and tablespoon of honey, and mix until incorporated. Slowly add liquid to the dry ingredients, stirring several times until it forms a thick dough. If your dough is too dry, add a few drops of water. You'll know it's too dry if the drops crumble and fall apart. If too wet, add a pinch of powdered peel. You want the dough workable, and not too sticky.

With a spoon, section off a thumbnail-sized piece of dough and roll between your palms. Roll it in your extra citrus peel for coating and set on a wax paper sheet to dry. If you'd like them to dry a little faster, flatten the drops with the back of a spoon until they're 5 millimeters thick.

Linden tastes like sweet black cherries, so if you don't like lavender or ginger syrup, try linden glycerite. A glycerite is glycerine that has herbs infused into it. It's a similar idea to tincturing, but no alcohol is used. You get a cleaner flavor (clean in that it's true to the plant material, not a value judgment) of the plant material in glycerine, so you'll have a more pronounced black cherry flavor.

Linden is a popular ingredient in throat-soothing drops and is aligned with justice magic, so consider making these before heading out to a protest to soothe your throat between chants or after the rallying cries are done.

MARJORAM

Scientific Name: *Origanum majorana*

Botanical Family: Lamiaceae

World Origin: France, Greece

Plant's Oil: Leaves

Scent Description: Sweet, earthy, lemony, loamy

Evaporation: Middle note

Scent Impact: Relieves grief, anxiety, and stress; soothes emotional burn out

Magical Correspondences

Application: Diffuse, dilute, direct inhalation

Element: Air, Fire

Day: Sunday, Friday

Magical Uses: Protection, happiness, health

Planet: Sun, Venus

Astrological Sign: Leo, Taurus

Suggested Crystal: Moqui balls/Maqui marbles—ruled by Aries, Libra, Aquarius, protection, self-realization

Deity/Spirit: Hermes—god of communication and messages

Herbal Lore/Uses

It is no surprise with a name like "sweet" marjoram that its epithets include "Joy of the Mountain" or "herb of happiness." This member of the mint family has been beloved for centuries, as it first appeared in *De Materia Medica* by Dioscorides in 78 CE. This sweet and woody perennial grows to a height of about twenty-four inches and smells like the rich soil of its birth, with a hint of lemon and molasses. It's used to relieve many different kinds of physical and emotional pain. It can be added to your nightly lotion to lull you to sleep, overcoming insomnia. It can relieve muscle spasms and abdominal cramps. It excels at helping to process grief, especially if paired with lemon balm (*Melissa officinalis*) or parsley (*Petroselinum sativum*).

Spells

Ancestor communication—To establish communication with an ancestor, gather incense charcoal tablets, dried marjoram, a lighter, fireproof dish, tongs, and a spoon. Hold the charcoal tablet with the tongs and light. Place into fireproof dish. Sprinkle marjoram on the burning disk with a spoon. Speak the name of the ancestor with whom you'd like to speak/establish communication. *Remember:* not all communication is verbal; 70 percent of communication is facial expressions, even among the dead. If you choose to limit communication, state those stipulations during your request. For instance, "I'd love to talk to you in my dreams." Dreaming is one of the easiest ways for us to accept communication from the deceased. They don't have to cut through the noise of your daily life to come through. We're more receptive in our dream states. If you've ever dreamed that your deceased loved one is alive and well and their death was just a bad dream, congratulations, you've likely had a spirit visit. If they make contact in your preferred way, make sure to thank them so they know they were heard. Perhaps set up an ancestor altar and leave them things they enjoyed in life, like coffee, alcohol, or sweets. You need only leave them 1–3 days; no one wants a moldy offering.

Angelic visions—To inspire visions of the angelic, diffuse 1 drop of marjoram essential oil in 100 ml of water. Sit or lie in a comfortable position and relax your body starting at your toes and working your way up to your head. When you reach the top of your head, see a small door open in the crown of your head for angelic visions to appear and communicate. If you have any reservations about the communication you might receive, add a drop of angelica essential oil to the marjoram, as angelica (*Angelica archangelica*) is associated with Archangel Michael. Thank them if communications, visions, or other messages come through and remember to seal off the funnel you opened for their communication. They can still reach out in other ways and you aren't tempting other spirit beings with an open door.

Astral travel—To open yourself to astral travel, diffuse 1 drop of marjoram essential oil in 100 ml of water. Sit or lie in a comfortable position and relax your body starting at your toes and working your way up to your head. When you reach the top of your head, see a small door open in the crown of your head to allow your spirit to exit your body and wander off to parts known or unknown. Before leaving your body alone to wander about, envision a small night-light burning in your heart to keep your body safe until your return. Once you're back in your body, remember to seal off the door you opened for your travel. That way you aren't tempting other spirit beings with an open door.

Attraction, desire—To inspire attraction and desire within yourself, find a pink (romantic love) or red (lust) candle and with a ballpoint pen, inscribe the word "desire" on the surface of the candle. Anoint the candle with diluted marjoram essential oil and place into a candleholder. Burn until complete. Best if done on a Friday.

Balance, harmony—To inspire harmony in your surroundings, place 1 drop of marjoram essential oil onto a cotton or wool pad for an aromatherapy necklace and place the fiber inside. As your body warms the locket, you'll experience the sweet, woody fragrance of the herb, and you'll notice it throughout the day. When the scent wafts up to your nose and your notice, take a moment to center yourself and remind yourself that you are in control and you are attuned to your surroundings.

Channeling—If you'd like to channel spirits, ancestors, ascended masters, and the like, diffuse 1 drop of marjoram essential oil in 100 ml of water. Grab a notebook and a pen. Sit in a comfortable position and relax. Start writing a letter to the entity you'd like to contact. Talk about the things you'd like to learn from them, any feelings you have and what you hope communication will bring. "I miss you, Judy." Or, "I hope you can teach me about my ancestors." "What is our hope for mankind?" When you're finished writing your letter, start writing their responses. It's doubtful that there will be a booming voice from the heavens instructing you. Likely it'll be a still, quiet voice that tells you what is happening, what will happen, or what has happened. "How will I know if I'm just making it up?" The easiest clue for projection versus a true channeling or journey is the element of surprise. If you feel genuinely surprised at the information you receive, you'll know it was a true sharing. If it reads like a fairy tale with lots of predictable plot points, it was likely a projection. "My great grandma was a princess and had lots of candy and favors from admirers, the end." You can close the session by turning off the diffuser and thanking the spirit with whom you spoke.

Clarity—To find clarity in a situation, find a blue (clarity of emotion) or yellow (clarity of thought) candle and inscribe "clarity" along the surface of the candle. Anoint the candle with diluted marjoram essential oil and place in a candleholder. Light and allow to burn completely. Best if done on a Sunday (fast luck).

Comfort—To seek comfort, take dried marjoram or a cotton pad with a drop of marjoram essential oil on it, and place it into a small bag (blue for emotional comfort or green for physical comfort). Cleanse the bag with the elements of earth with salt, air with your breath, fire with a candle, water from the sink, spirit with a waft of incense smoke. Tell the bag (out loud is fine) what comfort they can provide, and for whom the charm is intended.

Concentration—If you're struggling with concentration, take a nasal inhaler tube (you can use an old chapstick tube, too!) and make sure the cap is in place tightly. Into the open bottom, place the included cotton and place 7–10 drops of marjoram essential oil. Place the stopper in the bottom and lay on its side for 10 minutes before using. Remove the cap, place the open end under one nostril, and gently breathe in through your nose and out through your mouth. Repeat on the other side. Feel the scattered energy in your body come together in the center of your chest and remind you of your focus. Repeat in 2–4 hours if needed.

Dead, bring joy, comfort—To bring comfort to the deceased, take a white candle (purity of intent) and write their name on it with a ballpoint pen.

Anoint the candle with diluted marjoram essential oil and place into a candleholder. Burn until complete. Best if done on a Saturday (banish sadness or heavy emotions).

Defense—To defend yourself against hexes or malefic magic take a 10 ml roller bottle and add a drop of marjoram essential oil. Fill the rest of the way with fractionated coconut oil (inner peace). Place the roller ball and cap. Roll between the palms to blend. Anoint the bottoms of feet, belly, heart, hands, and forehead with a spot of diluted marjoram oil. Connect the dots in your mind to form a shield against any ill will directed your way.

Depression—To magically banish symptoms of depression, diffuse a drop of marjoram essential oil while sitting quietly for a minimum of 10 minutes. This won't resolve your depression permanently. Do not discontinue any medications without talking to a healthcare provider. This will lessen symptoms and allow you to forge ahead for a time.

Divination—To open your intuitive senses, take a notebook and pen, a dark glass bowl, a glass of water, a bottle of marjoram essential oil, and a candle to a place where you won't be disturbed. This works best in a darkened room, on a cloudy day or at night. On your working surface place the bowl in front of you, the candle in a candleholder behind the bowl, and the bottle and water on either side of the bowl. Light the candle and, if appropriate, ask for the guidance of the universe, ancestors, gods, and so forth to see beyond the scope of the every day. Pour the water into the bowl to create your scrying surface. Add 3 drops of marjoram essential oil. Oil and water do not mix, so the marjoram will sit on top of the water, creating a visual to concentrate your focus on, as well as perfuming the air with the magic of marjoram. Softly focus your eyes, so that the oil droplets on the surface of the water are blurry, or if you have difficulty, look through the drops to the bottom of the bowl. By giving your eyes something to focus on, it allows your mind to tune into the experience it is having without visual input. Allow your mind to wander. Gently direct your attention to your area of divining (travel, job, friends, home, finance, or the like) as you would a paper boat on a lake surface. Allow any impressions to come to you. Write down any impressions you received when you come back to awareness.

Grief, comfort—To comfort the grieving, take a small gray bag (you can find them in craft stores, rock shops, and with cheap jewelry supplies), and place dried marjoram inside; you can substitute a cotton ball with a drop of marjoram essential oil on it. *Optional:* add a pinch of lavender (grief, calming) to the bag, or a drop of lavender essential oil. Bless the bag with the elements, and tell it what you hope to gain: "Please help me grieve the loss of my Nana," thereby letting the bag know what you need.

Happiness—To increase joy and happiness, take a yellow (joy) candle and carve the word "joy" into the surface with a ballpoint pen. Anoint with diluted marjoram essential oil and place into a candleholder. Light the candle and allow to burn completely. Best if done on a Sunday (success).

Health/healing—To promote healing, diffuse marjoram essential oil, 1 drop in 100 ml of water, in the room of the sick or injured person.

Hex breaking—Make a 1 percent dilution of marjoram essential oil. Place 1 drop of marjoram essential oil into a 10 ml roller bottle. Fill the rest of the way with jojoba oil (hex breaking). Insert the roller ball and cap. Roll gently between the palms to mix so as not to introduce more air to the oil than necessary. Don't forget to label! Take a black candle and write "hex breaking" along the side with a ballpoint pen. Anoint the candle with the diluted marjoram essential oil. Push out any lingering negativity as you anoint. Place the candle into a candleholder and burn. Never leave a burning candle unattended. For best results burn on a Saturday (endings).

Innocence, maintain—To maintain innocence of thoughts, take a yellow candle (thoughtful, clear focus), write the name of the intended along the side of the candle and anoint with diluted marjoram essential oil. Burn on a Sunday (success) for best results.

Joy—Diffuse marjoram essential oil, 1 drop in 100 ml of water. *Optional:* add a drop of tangerine or mandarin essential oil to the water for ease in communication. Sit in the room with the diffuser, while breathing gently, in through the nose and out through the mouth, picturing or feeling joyful memories. Remind your body what joy feels like.

Loneliness, to banish—Gather a yellow (thought, will) candle and a 10 ml roller bottle. Add 1 drop marjoram essential oil and 1 drop grapefruit essential oil (self-esteem, joy) to a 10 ml roller bottle, top with fractionated coconut oil, (goal-oriented magic), and cap. Label your new Empowerment roller. Carve the name of the lonely person (if not yourself) and anoint with your new roller. Place into a candleholder and burn until complete. Best on a Sunday for success.

Love, to dream—To dream of your true love, gather a pale-blue (dreams, calm, comfort) candle, dried or fresh marjoram, and a candleholder. Set up your candleholder on a fireproof surface. I recommend a chime candle so you aren't waiting all night to fall asleep. Carve "true love" into your candle surface, anoint with sweet almond oil (love), and sprinkle dried marjoram in a circle around the base of the candleholder. Burn until complete. You will dream of the love you are seeking.

Lust, avert/repel—Place ¼ cup fresh marjoram or ⅛ cup dried marjoram into a jar and add 1 cup boiling water. Cover the jar loosely to collect steam (don't lose all those beautiful volatile oils to the air!). Once the jar is room temperature, anoint any door that leads to the exterior of the home. Make sure to include doors that lead to the garage, patio, or back deck, and windows that lead to the fire escape. Imagine/feel a lead apron coming down over doors to protect you inside the home. Remember, Cupid/Eros used lead arrows to kill the lust in his targets.

Marriage, happy—Diffuse a drop of marjoram essential oil in 100 ml of water once a month to ensure happiness continues in the marriage. All relationships need maintenance of some kind. No matter the depth of love a couple or a group has for each other, each member has to wake each day and choose to be present.

Memory—Sit in a darkened room, particularly auspicious if before the new moon appears in the sky. In front of you place a candle (taper or chime is recommended for best light reflection) and a dark bowl, preferably black, to absorb as much light as possible below the surface of the water, with a bottle of marjoram essential oil. Light the candle and turn as many lights off as possible. Close your eyes and center yourself. Connect with your inner voice through deep-breathing practices. Open your eyes and concentrate on the reflection of the flame on the water's surface. Place 3 drops of marjoram essential oil on the surface of the water. (Oil and water don't mix, so the water will support your visions while marjoram helps to unlock the memories you seek.) Watch the reflection of the candle flame, and if you can, softly focus or unfocus your eyes until the flame is a blur and allow your mind to project images of your memories onto the surface of the water. This separation of body and mind through the reflective surface will allow your mind to protect your body from any painful memories that may surface during this exercise. When you're finished, record your revelations, and extinguish the candle.

Peace—Take a pale-blue (calm) candle, and inscribe the word "peace" on the surface with a ballpoint pen. Place 1 drop of marjoram essential oil into a 10 ml roller bottle. Fill the rest of the way with meadowfoam oil (proliferation). It's a little pricier than olive oil, or sweet almond, but its shelf life is much longer than coconut and jojoba. Sweet almond oil (sweetness, positive regard) makes a good substitute if you're out of meadowfoam oil. Insert the roller ball and cap. Roll gently between the palms to mix so as not to introduce more air to the oil than necessary. Don't forget to label! Anoint the candle, pushing away anything that harms your peace. Place into a candleholder and light. Best done on a Monday (emotional support).

Prosperity—Gather a green (prosperity) or brown (stability) bag, and place a teaspoon of dried marjoram or a cotton ball with a drop of marjoram essential oil inside.

Protection—To make protection bath salts, add a total of 30 drops of essential oils including marjoram, bay, basil, clove, cypress, eucalyptus, geranium, lavender, neroli, or myrrh to a glass dish. If you're blending on the go, place the lids to any essential oils you're considering on a flat surface to smell together to see if they work as a team, before blending the oils together. Once you have the blend you want, add 2 cups of the salt of your choice to the oil in the glass bowl. Stir well. Start a bath and add the desired amount of salt to a warm running bath. Store any unused bath salts in a glass airtight container. Will keep up to a year.

Protection, business—Place a drop of marjoram essential oil on a cotton round and place inside the register. It will protect your business from magical sabotage.

Protection, home—Gather fresh marjoram if possible, or dried in the spice aisle in your local grocery store. Sprinkle around the outside of your home to create a border of protection for anyone taking shelter inside.

Protection, psychic—Place 1 drop of marjoram essential oil into a 10 ml roller bottle. Fill the rest of the way with jojoba oil (overcoming obstacles). Insert the roller ball and cap. Anoint the center of your forehead, directly over the pituitary gland, thought to be the center of psychic gifts. Feel a steel door cover your forehead from psychic intrusion whenever the danger presents itself. You can use as an all-purpose protection perfume, too. Consider adding a drop of oakmoss absolute (hex breaking) or neroli (protection) to raise the vibration of the single note oil.

Psychic awakening/protection—Take a 10 ml roller bottle and remove the roller cap. Add a drop of marjoram essential oil to the bottle, along with 2 drops of lavender essential oil (reveal secrets) and 1 drop of vetiver essential oil (psychic dreams, psychic protection). Fill the bottle the rest of the way with the carrier of your choice. Place the roller ball and lid, and make sure to label the bottle. Anoint the palms of both hands, as well as the center of the forehead to form a pyramid of knowledge that leads to the seat of intuition.

Relaxing—Diffuse 1 drop of marjoram essential oil in 100 ml of water where you will be sitting to relax. Marjoram connects to the stress centers in your mind to unravel the snarls that cause excess stress.

Release enchantment—If you think you've been hexed, cursed, or jinxed, take a piece of paper and draw a human figure, roughly shaped like a gingerbread man. No need for anything fancy, we're just going for person-shaped. However, if you're artistically inclined, feel free to make it more detailed or include your face on the person shape. Across the stomach, write your name and date of birth. We're personalizing this poppet to you. If you have access to a printer, you can print out a photo on plain paper (don't use photo paper; it's too glossy and won't work well for what we're doing). Take a 10 ml roller ball filled with diluted marjoram essential oil and draw a border around the figure a centimeter or so from the edge. Seal it up tight so nothing can get in. Once the edge is sealed and nothing is getting in there, switch to another 10 ml roller ball bottle with either diluted ginger essential oil (hex-breaking, purification, protection) or pink grapefruit essential oil (healing, protection, joy, self-esteem) inside. Color the inside of the figure or photo from head to toe. If there's any malicious magic lurking in your body, it will be destroyed. Energy itself can't be created or destroyed, but you can smash that malefic charm and send any included energies back out into the universe, never to bother you again. Feel free to substitute an illustration of your home instead of a photo of yourself to banish any nasty magic lurking in your home.

Restorative sleep—Diffuse 1 drop of marjoram essential oil in 100 ml of water 10 minutes before going to sleep to allow the scent to permeate the room. It'll soothe jangled nerves and allow you to fall asleep without the last minute leap to handle forgotten tasks. They can wait until morning.

Shield against evil—Place a drop of marjoram essential oil into an aromatherapy locket. Place around your neck and feel the aroma engulf your person in a shield of light and might. It'll last as long as the smell still remains in the locket (a day or two). Renew if needed. Consider adding the psychic awakening oil recipe above for an alternate helper.

Sorrow, to banish/overcome—To banish sorrow, craft a letter containing the object of your sadness and grief. Pour your heart out, as no one will see this but you.

Tarot—Before starting your reading, take the cap off your marjoram essential oil and waft the bottle under your nose to cleanse yourself of psychic cobwebs, low energy, and miasma so your best readings can be had without hesitation.

Transformation—To change your circumstances, take a gold (success) colored candle, and carve the word "transformation" into the surface of the candle with a ballpoint pen. Take diluted orange essential oil (transformation, strength, happiness) and anoint the candle. Light and burn until complete; best if done on a Sunday (success, protection).

Unite psychic and conscious mind—Place 1 drop of marjoram essential oil, 1 drop angelica essential oil (psychic protection), and 1 drop rosemary essential oil (conscious mind) into a 10 ml roller bottle. Fill the rest of the way with jojoba oil (overcoming obstacles). Insert the roller ball and cap. Make sure to label. Anoint pulse points when working to connect mind and body. Use caution with angelica and direct sunlight as it can be phototoxic.

Uplifting—Diffuse 1 drop marjoram essential oil with 1 drop tangerine essential oil (awaken joy, uncrossing) in the room where you'll be for the next half an hour or so. Your nose will tune out the fragrance after a few minutes, but your heart and mind will keep doing the hard work to uplift your spirits.

Recipe: Protect Your Peace Roller

- ❋ 3 drops marjoram essential oil (*Origanum majorana*) averting harmful people

- ❋ 6 drops lavender essential oil (*Lavandula angustifolia*) for protection, peace

- ❋ 3 drops Roman chamomile essential oil (*Chamaemelum nobile*) for aura balancing, protection

- ❋ 2 drops vanilla CO2 essential oil (*Vanilla planifolia*) for relaxing, happiness, peace, inspiration

- ❋ 9 ml +/- Jojoba carrier oil (*Simmondsia chinensis*) for overcoming obstacles

Blend the essential oils in a 10 ml roller bottle and then fill the rest of the way with jojoba oil. Place the roller ball and cap. Roll between the palms to blend. Use this sweet, empowering roller to remind yourself of your strength, your boundaries, and your bodily autonomy.

MAY CHANG

Also Known As: Mountain Pepper, Tropical Verbena

Scientific Name: *Litsea Cubeba*

Botanical Family: Lauraceae

World Origin: China, Indonesia, Taiwan

Plant's Oil: Fruit, leaves

Scent Description: Lemony, sweet, sharp

Evaporation: Top note

Scent Impact: Feelings of tranquility, relaxation

Magical Correspondences

Application: Diffuse, dilute, topical

Element: Water

Day: Monday

Magical Uses: Meditation, prayer, emotional strength, closure, uplifting

Planet: Moon

Astrological Sign: Cancer

Suggested Crystal: Golden topaz—Ruled by Sagittarius, Leo, Pisces: renews energy

Deity/Spirit: Bao Gu: Chinese Healing Goddess

WARNING
Use in 1 percent concentration on those with a history of sensitive skin irritations due to astringent action. Low risk for irritation.

Herbal Lore/Uses

From the mountains in southern China, this member of the Laurel family has been used in traditional Chinese medicine for hundreds of years; it's only recently (the 1950s) that the aromatherapy community has discovered this sweeter lemony aroma. It has a higher vibrational scent than lemongrass and is used to relieve tension headaches, muscle pain, and tightness.

That lemony aroma sends signals to the brain and olfactory sense, stimulating salivary glands and digestive enzymes, promoting digestive health. Its stress relieving properties and increased blood flow have shown heart-health benefits due to the reduced load on the physical structures, and results were verified with ECG profiles of cardiac arrhythmia in animals.

Its astringent properties help skin health, with antimicrobial and antifungal actions as well as clearing acne from skin. It has also shown in studies that it is effective against carcinogenic bacteria as well. It is a popular additive to cosmetics due to the benefits for hair, skin, and body as well as its citrusy aroma, which doesn't carry the same photosensitive warnings as the many citruses used in aromatherapy.

Spells

Calm—To promote peace in the heart, diffuse 1 drop of May Chang essential oil in 100 ml of water, while breathing steadily in through the nose and out through the mouth. As you continue to focus on your breath, feel excess energies spilling down your legs to join with the energy of the earth, who can use it much more effectively than we can. Allow the lemony scent to soothe the frayed ends of your nerves and bring you peace.

Energy—This sweet oil has a calming influence, but is energizing because it clears away the cobwebs cluttering our minds and heart. Take a nasal inhaler tube and make sure the top cap is on securely. Into the tube place the cotton pad and pour in 7–10 drops of May Chang essential oil. Insert the stopper into the bottom and lay on its side to rest for 10 minutes. Once the oil has been absorbed, take the cap off of the tube, rest it against one nostril, and breathe gently in through the nose and out through the mouth. Repeat on the opposite nostril. Replace the cap tightly and repeat in an hour if needed.

Let go—Place two cups of salt or Epsom salt into a glass bowl, and add 5 drops of May Chang essential oil and stir to incorporate. Draw a warm bath and halfway through filling, sprinkle as much salt as desired into the water. Keep any remainder in an airtight glass container. As you step into the bath, feel yourself letting go of anything that no longer serves you as you sink into the water. Stay as long as you like in the knowledge that it'll be gone when you emerge triumphant.

Meditation—Diffuse 1 drop of May Chang essential oil in 100 ml of water, while breathing steadily in through the nose and out through the mouth. As you continue to focus on your breath, feel your awareness of the outside world melt into the ground as you center yourself within your body, or your inner landscape.

Mental clarity—Take a light-blue candle and carve the word "clarity" into it with a pen. Anoint it with diluted May Chang essential oil, and place into a candleholder. For best results burn on a Wednesday.

New Beginnings—On a Saturday (endings), take a white candle (clarity of purpose) and write "new beginning" or a symbol to represent beginnings on it. Anoint it with diluted May Chang essential oil, and place it into a candleholder. Burn until complete.

Prayer—Anoint your wrist pulse points with diluted May Chang essential oil and rub into the skin with clockwise circles to increase feelings of connection before prayer. The scent will calm you and establish a sense of peace before connecting with the divine.

Rejuvenation/Renewal—The youthful energy of May Chang can be used here to increase vigor and emotional equilibrium as well as aid in magical renewal. Take an orange (adaptability) candle and write "renewal" along the surface. Anoint with diluted May Chang essential oil and place into a candleholder. Burn until complete. Best if performed on a Saturday (transformation).

Strength—Take a peach (strength) candle and write "strength" along the surface. *Optional:* take a piece of paper and lay out the situation you need strength to deal with. Anoint the candle with diluted May Chang essential oil and place it into a candleholder. Burn until complete. Best if performed on a Tuesday.

Recipe: Once More, with Feeling

- ❈ 12 drops May Chang essential oil (*Litsea cubeba*) for renewal, mental clarity, and new beginnings

- ❈ 5 drops cardamom essential oil (*Elettaria cardamomum*) for concentration, confidence, and purpose

- ❈ 15 drops bergamot essential oil (*Citrus bergamia*) for alertness, concentration, asking for help

Blend in a 2 ml bottle, place the reducer, cap, and label. Diffuse 1 drop in 100 ml of water when feeling soul-tired, burned out, or experiencing compassion fatigue, to renew vigor, emotional connection, and concentration on the work ahead.

Recipe: Help Wanted

This bright, sweet-smelling oil is a beacon to shine for your business's employment listings.

- ❈ 5 drops May Chang essential oil (*Litsea cubeba*) for renewal, strength, calm, antianxiety, and balanced emotions

- ❈ 5 drops black pepper essential oil (*Piper nigrum*) for courage, mental alertness, justice

- ❈ 8 drops lemon essential oil (*Citrus limon*) for business acumen, banishing fatigue

- ❈ 4 drops ylang-ylang essential oil (*Cananga odorata*) for harmony, balance, strength of spirit

- ❈ Yellow candle

Carefully combine the essential oils in a 2 ml bottle, place the reducer cap, top, and label. Diffuse the synergy when crafting your perfect employment listing, or add 2 drops of synergy to a 10 ml roller bottle, fill the rest of the way with a carrier oil, then place the roller ball, lid, and label. Anoint your job listing, or carve "new hire" into a yellow (thought) candle and burn until complete. Best if done on a Tuesday (Victory).

MYRTLE

Scientific Name: *Myrtus communis*

Botanical Family: Myrtaceae

World Origin: Morocco, Tunisia

Plant's Oil: Leaves

Scent Description: Herbaceous, green, yellow, sweet, reminiscent of fresh olive oil

Evaporation: Top note

Scent Impact: Comforting, sedative, rapturous, joyful, uplifting

Magical Correspondences

Application: Diffuse, dilute

Element: Water

Day: Friday

Magical Uses: Love, fidelity, grief, eloquence

Planet: Venus

Astrological Sign: Taurus and Libra

Suggested Crystal: Green aventurine—Ruled by Taurus: heart opening

Deity/Spirit: Apis—god of fertility, death, and the underworld

> ### WARNING
> Decongestant. Thyroid stimulant, liver stimulant. Contains 1,8-Cineole, can harm children under twelve and pets. If topical dryness or irritation appears, use a 1 percent dilution (5 drops per tablespoon, 1 drop per 10 ml). Oil expires after four years—oxidized oil can irritate skin. I recommend placing an expiration date on the bottle when purchased for safety. Avoid diffusing if asthmatic due to eucalyptol content.

Herbal Lore/Uses

It is the flower of Greek myth, sacred to Aphrodite, symbolizing love, loyalty, commitment, and devotion so ingrained that myrtle is still used in wedding bouquets today, including Greek and Jewish weddings. Even Queen Victoria carried myrtle on her wedding day.

The leaves were sacred to Demeter to symbolize devotion, to both the homestead and the land through farming. In Jewish tradition myrtle is used to celebrate the festival of Sukkot due to its association with agriculture. There's even a story in Zechariah Chapter 1 where a prophet of God was shown to be standing in a grove of myrtle trees.

In traditional Greek and Persian medicine, myrtle is used for clearing lung and bladder infections. The oil is very thin and reddish and settles an overactive nervous system. Diffusing in a room has helped those with low thyroid function.

Spells

Absent love—To send feelings of love to one who is absent (through both distance and time) write the name of the one absent on a tissue or flash paper. Anoint the four corners of the paper, place in a fireproof container, and light. Flash paper is a tissue paper impregnated with potassium nitrate, also called saltpeter. It ignites immediately in a flash of light, without smoke or leaving ash behind. The energy generated (energy cannot be created or destroyed) will be directed toward the person you're missing.

Afterlife—To connect with the spirit of those in the afterlife, carve the name of the deceased into a white (all-purpose) candle. Then anoint the candle with diluted myrtle essential oil (1 drop in 10 ml of carrier oil). Turn any overhead lights off, and settle somewhere comfortable. Soften your eyes until the candle flame is unfocused, and breathe deeply in through your nose and out through your mouth until you feel yourself transitioning into a trance state. Allow messages from your loved one to come through the candle flame. Put the candle out when you are done. Keep the candle for subsequent conversations with them if desired. (One candle per person.) Record any impressions for later review.

Creativity—To spark creativity within you, diffuse 1 drop of myrtle essential oil in 100 ml of water for 10 minutes in your creative space before you come in to begin work. It'll give the water droplets that disperse the fragrance time to suffuse the air with myrtle.

Dead, to prepare the—With the rise in green burials, death doula care, and home funerals, it's more commonplace for home funerals and immediate family preparing the body for its eternal rest. If you have access to fresh myrtle leaves, place a myrtle leaf into the water that the deceased is prepared with. Leave to infuse as long as you can. If you don't have access to fresh leaves, place 1 cup of the salt of your choice into a glass bowl (plastic is porous and will retain some of the essential oil in the plastic) and add 3 drops of myrtle essential oil. *Optional:* add 1 drop of angelica essential oil to aid in the grief process. Wash the body according to your tradition or beliefs.

Death rituals/Funerary rites—Diffuse the essential oil of myrtle in funerary spaces to start the grieving process, a drop in 100 ml of water. *Optional:* include 1 drop tangerine essential oil to uplift mourners and help them remember better times with the deceased.

Eloquence—On a day where wit and delivery need to be at their highest, place a drop of myrtle essential oil onto the wool or cotton insert for an aromatherapy locket. *Optional:* add a drop of fennel essential oil for eloquence and protection.

Favors from Aphrodite—Wreathe a statue of Aphrodite with fresh myrtle leaves, or scent sea salt (Aphrodite was said to be born of sea foam) with myrtle essential oil and place at the foot of her votive statue. If no statue is available, place the salt next to the bedside; include a red or pink candle if possible.

Fertility—Diffuse 1 drop myrtle essential oil in the bedroom during sexual activity to boost fertility and good luck in your family planning.

Fidelity—To nurture fidelity, anoint a human-shaped figure candle that matches your gender presentation and anoint it with diluted myrtle essential oil. Colors best suited to fidelity magic are red (lust), pink (romantic love), yellow (clarity of thought), and blue (peace). Best if done on a Friday.

Fortune, good—To bring good fortune into your home, dilute myrtle essential oil, 1 drop in 10 ml carrier oil, and use it after cleansing the home with other mediums such as smoke, sound, or diffusing essential oils. Anoint doors, windows, the backs of mirrors, and the central or main water valve into your home. Remember to keep anointing oil on surfaces like glass and metal, as oils can damage the finish on wood.

Heartbreak, to mend—Heartbreak can feel as though it has no end, but with myrtle by your side, you can begin to grow around the grief. Add 1 drop of myrtle essential oil to a 10 ml roller bottle. Fill the rest of the way with fractionated coconut carrier oil to direct your energy. Place the roller ball and cap the bottle. Roll between your hands to mix. Sit or lie comfortably. With your dominant hand, anoint your heart center by drawing an "X" over your heart, "stitching it" closed around the wound. With your nondominant hand, rub the oil into the skin in banishing circles (counterclockwise) to ease the heartbreak out of your system. See or feel the heart warming up and filling with light as it starts the healing process anew. This will help both at onset of grief, and if grief process seems stalled or lagging. You deserve joy, wholeness, and light again. Repeat if needed.

Innocence, to preserve—To protect innocence, gather myrtle essential oil and sweet almond oil. Place 1 drop of myrtle essential oil into a 10 ml bottle. Fill the bottle the rest of the way with sweet almond oil (substitute with fractionated coconut oil if you're allergic to almond) carrier oil to protect their heart. Label a pink (innocence) candle with the child's name. *Optional:* ask Artemis (protectress of children) to protect the innocence of the child mentioned in the spell. Burn on a Friday for protection of innocent, loving relationships or Monday to preserve emotional innocence.

Love—To draw a new loving relationship to you, make a list of the traits you hope to attract in a new loving relationship. Onto a pink candle (romantic love) inscribe "bring me love" or "love" onto the surface of the candle with a ballpoint pen. Anoint with diluted myrtle essential oil. Take a candleholder appropriate for the candle you've chosen, and place a pinch of ground clove or a drop of diluted clove essential oil (bring luck into the home) into the cup of the candleholder. Place the candle into the holder and light. Burn until candle is complete. Best if done on a Friday (love).

Magical charms—to bless magical charms, place 1 cup of the salt of your choice into a glass bowl. Add 3 drops of myrtle essential oil and stir thoroughly. Transfer to an airtight container with a label. When blessing magical charms, place a pinch of salt into 1/3 cup or 2½ ounces of warm water. Stir to dissolve and charge water as appropriate. Sprinkle charged water over magical charm.

Marriage—Marriages have been blessed by myrtle for thousands of years. To petition for a marriage proposal, create an invitation to the big event. Let your imagination and creative drive out in full force for this craft project: water colors, markers, pens, and that wax seal kit you ordered at three a.m. for some reason. If you're in a relationship, make sure to include the name of your intended. This spell isn't designed to overwrite the free will of anyone, but to signal to the universe that you're ready to have that relationship. If you're petitioning the universe for a marriageable partner, include the qualities you hope to attract in a partner worthy of joining in matrimony. Anoint the invite with diluted myrtle oil and place it in a safe place until your spell comes to fruition. Burn the invitation after your spell manifests.

Money/prosperity—Anoint a dollar bill at the four corners with diluted myrtle essential oil. Fold the dollar bill and place it where it is less likely to be spent, so it can attract prosperity to your wallet long term. Don't worry, you can spend it in an emergency, just remember to replace it as soon as possible.

Release—We know closure isn't always possible, but releasing emotional burdens can be. Contrary to what you might have heard, forgiveness isn't mandatory for healing and growth. However, release can be nourishing for the soul. Fill an aromatherapy diffuser with 100 ml of water. Add 1 drop of myrtle essential oil to the diffuser. Whisper the name of that which you'd like to release over the top of the solution, diffuse, and watch it disappear into the ether.

Sorrow, to overcome—To banish sorrow, grab a bayberry taper candle (happiness). Carve "release sorrow" onto the surface of the candle with a ballpoint pen. Anoint the candle with myrtle diluted in sunflower oil (happiness) on a Sunday (success).

Tower Card—Myrtle carries big Tower Card energy, meaning upheaval, destruction, disarray, cataclysmic ending. It's not just the end of the road; there are no more roads. To offset the sharp edges of your personal "end times" place a tissue into a black (endings) charm bag and add a drop of myrtle essential oil. Close the bag and tie it to seal in the good fortune. Tell the bag exactly what you need from it. Empower it with your breath or energy. *Optional:* add a frankincense tear to the bag to amplify the power it has. Keep the charm active by feeding it frankincense, or renewing the myrtle scent when it starts to fade.

Underworld—As myrtle prepares the dead for the underworld, so can it prepare the living who must journey there for understanding, enlightenment, and education. Find a taper candle, and anoint it with myrtle diluted in sweet almond oil (protection). Gather symbols of the underworld from your culture, or apple (any form), mistletoe, or owls. Darken the room as much as possible and take a few deep breaths before lighting the candle. Softly focus your eyes until the candle flame is fuzzy or out of focus. Continue to breathe deeply to settle into a trance state; allow the candle flame to give you the feedback. Allow your mind to wander to the underworld to find the information you seek. Whether it's a divination of the future, past, or present, many spirits in the underworld will give you the information you seek. If you have a particular truth you're seeking, feel free to use the sweet almond oil as a carrier for diluting other essential oils, lavender to divine the secrets of another, black pepper to drive away evil, geranium for love divination, or myrrh for success and prosperity, and so on.

Wedding—To bless a wedding, turn to myrtle sacred to Aphrodite. Add 1½ ounces of rubbing alcohol or witch hazel to a spray bottle. To the bottle, add 5 drops of myrtle essential oil. Fill the rest of the way with water. Cap the bottle and give it a shake to mix. Spray liberally to invite the blessings of Aphrodite for a loving marriage. If you seek Hera's blessing, include orange blossom water or add a drop of Neroli essential oil to the room spray. Color test for delicate fabrics; use with care.

Work, dedication—To renew your dedication to your work, diffuse 1 drop of myrtle essential oil in 100 ml of water in your workspace. If you are concerned about water vapor around electronics, add 3 drops of myrtle essential oil to a cup of salt and place near your workspace. Then allow to diffuse over time.

Recipe: Power Up Anointing Oil

This anointing oil has the heavy lifting built in! Consecrate magical objects and imbue them with the power to do anything.

- ❋ 5 drops myrtle essential oil (*Myrtus communis*) to empower magical charms, wealth, good fortune

- ❋ 20 drops benzoin essential oil (*Styrax tonkinensis*) for concentration, purification, wisdom

- ❋ 12 drops orange essential oil (*Citrus sinensis*) for good luck, strength, prosperity, material objects

Blend the oils in a 2 ml bottle and secure the cap. Roll the bottle between your palms to blend. Label. Next add 2 drops of your Power Up synergy (blend of essential oils) and add it to a 10 ml roller bottle. Fill the rest of the way with a carrier oil that has a long shelf life for best longevity. Meadowfoam oil, fractionated coconut oil, or jojoba are the best options. Add the roller ball and cap, then roll between your palms to blend. Anoint ritual tools, magical charms, devotional jewelry, and other magical items to cleanse, empower, and dedicate tools for use.

PARSLEY SEED

Scientific Name: *Petroselinum crispum, Petroselinum sativum*

Botanical Family: Apiaceae

World Origin: France, Morocco, Greece

Plant's Oil: Seed

Scent Description: Dry, warm, the scent of a dry riverbed baking in the heat

Evaporation: Middle note

Scent Impact: Release of negative emotions and thought patterns

Magical Correspondences

Application: Diffuse, dilute

Element: Air

Day: Tuesday, Wednesday, Friday

Magical Uses: Affection, concentration, honor, memory, relaxation

Planet: Mars, Mercury, Venus

Astrological Sign: Gemini

Suggested Crystal: Rhodochrosite—Ruled by Leo & Scorpio: promotes balanced love

Deity/Spirit: Dionysus—god of love, indulgence, and pleasure

WARNING

Avoid parsley during pregnancy. Oil is potentially toxic to liver and kidneys; do not use internally.

Spells

Affection—To feel more affectionate, place a drop of parsley seed essential oil on the cotton or wool pad for an aromatherapy locket. During the day when you find yourself noticing the fragrance, stop and remind yourself that you are loved.

Alertness—To stimulate the mind, take a nasal inhaler tube and make sure the cap is tightly sealed. Add 7–10 drops of parsley seed essential oil to the cotton. Place the stopper in the bottom securely. Lay on its side for 10 minutes to absorb. When needed, remove the cap and place the open end over one nostril and breathe gently, in through the nose and out through the mouth. Repeat on the other side. May repeat in 2–4 hours if needed.

Astral Travel—To intentionally leave your body, diffuse 1 drop of parsley seed essential oil in 100 ml of water while you close your eyes and concentrate on relaxing every muscle from your toes to the top of your head. Once you reach the top of your head, imagine a window opening there where your essence is able to slip out and journey about. Don't forget to leave a magical night-light burning inside your heart so it looks like someone is home and negative spirits don't get interested in what you've left behind. Consider having selenite or citrine nearby for pure intentions.

Attractiveness—To feel more attractive, place a single drop of parsley seed essential oil in a 10 ml roller bottle, and fill with fractionated coconut oil (love, lust, courage) because it's liquid at room temperature. Anoint the heart center and massage into the skin in clockwise (increase) circles. Don't forget to label your 10 ml bottle!

Concentration—Diffuse 1 drop of parsley seed essential oil in 100 ml of water while working. If a test is involved, anoint a tissue or aromatherapy locket with parsley seed essential oil the day of the test to help remind you of what you have studied.

Conquering—Write out what is in need of conquering on a small piece of paper. Anoint the four corners of the paper with diluted parsley seed essential oil. Take a peach (strength) or black (banishing) candle and carve "victory" on the surface of the candle with a ballpoint pen. Anoint the candle with diluted parsley seed essential oil and place into a candleholder. Light

Blackthorn's Book of Sacred Plant Magic

and allow to burn completely. Best if done on a Tuesday (victory) or Saturday (banishing, ending).

Death—Parsley was planted on graves to honor the dead. If you are missing someone consider growing parsley on your windowsill or in a garden. Cutting the leaves and adding them to your cooking is a reminder that this person loved you.

Evil—To banish evil forces, burn parsley seed over incense charcoal tablets. To invoke protection of the angels, consider diffusing angelica essential oil after you're done.

Fertility/conception—Place a green (fertility) bag containing parsley seeds or a cotton ball with 2 drops of parsley seed essential oil on it under your pillow.

Grief—Anoint a white (purity of intent) candle with diluted parsley seed essential oil and place it into a candleholder. *Optional:* carve the loved one's initials into the surface of the candle with a ballpoint pen. Light and allow to burn completely.

Honor—To invoke someone's sense of honor, write their name on a piece of paper with any other biographical data you have, like date of birth, in the center of the paper. Place 1 pinch of parsley seed in the center of their name. Fold up the paper around the seed so it cannot escape, as small as you can get it. Place a heavy object on it like a thick book. Leave it there until they honor their commitment or make it right.

Illness, reduce—To reduce illness in your home, diffuse 1 drop of parsley seed essential oil in 100 ml of water.

Love/lust—Place a paper tissue in a red (lust), pale-pink (romantic love), or white (platonic love/friendship) muslin bag and add 1 drop of parsley seed essential oil. Tie the bag closed. Take a pink (romantic/innocent love) or red (lust) candle, write your intention on the surface of the candle with a ballpoint pen, and anoint with diluted parsley seed essential oil. Place the bag as close to the candle as is firesafe to allow it to charge with the burning candle. Tell the burning candle and charging bag about your ideal relationship that you want to attract, not a person you want to attract. Letting the universe know what you're looking for is a great way to make sure you get what you're looking for.

Physical and emotional traits, hobbies, all of it. Taking away someone's free will should be done only in the direst circumstances, and loneliness isn't one of them. Burn until complete and carry the charm on your person until you find the person you asked for. Best if done on a Friday (love).

Memory—Make a diluted parsley seed essential oil roller bottle. Place 1 drop of parsley seed essential oil into a 10 ml roller bottle. Fill the rest of the way with jojoba oil (overcoming obstacles). Insert the roller ball and cap. Roll gently between the palms to mix so as not to introduce more air to the oil than necessary. Don't forget to label! *Pro tip*: parsley seed has a dry musky smell that can be a little much, so feel free to add a drop of tangerine (protection of memory), neroli (release negative emotions tied to memories), or sweet orange (reclaim the power of your memories) to brighten up the mix without risk of phototoxicity. Apply to pulse points and inhale when you think of something you would like to remember. Repeating this process will encourage memories you'd like to keep in the front of your memory.

Misfortune, banishing—Diffuse 1 drop of parsley seed essential oil in 100 ml of water to cleanse the space of any misfortune plaguing you. Do this monthly, rotating essential oils that also banish misfortune to keep the home free and clear of negativity, misfortune, and ill luck. Rotating the oils will make sure that all of the energetic nasties are removed, not just the ones that don't like parsley seed.

Money—Anoint a dollar bill in your wallet on four corners with diluted parsley seed essential oil. Place the bill in an unused or low traffic area of your wallet, like behind your driver's license, so you won't spend it by accident. It'll attract money while it is inside your wallet, but don't fear, if you have to spend it, you can repeat the process with a different bill, and the first one will go on to bring prosperity to anyone who handles it. It's a win for everyone.

Nervousness—Add a drop or 2 of parsley seed essential oil to the wool or cotton pad of an aromatherapy necklace. The woody fragrance of parsley seed will add a grounding for any excess energy that could be distracting you from the work at hand. Consider adding a drop of holy basil essential oil (*Ocimum tenuiflorum*) to reduce stress and anxiety. You won't smell it every minute of the day, just for the first few minutes before your nose discounts the fragrance as not harmful, and you'll catch a whiff of it every so often during the day. When you notice the smell, stop and take a centering breath, in through the nose and out through the mouth. Connect with the spirit of parsley and know it is cheering you on.

Relaxation—As noted above, parsley seed can help calm nerves, but also actively encourages the relaxation that we need. To take some time for your relaxation, take 2 cups of Epsom salts (magnesium will help you sleep, too!) or salt of your choice, add 5 drops of parsley seed essential oil, and stir well. Sprinkle salt under a running bath and allow the aroma to ground any excess energy and suffuse you with warmth. Let go of anything weighing you down, and release it into the water. Once you're done, give a light rinse, as salt can dry your skin and cause itchiness, and feel any lingering issues following the water down the drain.

Stamina—To increase stamina, place 1 pinch of parsley seed in the bottom of your shoes and ask the blessing of your favorite fleet-footed god. Mercury and Hermes are popular choices, but find the best messenger suited to you.

Truthfulness—When seeking the truth, sprinkle parsley seed on your front porch (or around the front door for apartments and other housing styles that don't include a porch) to bring the truth to your door. If the lies are happening within the home, diffuse a drop of parsley seed essential oil. *Optional:* you can add a drop of lavender essential oil as well, to reveal secrets.

Victory—With a taper or chime candle in hand (red preferred, action color), carve the word "victory." Place 1 drop of parsley seed essential oil into a 10 ml roller bottle. Fill the rest of the way with jojoba oil (overcoming obstacles). Insert the roller ball and cap. Roll gently between the palms to mix so as not to introduce more air to the oil than necessary. Anoint the candle with the diluted parsley seed essential oil. Place into a candleholder and burn until complete. Best if done on a Tuesday.

Work, concentration at—Diffuse 1 drop of parsley seed essential oil in 100 ml of water to scent your immediate area with the grounding fragrance to aid your concentration. If you're concerned about water around electronics, add 5 drops of parsley seed essential oil into a cup of salt and stir well. Place in an open container like a dish or custard cup to concentrate the aroma in your area, especially in fragrance-conscious workspaces. It will aid your focus and help redirect your focus if you become distracted easily.

Recipe: Astral Air Miles

If you're looking to astral travel, this is the blend for you.

- ❁ 4 drops parsley seed essential oil (*Petroselinum sativum*) for astral travel, victory, stamina

- ❁ 2 drops black pepper essential oil (*Piper nigrum*) for mental alertness, courage, stimulation

- ❁ 1 drop oakmoss essential oil (*Evernia prunastri*) for clairvoyance, contacting other planes

- ❁ 3 drops ylang-ylang essential oil (*Cananga odorata*) for calming, harmony, strength of spirit

Diffuse this synergy 1 drop in 100 ml of water 10 minutes before you enter the room to meditate, to allow the fragrance to spread and your spirit to take flight. Wind to your wings.

PRACTICAL TESTS FOR OIL INTEGRITY 11

With many shops looking to provide affordable supplies to support their customers, it can be difficult to tell what kind of materials you have in your local shop.

THINGS TO LOOK OUT FOR

Clear glass bottles—This means they're not protected from the sun, so the manufacturers aren't expecting the oil to be around long enough to benefit from UV-blocking glass like amber, green, cobalt, violet, or other colored glass.

Same price—When all the oils are the same price, it means they have been diluted enough that they can absorb the cost differences between varieties of oil, which saves on the wallet, but means heavy dilution rates and potential shelf-stability issues. Use these oils before the carrier oil goes rancid.

Extra packaging (Crystals, stones, herbs, colorful drawstring bags, and so forth)— While not a huge red flag, this is a good indication that there is a lower quality oil inside, otherwise it wouldn't need so much window dressing, especially when you compare it to price.

Home-computer-printed labels of low quality—Independent businesses are the backbone of the Pagan community, but it indicates that the product has passed through a few hands before it got to yours, and it has likely been diluted. Make sure the label tells you what it was diluted with, both for allergy purposes and for estimating the shelf life of your product. A cheaper oil will mean the shelf life isn't as long as you hoped for, and should come with a cheaper cost.

Words like therapeutic grade, pure, certified, and other official-sounding terms on the label—If you look closely at labels bearing words like this, you'll see the ™ symbol at the end of these claims, letting you know that it's a trademarked phrase, *not an official designation* of any kind. There is no such thing as an official governing body that certifies essential oils or grades them in any way.

None of these by themselves indicates a bad product, but all of them start adding up quickly. Budgetary concerns are a huge driving force in purchases, and shops have to keep the budget of the consumers in mind when making shop decisions.

Alcohol Testing Method

Since the global COVID-19 pandemic started, the availability of alcohol-based hand sanitizer in small portable bottles has skyrocketed. This is great for a Witch looking to test the oil they purchased for their magical apothecary.

1. To a small bottle of hand sanitizer, add 2–3 drops of your favorite essential oil to test. Give the bottle a shake and observe the results.

2. If it looks like nothing happened, congratulations! It's unadulterated essential oil.

3. If it looks cloudy or murky, it's been adulterated with an emulsifier to dilute with water. There is no therapeutic benefit to this.

4. If it looks soapy inside, it's been diluted with carrier oil.

Water Testing Method

With a small amount of water we can also test to see whether or not the oil sample contains oil or water. An ethical company will tell you 10 percent frankincense in jojoba or other such information. They are diluting the oil to reduce your cost and increase their profit. But for that to be ethical, they have to tell you what the ingredients are. An unethical company will add things like food coloring (there is no therapeutic use for this) or emulsifiers so that they can dilute the oil with water.

In an empty water bottle headed to the recycling bin, place a small amount of water, ¼ cup or 2 ounces. Add 1 drop or 2 of your essential oil to test, place the cap, and give it a shake. Bubbles or cloudy water mean there's an emulsifier present to water down your oil. If they used carrier oil, the inside of the bottle will look slimy or greasy. If there's no change, it's unadulterated essential oil.

Paper Testing Method

This is the only method with a specialty item for testing. I use a watercolor paper notebook that's 4" x 6". Draw a small square on a sheet of paper in your notebook and label it with the name of the brand, for example, "John Doe's Awesome Oils." Make sure to include the oil's common name and Latin name if the bottle includes it, and bonus points to the company if they do.

Place a drop of the oil to be tested in the square you've drawn. Observe the drop; take note if there are glaring issues like color. Some companies will add things like food coloring to their oils to distract consumers from their adulterations to the product. One company I've seen colors their lemongrass with green food coloring. It's quite silly as lemongrass essential oil isn't green. It's closer to a yellow.

Leave the notebook open to your testing page overnight. Come back to it in twenty-four hours. Compare to other versions of the same or similar oils in the notebook if you have tested them before.

1. *What does it look like?* If you have an oil that's been adulterated for ethical reasons, like frankincense, compare the oily spot on the page to other oils that you are testing to see what oil-stained paper looks like. It'll have the glossy clear section on the paper the way paper bags full of French fries will have glossy splotches.

   If the paper has small wrinkles close together and only in the square and close by, the manufacturer used an emulsifier to water down the oil you tested. Your square should have little to no color. The exception is expressed citrus oils, because the oil can be stained by the citrus peel the oil was extracted from. For instance, an expressed orange oil will stain the paper orange, and possibly the lid as well (depending on original color).

2. *What does it smell like?* After twenty-four hours a good amount of essential oil's volatility will have been expended and it should only be a faint

whiff of its original aroma. The exception to this can be a *really* viscous patchouli or vetiver-type base note.

If you come back and it smells like rancid oil, we know that the essential oil has evaporated and left a particularly funky carrier oil. Because carrier oils have a much different structure, it's important to use diluted essential oils like this sooner rather than later, as once the carrier oil is rancid, it's garbage.

BIBLIOGRAPHY

Author's note: Times change and so do personal beliefs. It is my responsibility as an author to cite works utilized in the creation of this work; however, this does not guarantee that I will co-sign the words of the authors of those works now or in the future. Problematic views can crop up years after publication of any work. It is my aim to stand alongside marginalized people and the disenfranchised, always.

"The 38 Remedies Quick Reference Guide." The Bach Centre, April 14, 2021. *bachcentre.com.*

Blackthorn, Amy. *Blackthorn's Botanical Brews: Herbal Potions, Magical Teas, and Spirited Libations.* Newburyport, MA: Red Wheel/Weiser, 2020.

Blackthorn, Amy. *Blackthorn's Botanical Magic.* Newburyport, MA: Weiser, 2018.

Blackthorn, Amy. *Blackthorn's Botanical Wellness: A Green Witch's Guide to Self-Care.* Newburyport, MA: Weiser Books, 2022.

Blackthorn, Amy. *Blackthorn's Protection Magic: A Witch's Guide to Mental and Physical Self-Defense.* Newburyport, MA: Red Wheel/Weiser, 2022.

Cabot, Laurie, and Thomas Dale Cowan. *Power of the Witch.* London, England: Arkana, 1992.

Caduto, Michael J., Joseph Bruchac, John Kahionhes Fadden, and David Kanietakeron Fadden. *Keepers of Life: Discovering Plants through Native American Stories and Earth Activities for Children.* Told by Joseph Bruchac. Saskatoon, Sask.: Fifth House Publishers, 1995.

"Davana Leaves." *Davana Information and Facts,* January 1, 1996. *specialty produce.com.*

Densmore, Frances. *Strength of the Earth: The Classic Guide to Ojibwe Uses of Native Plants.* St. Paul: Minnesota Historical Society Press, 2006.

Devlin, Caitlin. "May Chang Essential Oil: History, Uses, and Benefits." Nikura, January 26, 2022. *nikura.com*.

Easley, Thomas, and Steven H. Horne. *The Modern Herbal Dispensatory: A Medicine-Making Guide*. Berkeley, CA: North Atlantic Books, 2016.

Eby, Margaret. "A Guide to Every Kind of Peppercorn and How to Use Them." Food & Wine, March 10, 2023. *foodandwine.com*.

Essential Oils Desk Reference. Third ed. Marble Hill, NY: Essential Science Publishing, 2006.

Ferber, S. G., D. Ken-Shoval, G. Eger, H. Koltai, G. Shoval, L. Shbiro, and A. Weller. "The 'Entourage Effect': Terpenes Coupled with Cannabinoids for the Treatment of Mood Disorders and Anxiety Disorders." *Current Neuropharmacology*, February 18, 2020. *pubmed.ncbi.nlm.nih.gov/31481004/*.

Gaumond, Andrew. "Myrtle Flower Meaning, Symbolism, Myths, Folklore, and Cultural Significance." *Petal Republic*, November 3, 2023. (updated March 23, 2024). *petalrepublic.com*.

Grescoe, Taras. "This Miracle Plant Was Eaten into Extinction 2,000 Years Ago—or Was It?" *History*, September 23, 2022. *nationalgeographic.com*.

Harrison, Karen. *The Herbal Alchemist's Handbook: A Complete Guide to Magickal Herbs and How to Use Them*. Newburyport, MA: Weiser Books, 2011.

Hart, Carl L., and Charles Ksir. *Drugs, Society, & Human Behavior*. New York: McGraw Hill Education, 2022.

Hennessy, Alena. *The Healing Guide to Flower Essences: How to Use Gaia's Magick and Medicine for Wellness, Transformation, and Emotional Balance*. Birmingham, AL: Sweet Water Press, 2020.

Holland, Eileen. *Holland's Grimoire of Magickal Correspondences: A Ritual Handbook*. Franklin Lakes, NJ: New Page Books, 2006.

Horne, Roger J. *Folk Witchcraft: A Guide to Lore, Land, & the Familiar Spirit for the Solitary Practitioner*. United States: Moon over the Mountain Press, 2021.

Illes, Judika. *Daily Magic: Spells and Rituals for Making the Whole Year Magical*. New York: HarperOne, 2021.

Inaba, Darryl, and William E. Cohen. *Uppers, Downers, All Arounders: Physical and Mental Effects of Psychoactive Drugs*. Medford, OR: CNS Productions, 2014.

Jacobs, Michael. "The Difference between Cannabinoids and Terpenes." *Analytical Cannabis*, November 25, 2021. *analyticalcannabis.com*.

Keniston-Pond, Kymberly. *Essential Oils 101: Your Guide to Understanding and Using Essential Oils*. Avon, MA: Adams Media, 2017.

King James Bible. "Exodus Chapter 30." King James Bible Online, accessed August 14, 2023, *kingjamesbibleonline.org*.

"Lime Blossom (Linden)." The Perfume Society, September 9, 2019. *perfume society.org/*.

"Linden Flower Extract." Atlantis Skincare. Accessed July 15, 2023. *atlantis skincare.com*.

Martin, Deborah J. *Baneful! 95 of the World's Worst Herbs*. The Herby Lady, LLC, n.d.

Martin, Deborah J. *Herbs: Medicinal, Magical, Marvelous!* Winchester, UK: O Books, 2010.

Melody. *Love Is in the Earth: A Kaleidoscope of Crystals*. Wheat Ridge, CO: Earth Love Publishing House., 1995.

Olszewski, Edward. "Dionysus's Enigmatic Thyrsus." *Proceedings of the American Philosophical Society*, June 1, 2019. *jstor.org/stable/45380627*.

Orhan, Ilkay Erdogan, and Ibrahim Tumen. "Potential of *Cupressus Sempervirens* (Mediterranean Cypress) in Health." *The Mediterranean Diet*, 2015, 639-47. *doi.org/10.1016/b978-0-12-407849-9.00057-9*.

Pearson, Nicholas. *Flower Essences from the Witch's Garden: Plant Spirits in Magickal Herbalism*. Rochester, VT: Destiny Books, 2022.

Prete, Giovanni. "Miracle Plant Used in Ancient Greece Rediscovered after 2,000 Years." Greek Reporter, August 13, 2023. *greekreporter.com*.

Roth, Harold. "Alchemy Works Oils, Incense, Herbs, and Seeds for Magic." Alchemy Works, January 1, 2000. *alchemy-works.com*.

Satyal, Prabodh, Brittney L. Murray, Robert L. McFeeters, and William N. Setzer. "Essential Oil Characterization of *Thymus Vulgaris* from Various Geographical Locations." Foods (Basel, Switzerland), October 27, 2016. *ncbi.nlm.nih.gov*.

Saunders, Chas, and Peter J. Allen. "Snoqualm—The Snoqualmie God of the Moon (Native American Mythology)." Godchecker, October 23, 2018. *godchecker.com*.

Selemin, Julian. "Angel's Trumpet Poisoning: Common Symptoms and What to Do." WebMD, November 2, 2022. *webmd.com*.

Sharifi-Rad, M., E. M. Varoni, M. Iriti, M. Martorell, W. N. Setzer, M. Del Mar Contreras, B. Salehi, et al. "Carvacrol and Human Health: A Comprehensive Review." *Phytotherapy Research*, September 1, 2018. *pubmed-.ncbi.nlm.nih.gov*.

Sicard, Cheri. "How to Calculate THC Dosages for Homemade Edibles." High Times, February 28, 2018. *hightimes.com*.

Sommano, Sarana Rose, Chuda Chittasupho, Warintorn Ruksiriwanich, and Pensak Jantrawut. "The Cannabis Terpenes." Molecules, December 8, 2020. *ncbi.nlm.nih.gov*.

Stein, Diane. *Healing with Flower and Gemstone Essences*. Twin Lakes, WI: Lotus Press, 2012.

Sédir, Paul, and R. Bailey. *Occult Botany: Sédir's Concise Guide to Magical Plants*. Rochester, VT: Inner Traditions, 2021.

Trinklein, David. "The Intriguing Disappearance of Silphium." Integrated Pest Management, University of Missouri, September 22, 2022, *ipm .missouri.edu*.

Weber, Jane. "Chronological History of Oranges." *Citris County Chronicle*, January 8, 2020. *chronicleonline.com*.

Ethos Cannabis. "How Terpenes Shape Cannabis Flavor, Scent, and Experience." Ethos Cannabis, December 7, 2023. *ethoscannabis.com/how-terpenes-shape-cannabis-flavor-scent-and-experience/*.

Woodward, Laurel. *Kitchen Witchery: Unlocking the Magick in Everyday Ingredients*. Woodbury, MN: Llewellyn, 2021.

Young, Pandora. "The Lore of Our Trees." Longwood Gardens, March 19, 2015. *longwoodgardens.org*.

Zhang, Shu-Dong, Jian-Jun Jin, Si-Yun Chen, Mark W. Chase, Douglas E. Soltis, Hong-Tao Li, Jun-Bo Yang, De-Zhu Li, and Ting-Shuang Yi. "Diversification of Rosaceae since the Late Cretaceous Based on Plastid Phylogenomics." New Phytologist Foundation, February 10, 2017. *nph.onlinelibrary.wiley.com*.

PLANT INDEX

About the Author

Amy Blackthorn is a professional intuitive and the bestselling author of several books on botanical magic, including *Blackthorn's Botanical Magic, Blackthorn's Botanical Brews*, and *Blackthorn's Botanical Wellness*. The founder of Blackthorn's Botanicals, she has a certification in aromatherapy and has been ordained by the Order of the Golden Gryphon. Amy lives in Delaware. Keep up with Amy's book news at *amyblackthorn.com* and view her tea shop at *blackthornsbotanicals.com*.

To Our Readers